CONJURING

Conjuring

Black Women, Fiction, and Literary Tradition

Edited by

Marjorie Pryse

and

Hortense J. Spillers

INDIANA UNIVERSITY PRESS

Bloomington

Manufactured in the United States of America

Library of Congress Cataloging in Publication Data
Main entry under title:

Conjuring: black women, fiction, and literary tradition.

Bibliography: p.
Includes index.
1. American literature—Afro-American authors—History and criticism—
Addresses, essays, lectures. 2. American literature—Women authors—His
tory and criticism—Addresses, essays, lectures. 3. Afro-American women in
literature—Addresses, essays, lectures. 4. Women in literature—Addresses,
essays, lectures. I. Pryse, Marjorie, 1948-   . II. Spillers, Hortense J.
PS153.N5C63   1985   810'.9'896   84-43171

ISBN 0-253-31407-0

1 2 3 4 5   89 88 87 86 85

Contents

CONJURING

Introduction

Zora Neale Hurston, Alice Walker, and the "Ancient Power" of Black Women

MARJORIE PRYSE

> I thank everybody in this book for coming.
> A.W., author and medium

With this closing note in her most recent novel, *The Color Purple*, Alice Walker associates authorship with magic. "Everybody in this book" has helped her write it; she herself has served as "medium" or midwife and she implicitly disclaims genius. Why would she choose not to give herself full credit, even in a humorous way, for writing one of the most original works of fiction to appear in contemporary literature? For *The Color Purple* is certainly "original," effectively revising the requirements for authorship that literary historians link with the rise of the English novel. Beginning with letters to God and continuing in epistolary form, the book pays lip service to the eighteenth-century roots of the genre. Yet, in the hands of Alice Walker, the storyteller as *The Color Purple* opens is a fourteen-year-old girl who lacks a formal education and who writes her letters (and the novel) in the colloquial English of southern, black, poor, and barely literate country people.

Celie's authority as storyteller results from no mere sleight-of-hand; Walker seems to be saying that Celie's ability to write her story is a precondition for her own ability as a novelist.

The conditions under which Celie "writes" *The Color Purple* resemble those Walker's nineteenth-century antecedents would have known. By disclaiming some of the originality that informs her novel, Walker suggests that the black woman novelist cannot view herself as extraordinary, a late fluke of twentieth-century American culture. If the lasting effects of the "peculiar institution," the lack of formal education, and sexual abuse have historically limited their literary productions, nevertheless black women have been telling and writing their stories for more than a century. If there is magic involved in Walker's perception of herself as a "medium," it is women's magic, the origins of which are as old as women themselves—and which, in the black community, has often taken other forms but has also long included literary expression. Black folk and community life gives Walker her context in *The Color Purple*; and she, like Zora Neale Hurston before her, sees folk magic as art and fiction as a form of conjuring. By making her statement, then, Walker purposely gathers together all the creative force of her black and female forerunners. By acting as "medium" for Celie, she gives them voice as well.

What, then, has happened to explain the emergence of the southern black woman as major novelist? Precisely who is "everybody in this book"? In what relation does Walker herself stand to the source of creative power for which she calls herself a "medium"? And does she stand alone? These are just a few of the questions *The Color Purple* raises, and any attempt to answer them will take us a long way back. We have to go, as Walker suggests in the title of her collection of essays, "in search of our mothers' gardens."

The way back links black women's biological heritage with their powers of naming each other as literary models. Throughout her childhood, "the artist that was and is my mother" revealed herself to Walker in the "ambitious gardens" she planted, so that "her fame as a grower of flowers spread over three counties." Her mother turned to gardens because although she also liked to tell stories, stories "were subject to being distracted, to dying without conclusion. Dinners must be started, and cotton must be gathered before the big rains." Her mother, quilt maker as well as gardener, turned domestic necessity into the occasion for art, and it would take her daughter years to recognize the literary heritage her mother also gave her. "Only recently did I realize this: that through years of listening to my mother's stories of her life, I have absorbed not only the stories themselves, but something of the manner in which she spoke, something of the urgency that involves the knowledge that her stories—like her life—must be recorded."[1] Her sharefarmer mother lived, when Walker was growing up, far removed from even the fringes, much less the center, of literary culture, can hardly be described as middle class (one of the "conditions" literary historians have ascribed to the rise of the novel[2]), and derived her fame as artist from a "green thumb" rather than from the hand that holds a pen; despite those facts, Walker names her mother as one source of her own creative power.

Black women have long possessed "magical" powers and told their daughters stories. Writing out of the urgency to record her mother's life, Walker discovers her ability to write her "mothers' " lives. Who are these other mothers? Are they related to biological mothers? Why didn't more of them write their own stories? What made it possible for some black women long before Walker herself to begin to write them down? And what made them want to? The history of black women's tradition as fiction writers—as yet unwritten—contains strategies by which individual women overcame every conceivable obstacle to personal evolution and self-expression. Studying the forms and themes in which black women have chosen to record their struggle, preserving in fiction the strengths they have long orally and personally passed down to each other as fact, can provide students and scholars alike with a laboratory for examining the origins and patterns of development that characterize literary traditions in general.

For Alice Walker, some of those "other mothers" include Zora Neale Hurston, Flannery O'Connor, Virginia Woolf, Jean Toomer, and Martin Luther King, Jr., a few of the many influences she cites in *In Search of Our Mothers' Gardens*. Even more significantly, they also include the few nameable and the many nameless nineteenth-century black women who kept alive the way back. Whether known or not to Alice Walker personally, or to Toni Cade Bambara, Octavia Butler, Alice Childress, Rosa Bird Guy, Kristin Hunter, Gayl Jones, Audre Lorde, Paule Marshall, Louise Meriwether, Toni Morrison, Gloria Naylor, Ann Allen Shockley, or Joyce Carol Thomas (to name just a few of the many black women writing fiction during the 1970s and 1980s), those nineteenth-century "mothers" who preserved biological lineage and connection by telling their stories as autobiographies or slave narratives made fiction writing possible for black women.

Susie King Taylor's *Reminiscences* (1902) records at least one such lineage.

> My great-great-grandmother was 120 years old when she died. She had seven children, and five of her boys were in the Revolutionary War.

She was from Virginia, and was half Indian. She was so old she had to be held in the sun to help restore or prolong her vitality.

My great-grandmother, one of her daughters, named Susanna, was married to Peter Simons, and was one hundred years old when she died, from a stroke of paralysis in Savannah. She was the mother of twenty-four children, twenty-three being girls. She was one of the noted mid-wives of her day. In 1820 my grandmother was born, and named after her grandmother, Dolly, and in 1833 she married Fortune Lambert Reed. Two children blessed their union, James and Hagar Ann. James died at the age of twelve years.

My mother was born in 1834. She married Raymond Baker in 1847. Nine children were born to them, three dying in infancy. I was the first born.[3]

In these opening paragraphs from *Reminiscences* we discover that some black women growing up in the ninetcᵒnth century knew their grand-mothers—and their great-great-grandmothers—and that however fleetingly history recorded their lives, there existed a women's tra-dition, handed down along female lines. Susie King Taylor's knowl-edge of her heritage, going back generations, stands as an anomaly against the norm of severed family ties and the separation of children from their mothers by the "peculiar institution" of American slavery.

Alice Walker describes her own heritage in language that resembles Taylor's:

My great-great-great-grandmother walked as a slave from Virginia to Eatonton, Georgia—which passes for the Walker ancestral home—with two babies on her hips. She lived to be a hundred and twenty-five years old and my own father knew her as a boy. (It is in memory of this walk that I choose to keep and to embrace my "maiden" name, Walker.)

There is a cemetery near our family church where she is buried; but because her marker was made of wood and rotted years ago, it is im-possible to tell exactly where her body lies. In the same cemetery are most of my mother's people, who have lived in Georgia for so long nobody even remembers when they came. And all of my great-aunts and -uncles are there, and my grandfather and grandmother, and, very recently, my own father.[4]

Walker collapses at least part of the chronological distance that sep-arates her from her nineteenth-century "mothers."

Exploring the apparent anomaly of connection within a heritage of separation, black women novelists challenge the authenticity and ac-curacy of an American history that failed to record their voices and a literary history—written by black men as well as white—that has compounded the error of that neglect.[5] Black women, achieving par-tial literacy despite the prohibitions of slavery, began making their voices heard well before emancipation, published books that are clearly novels by the 1890s, and produced by the 1930s, in the figure of Zora Neale Hurston, a prolific and self-conscious novelist, folklorist, and essayist. In the 1970s and 1980s, black women novelists have become metaphorical conjure women, "mediums" like Alice Walker who make it possible for their readers and for each other to recognize their common literary ancestors (gardeners, quilt makers, grandmothers, rootworkers, and women who wrote autobiographies) and to name each other as a community of inheritors. By their combined recognition and mutual naming, based on magic, oral inheritance, and the need to struggle against oppression, black women writers enlarge our conventional assumptions about the nature and function of literary tradition. Focusing on connection rather than separation, transforming silence into speech, and giving back power to the culturally disenfranchised, black women writers affirm the wholeness and endurance of a vision that, once articulated, can be shared— though its heritage, roots, survival, and intimate possession belong to black women alone.

The essays included in the collection that follows attempt to raise questions about individual writers and works, and about the aggregate significance of their fiction, that will move us closer to assessing the influence and writing the literary history of black women novelists. The first two essays, by Frances Foster and Minrose Gwin, consider aspects of the nineteenth-century origins of the tradition, emerging from the autobiographical writings and slave narratives that must be our starting point. As Bert James Loewenberg and Ruth Bogin observe in *Black Women in Nineteenth-Century American Life*, it is not difficult to understand why so few narratives by nineteenth-century black women have survived.

> Literacy itself was exceptional. While this was particularly true in the antebellum South, opportunities for education in the North as well were often minimal. If the black male's words . . . were recorded only spasmodically, those of the black female were still less frequently set down on paper. And the more that black communities reared churches, schools, and traditions of family life on white America's models, the more it was the men, not the women, who gave expression to their history, their strivings, and their innermost feelings.[6]

Yet despite the obstacles to literacy and literary expression, nineteenth-century black women placed a high value on writing. Phillis Wheatley (1753–1784), poet born in Africa, and Ann Plato, early nineteenth-century poet and essayist, were by no means the only black

women writing before the twentieth century. In her brief career as a
writer and public speaker, Maria Stewart (1803–1879) very early addressed the problems facing black women who might want to write.
In a lecture delivered in Boston in 1832, Stewart describes the "miserable existence of servitude" that constituted life for most "of our
color . . . from the cradle to the grave." She then asks, speaking specifically to the condition of black women, "And what literary acquire-
ments can be made, or useful knowledge derived, from either maps,
books, or charts, by those who continually drudge from Monday
morning until Sunday noon?"[7] And as early as 1831 and 1832, black
female literary societies appeared in Philadelphia and Boston. Benjamin Quarles notes that "these literary societies sent reports of their
proceedings, along with examples of their creative writings, to the
abolitionist press."[8]

The recent republication of *Our Nig; or, Sketches from the Life of a Free
Black*, edited and introduced by Henry Louis Gates, Jr., gives us an
important early text that, while continuing to be autobiographical,
reflects formal and artistic consciousness on the part of its author.
Gates calls the work a "novel, a fictional third-person autobiography"
that first appeared on September 5, 1859.[9] While readers of *Our Nig*
will be debating for some time the question of whether the work is
fiction or autobiography, Gates is correct in calling the book a "missing
link" between the tradition of black autobiography and the "slow
emergence of a distinctive black voice in fiction." Referring to Frances
E. W. Harper's publication of her short story, "The Two Offers," also
in September 1859, Gates writes, "That two black women published
in the same month the first novel and short story in the black woman's
literary tradition attests to larger shared cultural presuppositions at
work within the black community than scholars have admitted before . . . . The transformation of the black-as-object into the black-as-
subject: this is what Mrs. Harriet E. Wilson manifests for the first time
in the writings of Afro-American women.[10]

Monroe A. Majors, in *Noted Negro Women* (1893),[11] and Mrs. N. F.
Mossell, in *The Work of the Afro-American Woman* (1894),[12] both record
extensive lists of nineteenth-century poets, journalists, and essayists.
An essay published by Lucy Wilmot Smith in *The Freeman* in 1889 and
included in Majors, discusses ten women journalists and mentions
another ten. She describes Mossell's own career, citing her as a writer
of short stories and essays "following the particular lines of race literature and the 'Woman's Question.' " Another "writer of rare
ability," Mrs. Lucretia Newman Coleman, produced among other
work "a novel entitled 'Poor Ben,' which is the epitome of the life of
a prominent A.M.E. Bishop," and "pronounced an excellent pro-

duction." While "Poor Ben" does not appear to have survived, perhaps some careful researcher in the period will be able to locate more evidence of its actual existence. A woman named Lillial Akbeeta Kewus, who wrote under the name of Bert Islew, is reported to have written shortly after her high school graduation an unpublished novel entitled "Idalene Van Therese." Others, writing even from a "faraway Dakota home," expressed their views on temperance and woman suffrage in the black press and wrote juvenile literature.[13] Claudia Tate turns her attention in her essay in this collection to reexamining Pauline Hopkins, novelist and contemporary of Frances E. W. Harper (whose novel *Iola Leroy, or Shadows Uplifted*, 1892, has long been considered the first novel by a black American woman) and cites the names of other women whose works have apparently disappeared.

Without doubt those nineteenth-century writers who belonged to the small black northern middle class had fewer difficulties conceiving of themselves as writers. Charlotte Forten Grimké, born into the leading black family in Philadelphia, received formal education in Salem, Massachusetts, and after graduation taught white pupils in the city's public schools. Enlisting through the Philadelphia Port Royal Relief Association, she volunteered to go to the island of St. Helena, off the coast of South Carolina, and there became one of the first Negro teachers to test abolitionist hopes that slaves could be taught literacy. During her stay on St. Helena she wrote "Life on the Sea Islands," two sketches published in the *Atlantic Monthly* in 1864.[14] And one of her friends from Salem, writer Sarah Parker Remond, was also, according to Loewenberg and Bogin, "exceptional among black females. Never a slave, never the unwilling concubine of a plantation lord, never the undeserving victim of brutality, she was well-bred, well-educated, well-clothed and well-housed."[15] Much as we need to learn about the perseverance of nineteenth-century black women writers in the face of seemingly insurmountable barriers to literary expression, we also need to recognize Charlotte Forten Grimké and Sarah Parker Remond as real-life cultural models for the affluent black characters in Jessie Fauset's novels and in Dorothy West's *The Living Is Easy* (1948). As Deborah McDowell discusses in her essay in Chapter 5, even by the time of the Harlem Renaissance Jessie Fauset exposed the "unduly limited possibilities for female development," a theme that places her "squarely among the early black feminists in Afro-American literary history." Achieving literacy and financial security did not in themselves allow black women to free their cultural imaginations. Charlotte Forten Grimké and Sarah Parker Remond, despite their advantages, had to contend with racism and sexism that certainly inhibited their expression and possibly curtailed their productivity.

For Jarena Lee and other nineteenth-century black women preachers, religious evangelism perhaps provided sufficient sanction of faith
to allow them to transcend proscriptions against women's expression.
As Frances Foster points out in her essay in Chapter 1, Lee invoked
"divine aid" in her writing. She justified herself by claiming, " . . . as
unseemly as it may appear nowadays for a woman to preach, it should
be remembered that nothing is impossible with God." Loewenberg
and Bogin note that many nineteenth-century preachers were itin-
erants, and that therefore, "somewhat apart from the organized
church establishments, such wanderers might be white or black. They
might also be female."[16] Afro-American female literary societies
might serve as self-improvement associations; black women preachers
might advance the cause of Christianizing the race; and, if the mis-
sionary impulse remained paramount, a novel written by a black
woman might also be put to the higher service of racial uplift. Therefore Frances Harper can conceive of writing *Iola Leroy*. Iola, though
white enough to receive an offer of marriage from a white doctor,
refuses the opportunity to "pass" and ends by marrying a black phy-
sician and going into the deep South to work for the "moral uplift"
of black people. As long as black women concentrated on "higher"
concerns, they might even write fiction. Harper recognizes the potential of her attempt in the "Note" with which she closes *Iola Leroy*.
"There are scattered among us materials for mournful tragedies and
mirth-provoking comedies, which some hand may yet bring into the
literature of the country . . . and thus add to the solution of our un-
solved American problem."[17]

Yet for all of Harper's (and her contemporary Pauline Hopkins's)
achievements, breaking into fiction by means of didactic "uplift"
themes would not in and of itself give black women literary authority
or provide the basis for a strong literary tradition. Ironically, the very
strategy that Jarena Lee and other nineteenth-century black women
preachers and writers employed to enable them to write at all, claiming that they spoke with divine aid, may also have limited their con-
fidence in their own voices and therefore also inhibited the development of artistic self-consciousness, a quality that would not begin
to characterize black women's fiction until Zora Neale Hurston. From
this perspective, by allowing her protagonist Celie to write her novel
as a series of letters to God and by viewing herself as "medium,"
Walker in *The Color Purple* establishes the question of literary authority
as central to the history of black women novelists. But the question
of literary authority has long occupied our attention, for it was one
of the problems that faced our culture's earliest white males. Although
the scope of this essay will not allow me to do more than briefly

sketch in the origins of literary authority in American history, the inquiry is relevant to our attempts to understand the chronology of the emergence of black women's fiction.

The struggle for writers in the early years of the Republic to find a place in American culture for imaginative literature, then to conceive of themselves as writing works that did more than imitate English poetry, and finally to produce artists capable of a *Scarlet Letter* or a *Moby-Dick* resembles the literary endeavor of nineteenth-century black women. Yet the white male writers with whom we are most familiar did not have the barriers to literary expression that were so formidable for black women. Even as colonials white males had more access to authorship than other cultural groups in America have ever had. Although the colonial white male aspiring to write would certainly, like nineteenth-century black women, have associated the act with the "magic" of divine authority, he would not have seen himself as an inappropriate receptacle or medium through which God might reveal his Providence. Therefore Edward Taylor can confidently say in his poem "Prologue" that if God will make his pen, then he will be able to "write in liquid gold." In the white male literary tradition, attributing one's authority as a writer to God may have delayed the evolution of indigenous American forms; Taylor's "liquid gold" reflects the influence of his other English "fathers" in his extensive use of the metaphysical conceit. Only after Puritanism loses its hold on the white male colonial imagination, by the late eighteenth and early nineteenth century, do we find writers capable of producing American books and, eventually, of inventing American poetic forms and expression.

The Puritans believed that the Bible was quite literally God's text, and since by the typological manner of their logic all written texts "suggested" the Holy Word, therefore they sanctioned only literature that addressed spiritual concerns. By the same typology, only the male descendants of Adam might be writers. Therefore, calling on God to "guide [his] pen to write aright" limited Taylor's originality but it certainly did not impair the authority of his poetic voice. Deriving the source of their own literary power (in sermons and journals as well as religious poetry) from the patriarchal genealogy by which the Bible transmits authority (Father to Son to Puritan minister to male head of household), the Puritans bequeathed to subsequent generations, long after the waning of Puritanism as theology, the association between formal authority and written texts; and that formal authority was male. During the Puritan period the kind of "primitive" authority folk cultures assign to their oral storytellers was considered heretical by the theologians, who persecuted the Quakers for their faith based on "inward light" and who exiled Anne Hutchinson for daring to speak with a female, and therefore unauthorized, voice.

In such an intellectual climate, in which literary authority derives from God and is only acceptable in written not oral form, the ability to locate in oneself the potential for literary expression is readily available only to those members of the culture who possess sanctioned power. It should come as no surprise to students of American literature that women writers, lacking that power, should have difficulty finding literary authority for their own expression. Taylor's contemporary Anne Bradstreet complains of being considered "obnoxious" as a woman trying to write poetry, even with a "mean" or common pen, in her poem "Prologue," and Phillis Wheatley expresses herself very rarely in personal imagery, writing instead of the fortunate Christianizing of black Africans. While the combined influences of the American Revolution and European romanticism served to help white male writers break the original association between divine authority and written texts by the middle of the nineteenth century, for all other cultural groups prevented full access to enfranchised power the ability to write remained a mystery they would continue to associate with God, or with white men.

Not until the novels and short stories of Charles Waddell Chesnutt in the late nineteenth century do we find a black writer capable of locating some other potential source than the Christian god for his own creativity. In stories in the *Atlantic Monthly* later collected and published as *The Conjure Woman* (1899), Chesnutt writes out of the "magic" of black folk life, thereby finding a form for black authority that can avoid challenging prevailing white assumptions about literary power (since it emerges, unlike Christianity itself, from an oral rather than a written tradition) yet at the same time allows him to portray black life on the plantation in realistic terms. Beginning with the first of these stories, "The Goophered Grapevine," Chesnutt creates an old black man and former slave, Uncle Julius, who entertains a northern white man (who is also the ostensible narrator of the stories, a device that serves further to defuse their actual source) and his wife with tales of Negro life before Emancipation. Sometimes successful and sometimes not in using his tales to get what he wants from the white narrator and his wife, Uncle Julius nevertheless tells stories at the white man's expense and with a particular moral. At the end of "Mars Jeems's Nightmare," for example, Julius concludes his tale by saying, " 'Dis yer tale goes ter show . . . dat w'ite folks w'at is so ha'd en stric', en doan make no 'lowance fer po' ign'ant niggers w'at ain' had no chanst ter l'arn, is li'ble ter hab bad dreams, ter say de leas', en dat dem w'at is kin' en good ter po' people is sho' ter prosper en git 'long in de worl'.' "[18] The white man's wife, showing that the story has effectively "conjured" her, ends by giving Julius's "grandson" a second chance at working for her, thereby making " 'lowance fer po' ign'ant niggers."

Although sometimes Aunt Peggy, the "cunjah" woman of the tales, uses the magic of conjure in such a way as to injure black men as well as white, conjuring, for Uncle Julius, is a useful way to try to make a white man do what he doesn't want to do. Therefore his own tales become a form of conjure of their own, both Uncle Julius and his creator Chesnutt himself trying to make some "magic" that will earn the sympathy of their respective (white) audiences. Even more important, the Aunt Peggy of Chesnutt's *The Conjure Woman* stories provides a connection between black women and literary authority. Although Aunt Peggy does not either tell the tales or write the fiction that appeared in the *Atlantic*, Chesnutt offers her and the actual conjure women who served him as models as a source of power that makes his own fiction possible.

Chesnutt established the conjuring that was a pervasive part of nineteenth-century black life as subject matter for black writing. Zora Neale Hurston took conjuring a great leap forward—and with it, transposed the terms of literary authority for black women writers. The key to Hurston's genius was her return to her birthplace in Eatonville, Florida, as a student of anthropology at Barnard College, in order to collect and transcribe the folktales or "lies" she remembered hearing growing up in the state's only incorporated all-black town. By writing down black folklore in a form that made it accessible for the first time to general readers, Hurston in *Mules and Men* (1935) called an abrupt halt to the cultural attitude that excluded black women from literature because it excluded them from other kinds of power. *Mules and Men* used the power of the written text itself as a form of magic. Many of the tales Hurston transcribes show black people trying to explain the riddles of the universe—why they are poor, why they are black, and where they came from. Hoodoo, which uses conjure to work "miracles," is actually, according to Hurston, a folk religion. But like other folkways, it remained part of the oral tradition until Hurston wrote it down. *Mules and Men* has the effect on Hurston's own fiction and thereby, through Hurston to Alice Walker, the effect on the black woman novelist's literary tradition, that the Bible had on the earliest white male colonials. It gave her the authority to tell stories because in the act of writing down the old "lies," Hurston created a bridge between the "primitive" authority of folk life and the literary power of written texts. The point is that she *wrote them down*, thereby break-ing the mystique of connection between literary authority and pa-triarchal power.

Therefore, although folklore would not become, for Hurston, ex-plicit subject matter in the way Chesnutt used it in his stories, it would do so much more. As Robert Hemenway writes, "her fiction repre-sented the processes of folkloric transmission, emphasizing the ways of thinking and speaking which grew from the folk environment."[19] In her best novel, *Their Eyes Were Watching God* (1937), Hurston would write out from folklore or hoodoo as a source of power and would be able to find for herself and invest her female protagonist Janie with the "magic" of authority that makes storytelling—whether in oral or written form—possible. Once again looking backwards through the eyes of Alice Walker, Hurston's literary daughter if not the actual biological niece she once claimed to be,[20] we can see that however important its nineteenth-century origins were—in slave narratives, black women speakers and preachers, the women who formed black literary societies and wrote for the abolitionist press, and in the oral tradition portrayed most realistically by Chesnutt's Aunt Peggy—the literary tradition of black women's fiction finds its second beginning, and first real flowering, in Hurston.

From the opening scene in *Their Eyes Were Watching God*, when Janie comes back to Starkville "from burying the dead," her very presence makes the storytelling "mood come alive." The porch sitters who watch her pass by had been "tongueless" until seeing Janie "as she was made them remember" and Hurston emancipates storytelling powers: "Words walking without masters; walking altogether like harmony in a song" (p. 10).[21] Janie has come home, and despite the general storytelling mood that prevails on the "bander log" among the porch sitters, without access to Janie's story "the porch couldn't talk for looking." What both the men and the women see in Janie is evidence of her strength. Most of the townspeople hope that they can use cruel questions and gossip to get Janie to "fall to their level some day." Janie's old friend Pheoby, with whom she has been "kissin'-friends" for twenty years, is alone able to enter the "intimate gate" with the food she has brought, to rejoice in Janie's good looks (" 'You looks like youse yo' own daughter' " p. 14) and to leave her husband and implicitly all men to their own devices. She serves as the ideal audience who, by becoming "eager to feel and do through Janie" (p. 18), mirrors back to her friend a faith in her power of agency that makes it possible for Janie to ease "that oldest human longing—self revelation"(p. 18). The black woman, in Hurston's novel, finds her authority as storyteller both by her ability to "conjure" up her past, and then to make storytelling itself serve as a connection between "kissin'-friends." The conjuring and the community of kissing give her the power white men once said only comes from "God."

From the beginning, Janie's story is entwined with her grandmother's history. She is raised by her grandmother, Nanny, who found herself with a one-week-old daughter, Janie's mother Leafy, when Sherman took Atlanta. In order to prevent her mistress from selling off her daughter, she escaped with Leafy and after the "Big Surrender" moved to West Florida and enrolled her daughter in school. But the school teacher rapes Leafy, and shortly after Janie is born, Leafy runs away, leaving Janie with Nanny. Janie sees her grandmother's head and face as "the standing roots of some old tree that had been torn away by storm. Foundation of ancient power that no longer mattered" (p. 26). When the old woman knows she is about to die, she marries Janie to middle-aged Logan Killicks, who she thinks will give her granddaughter "protection" in the world.

But although it takes Janie three marriages to figure it out, her grandmother had long ago given her all the "protection" she would ever need in that "ancient power." For Nanny, " 'born back due in slavery,' " wasn't able " 'to fulfill my dreams of whut a woman oughta be and to do. . . . But nothing can't stop you from wishin' ' " (p. 31). Unlike Jarena Lee, she couldn't even become a preacher. " 'Ah wanted to preach a great sermon about colored women sittin' on high, but they wasn't no pulpit for me. Freedom found me wid a baby daughter in mah arms, so Ah said Ah'd take a broom and a cook-pot and throw up a highway through de wilderness for her. She would expound what Ah felt. But somehow she got lost offa de highway and next thing Ah knowed here you was in de world. So whilst Ah was tendin' you of nights Ah said Ah'd save de text for you' " (pp. 31–32). "Saving the text" is precisely what Janie learns to do for Pheoby, and what Hurston does for the writers who would come after her.

Janie finds a different "highway" from the one her grandmother plans for her when she turns her over to Logan Killicks, but by the end of the novel she has indeed managed to "expound" what Nanny, and other black women, have felt. She fulfills a prophecy that Nanny makes even when she forces Janie to marry Killicks against her will: " 'You know, honey, us colored folks is branches without roots and that makes things come round in queer ways' " (p. 31). For Janie, development of autonomy requires her apparent separation from Nanny, both physically and emotionally. When her second husband

Jody dies and Janie tastes freedom for the first time, she lies awake at night wondering what to do with that freedom and "asking lonesomeness some questions."

> She asked if she wanted to leave and go back where she had come from and try to find her mother. Maybe tend her grandmother's grave. Sort of look over the old stamping ground generally. Digging around inside of herself like that she found that she had no interest in that seldom-seen mother at all. She hated her grandmother and had hidden it from herself all these years under a cloak of pity . . . . She hated the old woman who had twisted her so in the name of love. (pp. 137–38)

Yet although she professes to "hate" her grandmother, by coming back to Starkville after Tea Cake's death Janie actually does return home.

Janie's ability to love Tea Cake passionately but also to kill him (the novel presents it as self-defense, but Alice Walker concludes that Janie kills Tea Cake because he beat her and forced her to look as though she enjoyed the role of battered wife[22]) demonstrates the development of Janie's ability to act in her own behalf. Her story therefore becomes a mythology in the original meaning of the word: *Their Eyes Were Watching God* explains the beginnings and growth of Janie's autonomous self and her ability to create a world. Bringing back with her garden seeds to plant in her lover's memory, Janie associates her new inner strength with the "green thumb" of women's magic as well as with her ability to use storytelling to "conjure" up Tea Cake's memory. "Of course he wasn't dead. He could never be dead until she herself had finished feeling and thinking" (p. 286) and speaking and writing. The novel that ironically presents Janie as "hating" her grandmother actually provides a crucial link between generations of black women and establishes storytelling both in oral *and* written form as essential to passing down the "ancient power" that will enable black women to fulfill their dreams " 'of whut a woman oughta be and to do.' "

Finding her authority as storyteller gives Janie a profound influence on Pheoby, who says, " 'Ah done growed ten feet higher from jus' listenin' tuh you, Janie' " (p. 284). In the act of storytelling Janie has managed to preserve Nanny's "text" and to make her grandmother's "ancient power" matter again. Hurston makes artistic self-consciousness an integral part of the black woman's novel. The child abandoned by her mother restores the network of female connectedness in her long talk with Pheoby, who promises as Janie begins her story to report her narrative to others. One generation of storytellers bequeaths her power to the next. Janie gives Pheoby permission to tell the porch sitters about her life with Tea Cake, implicitly recognizing that there she, too, will become part of their folklore, because, as she explains, " 'Dat's just de same as me 'cause mah tongue is in mah friend's mouf' " (p. 17). *Their Eyes Were Watching God* recreates the tradition of female friendship and shared understanding and heals the lingering impact of separation imposed by slavery and sexism.

Still, in spite of the novel's frame and its ending, Hurston gives a lot of her fiction over to the process of separation. Hurston planned the garden, but it would take Alice Walker to plant it. If Hurston could have imagined a novel in which Janie had indeed gone home to look for her mother and "maybe tend her grandmother's grave," then she might have written Alice Walker's *The Color Purple*. Still, Walker has claimed about *Their Eyes Were Watching God* that *"there is no book more important to me than this one."*[23] Although there are other sources of influence on her writing, it is to Hurston herself that Walker claims her deepest literary kinship. Great-great-great-grandmother Walker walked from Virginia to Eatonton, Georgia. Alice walked backwards to move ahead in her art—from Eatonton to Eatonville, Florida, Hurston's childhood home and the model for the Starkville of *Their Eyes Were Watching God*. And, "Looking for Zora," as she titles one of her essays reprinted in *In Search of Our Mothers' Gardens*, Walker followed Hurston to her unmarked grave in Fort Pierce, Florida, placed a stone near that grave, and marked her literary foremother, borrowing a phrase by Jean Toomer, as "A Genius of the South."[24]

The Color Purple stands as yet another monument to Hurston, and to the tradition of black women novelists. For like Hurston, Walker also finds "magic" in combining folk and female material, transforming the power of the root-doctor's conjure. Unlike Chesnutt, who used conjuring in storytelling as a way of getting the white man to do something he didn't necessarily want to do—read realistic stories about the lives of black people—Walker allows her black characters to take folk and female magic into their lives and to "grow" just by listening to each other.

Walker's use of folk material has evolved considerably over the course of her career as a fiction writer. In "The Revenge of Hannah Kemhuff," a story from *In Love and Trouble*, Walker used a conjure woman, Tante Rosie, as "a weapon against oppression."[25] In this story, Hannah goes to Tante Rosie for a spell that will achieve her revenge on a white woman who, more than thirty years earlier, had publicly humiliated Hannah, refusing her request for food on the welfare line because Hannah had worn her best clothes for the occasion. Hannah traces her decline and the decline of her family to this moment, and in Walker's story, the conjure works. Tante Rosie promises Hannah Kemhuff that Sarah Sadler, the "little moppet" of the welfare line, will not outlive her by more than six months.

This happens. But Walker uses conjure in her story not merely to "kill off" her white character but also to revive Hannah Kemhuff's sense of pride. For Walker, like Hurston, has transformed the nature of black "magic." The story defines conjure as the power to reassert the self and one's heritage in the face of overwhelming injustice. Hannah Kemhuff tells Tante Rosie that she herself does not " 'care to be cured,' " but that she wants to help justice take its course. " 'God cannot be let to make her happy all these years and me miserable. What kind of justice would that be? It would be monstrous!' "[26] Tante Rosie achieves her real "power" by affirming Hannah Kemhuff's perception of injustice. Hannah therefore tells Rosie, " 'You are a true sister,' "[27] and when she leaves the rootworker's, she bears herself "grandly out of the room. It was as if she had regained her youth; her shawls were like a stately toga, her white hair seemed to sparkle."[28] The art of rootworking, for Tante Rosie, involves an actual spell and Walker uses as first-person narrator to "The Revenge of Hannah Kemhuff" a character who calls herself an "apprentice" to Tante Rosie, much as Zora Neale Hurston (to whom the story is dedicated "in grateful memory") apprenticed herself to hoodoo doctors in New Orleans.[29] And later in the story, the apprentice, claiming not to "know by heart" the curse-prayer "regularly used and taught by rootworkers," recites it, as from a Bible, "straight from Zora Neale Hurston's book, *Mules and Men*, and Mrs. Kemhuff and I learned it on our knees together."[30]

In other stories from *In Love and Trouble* such as "Strong Horse Tea" and "Everyday Use," and in the novel *The Third Life of Grange Copeland* (1970), Walker continues to use folk materials and to explore the ways the folk heritage can define human relationships. The actual conjure does not always have to "work" in order to make the rootworker's point. In "Strong Horse Tea," the baby dies before his mother returns with the still-warm horse urine "old Sarah" has told her to collect. And in "Everyday Use," the narrator must deny one daughter the quilts she wants to hang as art in recognition of her heritage in order to preserve them for the other daughter who plans "to put them to everyday use."[31] In both of these stories, the mother Rannie Toomer and the older daughter Dee (who has renamed herself "Wangero Leewanika Kemanjo") suffer the consequences of having earlier rejected black folk life. Rannie holds out too long for a "real" (white) doctor; and Dee rejected the quilts for her own use when she went away to college because they were "old-fashioned, out of style."[32]

"Everyday Use" makes the point that mere "stylishness" does not conjure up the genuine power of the folk tradition. In *The Third Life of Grange Copeland*, the grandfather in his last "life" becomes a root-worker of a different kind, telling his granddaughter Ruth the old stories but reinterpreting them within the context of the sixties and the Civil Rights movement.[33]

In *The Color Purple* Walker moves folk heritage further forward, into a context in which loving women becomes the most successful "conjure" of all. And she does so by simultaneously moving backwards, taking for her narrator a woman whose incorrect spelling and broken syntax place her firmly within the nineteenth-century tradition of black women for whom, as Sojourner Truth once claimed, "reading men and nations" was more important than mere literacy.[34] At the point in *The Color Purple*[35] at which Celie stops writing her letters to God and begins writing her sister, Walker uses the change in Celie's form of address to mark her radical internal transformation. Celie moves from being a terrorized, silenced victim of rape ("You better not never tell nobody but God. It'd kill your mammy," p. 3) who looks for a miracle ("a sign letting me know what is happening to me," p. 3) and writes letters to God to a woman who draws her strength and her authority both to live her life and to tell others about it from her love for a human woman, Shug Avery. In the process she stops writing "God" altogether (her last letter to "him" ends "You must be sleep," p. 151), rediscovers her lost sister (with Shug's help), begins writing to and for that sister, and manages to redefine her own concept of "God" as stars, trees, peoples, sky, "Everything" (p. 242). Her final letter, addressed to this new "God," celebrates all of the changes that culminate in Celie's family's reunion (Nettie, Samuel, Tashi, and Adam all return from Africa) and in her own reintegration. They hold their family party on July fourth, a day in which "White people busy celebrating they independence from England . . . so most black folks don't have to work. Us can spend the day celebrating each other" (p. 243).

The most significant catalyst in Celie's transformation is her love for Shug Avery. Initially Shug appears in Celie's life as a photograph of someone Celie's husband-to-be, Mr. _____, loves. "I ast our new mammy bout Shug Avery . . . . She git a picture. The first one of a real person I ever seen" (p. 8). Before she can know Shug as a real person, though, she sees her as a goddess of sorts: "The most beautiful woman I ever saw. She more pretty than my mama. She bout ten thousand times more prettier then me . . . . An now when I dream, I dream of Shug Avery" (p. 8). On her wedding night she fantasizes about Shug Avery ("I know what he doing to me he done

to Shug Avery and maybe she like it," p. 13) in order to endure the
time Mr. _____ is "on top of" her; she hears Mr. _____'s sister talking
about the fact that Shug Avery is "black as my shoe" and she imagines
her a "queen" dressed in purple and red; and when Shug Avery
finally comes to town to sing, she "just be thankful to lay eyes on
her" (p. 25).

But the "queen" turns out to be a real woman. When she gets sick,
rumor spreads that she has "some kind of nasty woman disease" and
"even the preacher got his mouth on Shug Avery, now she down.
He take her condition for his text" (p. 40). When Shug shows up at
Mr. _____'s house (at this point in the novel Celie remembers that
his first name is Albert), Celie begins to nurse her back to health. In
the process, she begins to nurture herself, for Celie, who wanted to
stand up for Shug when she heard the preacher, finds to her surprise
that Shug begins to stand up for her. And when she starts giving
Shug her bath, she thinks she herself has turned into a man. "I wash
her body, it feel like I'm praying. My hands tremble and my breath
short" (p. 45). Celie cornrows Shug's hair; Shug makes up a song and
calls it "Miss Celie's song" (p. 65); Shug shows Celie her "button"
and "wet rose" between her legs; Celie watches Shug sing and thinks
she "looks like a real good time" (p. 72). When they become lovers,
although Shug tells Celie she "don't know much" about it, Celie "feels
something real soft and wet on my breast (p. 97) that reminds her of
her own children's mouths. Pretty clearly there's a lot of what Shug
earlier called "finger and tongue work" going on.

The Color Purple is a novel, then, about speaking in tongues. Although Shug herself becomes the minister's patriarchal "text," the
spiritual center of the book radiates out from the connection between
Celie and Shug that is simultaneously outrageous, audacious, cou-
rageous, willful (all terms Walker uses in *In Search of Our Mothers'
Gardens* to define the "womanist" woman) and decidedly sexual.
Quite literally these are "kissin'-friends," whose tongues are in each
others' mouths. Shug Avery becomes a major focus for Celie's text,
her letters to God, and of Alice Walker's own. And Celie quickly
learns, from Shug's own love for trees, air, birds, and other people,
"to git man off [her] eyeball."

Shug describes her spiritual connection to the universe as "that
feeling of being part of everything . . . . It sort of like you know what,
she say, grinning and rubbing high up" on Celie's thigh (p. 167).
Celie's transformation, fully apparent by her last letter ("Dear Everything"), moves outward from her love for Shug. Real love—and moving fiction—finds form for the feelings that move us, whatever those
feelings are. Celie doesn't see herself as an artist, whether she is

quilting, making pants, or writing the letters that become Walker's novel, but her author implies that the tradition of black women's fiction finds its flowering and simultaneously begins again in the original development of Celie's self-consciousness. Celie becomes another "genius of the South," finding, like Hurston, authority and authorship in folk experience. Without formal education Celie can't know what Walker does, that the earliest novels in English were also epistolary. Therefore Celie is not writing an "epistolary novel." She has simply found the form in which to both express and share her deepest feeling, which is love for other black women and men like Albert who accept her newly discovered autonomy. By the end of the novel Albert joins Celie and Shug as the new porch sitters, replacing Jody Starks and his cronies in Hurston's novel. As Walker writes in *In Search of Our Mothers' Gardens*, "understanding among women is not a threat to anyone who intends to treat women fairly."[36] Albert is allowed to join in Celie's transformation.

Shug Avery is no conjure woman but she teaches Celie new meaning for the term. She tells Celie, "Man corrupt everything . . . . He on your box of grits, in your head, and all over the radio. He try to make you think he everywhere. Soon as you think he everywhere, you think he God. But he ain't. Whenever you trying to pray, and man plop himself on the other end of it, tell him to git lost, say Shug. Conjure up flowers, wind, water, a big rock." Celie finds this "hard work" and writes, in her first letter addressed not to God but to Nettie, "Every time I conjure up a rock, I throw it" (p. 168). Getting man out of her head changes her form of address, and it changes the direction of black women's fiction.

Alice Walker describes the difficulties she had trying to write *The Color Purple*. She knew that the germ of her story came from an anecdote her sister Ruth told her about a triangle of a man and two women in which " 'one day The Wife asked The Other Woman for a pair of her drawers.' "[37] Such a request, she thought, not only began her own story but also made *The Color Purple* a historical novel. While she doesn't elaborate on why this is the case, she does then describe what it took to get her characters to "talk" to her: it took her daughter's return (from spending a year with her father) and character Celie's need both to mother and to hug Alice's real daughter Rebecca. Only then, and because of Rebecca, would Walker's characters agree to "speak" to her. Partly out of the sense of her characters' having lives of their own, she therefore writes at the end of *The Color Purple* that "A.W., author and medium" thanks "everybody in this book for coming." Celie discovers her own authority through her love for women— Shug and her sister Nettie. Alice Walker discovers her most powerful fictional form to date in becoming a "medium" for another woman's voice. The novel begins with the patriarchal model (Celie writing "for" a sign from God), turns to "speaking in tongues" and conjuring woman-love to "git man off" Celie's eyeball, and ends when Celie writes, in her last letter, "By now my heart is in my mouth" (p. 242). This image offers the final and most compelling form feeling takes whether in life or in fiction; getting her heart in her mouth allows Walker to speak for Celie and for many other black women; and thus *The Color Purple* both affirms history and makes it.

Black women's fiction has moved light-years beyond the white-skinned heroines of Harper's *Iola Leroy* and Hopkins's *Contending Forces*, as well as the light-skinned protagonists of Harlem Renaissance novels by Nella Larsen and Jessie Fauset, to the black-skinned lesbian mother Celie who finds life, liberty, and the pursuit of happiness by getting man off her eyeball and finding again the "ancient power" of great-great-great-grandmother Walker (and all the other grandmothers) by loving women. In *The Color Purple* black history becomes firmly rooted in the network of female friendship. And wherever we find interest in folklore in novels by black women we also find stages in the tradition's emerging perception that women have the ability to reclaim their "ancient power."

While it would take a much more extensive discussion of the novels than this essay to document the varying degrees of commitment to folk life and its connection to vision for black women in novels since the Harlem Renaissance, readers interested in tracing that integration will find certain writers and works of particular interest. Before Hurston, Nella Larsen's *Passing* (1929), and after Hurston, Ann Petry's *The Street* (1946), both trace the cost of missing that connection. In recent decades, Louise Meriwether's *Daddy Was a Number Runner* (1970) and Toni Morrison's *Sula* (1974), along with many other works that Elizabeth Schultz discusses in her essay in Chapter 4, explore friendship between women, fully grounded in the black experience, as a means of liberation. If not finally from a world in which, as Meriwether writes, " 'either you was a whore like China Doll or you worked in a laundry or did day's work or ran poker games or had a baby every year,' "[38] female friendship at least eases the powerlessness that results from isolation. And Morrison's Sula stands as a major link between Hurston's Janie and Alice Walker's Celie.

The "ancient power" black women writers document in their fiction and express as the intersection of black, female, and folk vision serves as a predominant and unifying concern for the writers of many of the essays in this collection, as well as for the novelists themselves. Essays by Thelma Shinn, Elizabeth Schultz, Minrose Gwin on *Jubilee*, and

Gloria T. Hull all consider the influence of women as friends, mentors, and visionary guides for each other. The essays on Ann Petry by Bernard Bell and myself show Petry offering black folk wisdom as a corrective to white values in a world where black women can choose between individualism or women's community. Essays by Madonne Miner and Joseph Skerrett link speaking and storytelling to the process of self-definition—for black women and black men. And all of the essays, especially those by Claudia Tate, Deborah E. McDowell, Barbara Christian, and Hortense Spillers, which address the question of literary tradition or place individual writers within that tradition, implicitly argue that the fusion of black and female that has historically seemed to work against progress by doubly stigmatizing black women comes into its actual power in the tradition of black women's fiction.

In an interview she gave in 1973, Alice Walker describes teaching her earliest courses on black women writers at Wellesley College and the University of Massachusetts and the need she felt then "for real critical and biographical work on these writers." At the time she hoped "soon" to visit Hurston's birthplace and home. "I am so involved with my own writing that I don't think there will be time for me to attempt the long, scholarly involvement that all these writers require. I am hopeful, however, that as their books are reissued and used in classrooms across the country, someone will do this. If no one does (or if no one does it to my satisfaction), I feel it is my duty . . . to do it myself."[39] Without doubt, Walker envisioned then, and now, university study for all students that would do what her own daughter's nursery school did for her. She praises a woman named Mrs. Cornelius whose "school is the best I expect Rebecca to know, wherever she is in her life, because it was here that the culture and the curriculum matched serenely, where Rebecca learned to sing 'Ain't Gonna Let Nobody Turn Me 'Round' as readily as 'You Are My Sunshine,' where she could hear the story of Harriet Tubman read to her and see Harriet herself in her teacher's face."[40]

The following collection is intended to free writers like Walker from the necessity of writing critical and biographical work—or at least to encourage others to join in the task of doing so. For there remains almost everything yet to be accomplished, if we are going to work toward a world in which the culture and the curriculum can match serenely. Hortense Spillers and I offer the collection as a beginning in critical definition and hope that those who read these essays will be inspired to write their own. Examining black women fiction writers' literary tradition ought to generate at least the same excitement scientists feel when they find a new solar system in the making; we are privileged to have a chance to watch first-hand the process of evolution in the tradition. And a new solar system may save our present one from total eclipse. But we must be absolutely clear on one point: a lately evolved tradition in literary history tells us as much about our own past biases and blindness as it does about the literary production of any individual novel or writer within the tradition. The evolution of the tradition depends on the writers' ability to perceive that tradition; and the presence of at least a minimal body of criticism and scholarship surrounding the fiction is essential to help nurture the growth of new, young writers. "Whenever you trying to pray, and man plop himself on the other end of it, tell him to git lost, say Shug. Conjure up flowers, wind, water, a big rock." We propose our volume's title, *Conjuring*, as a tribute to the powers of Hurston and Walker, and as a reminder, both of the "magic" involved in writing literary criticism as well as fiction, and of the oath we all must take to continue the work of speaking with each others' tongues in our mouths, thereby illuminating women's lives.

Notes

1. Alice Walker, *In Search of Our Mothers' Gardens* (San Diego: Harcourt Brace Jovanovich, 1983), pp. 240–41.
2. See Ian Watt, *The Rise of the Novel* (Berkeley: University of California Press, 1957).
3. Susie King Taylor, *Reminiscences of My Life in Camp with the 33rd United States Colored Troops, Late 1st S. C. Volunteers* (Boston, 1902), pp. 1–2. Reprinted in Bert James Loewenberg and Ruth Bogin, *Black Women in Nineteenth-Century American Life* (University Park, P.: Pennsylvania State University Press, 1976), p. 90.
4. *In Search of Our Mothers' Gardens*, pp. 142–43.
5. In a bibliographical essay that first called this fact to my attention, Rita B. Dandridge observes that most references in literary history to black women writers have appeared in footnotes or cross-references and that the few existing bibliographies that list novels by black women are woefully incomplete. For example, a book that Dandridge terms "a valuable reference guide" to the study of black literature, *From the Dark Tower: Afro-American Writers 1900–1960*, by Arthur P. Davis (Washington, D.C.: Howard University Press, 1974), includes discussions and a "highly selective bibliography" of only six women writers (Jessie Fauset, Nella Larsen, Zora Neale Hurston, Margaret Walker, Gwendolyn Brooks, and Ann Petry). She notes further that "sources of information about the literary backgrounds and personal lives of Black women novelists are scarce and generally unpublished"; that "to my knowledge, no letters of a single Black American female novelist have been published"; that with the exception of Robert Hemenway's *Zora Neale Hurston: A Literary Bi-*

ography (Urbana, Ill.: University of Illinois Press, 1977) and Barbara Christian's *Black Women Novelists* (Westport, Conn.: Greenwood Press, 1980), there exists no full-length study of novels by black American women, either individually or collectively; that other book-length studies of Afro-American fiction give the women only "token respect," citing their works in mere paragraphs or at most one or two pages; and that critical essays on black women writers are almost entirely absent from the pages of scholarly journals. (Rita B. Dandridge, "On Novels By Black American Women: A Bibliographical Essay," *Women's Studies Newsletter* 6:3 [Summer 1978], pp. 28–30.) See also Dandridge, "Male Critics/Black Women's Novels," *CLA Journal* 23:1 (September 1979), pp. 1–11. Barbara Smith observes in "Toward a Black Feminist Criticism" (*Conditions* 1 [1977]: pp. 25–32) that even "Black male critics can also *act* as if they do not know that Black women writers exist . . . . Unfortunately there are also those who are as virulently sexist in their treatment of Black women writers as their white male counterparts." She mentions Darwin Turner's treatment of Hurston in *In a Minor Chord: Three Afro-American Writers and Their Search for Identity* (Carbondale, Ill.: Southern Illinois University Press, 1971) as one example. Without doubt the best source to consult in order to begin remedying the critical neglect of black women novelists is Gloria T. Hull, Patricia Bell Scott, and Barbara Smith, *But Some of Us Are Brave: Black Women's Studies* (Old Westbury, N.Y.: The Feminist Press, 1982).

    6. Loewenberg and Bogin, p. 5.

    7. Lecture by Maria W. Stewart, given at Franklin Hall, Boston, September 21, 1832, included in Dorothy Porter, *Early Negro Writing 1760–1837* (Boston: Beacon Press, 1971), pp. 136–40.

    8. Benjamin Quarles, *Black Abolitionists* (New York: Oxford University Press, 1969), p. 105.

    9. Henry Louis Gates, Jr., ed., [Mrs. Harriet E. Wilson], *Our Nig: or, Sketches from the Life of a Free Black* (New York: Vintage, 1983), p. xi.

    10. Ibid., pp. lii–lv.

    11. Reprinted by Freeport, N.Y.: Books for Libraries Press, 1971.

    12. Also reprinted by Freeport, N.Y.: Books for Libraries Press, 1971.

    13. Majors, pp. 61–67.

    14. See Ray Allen Billington, "Charlotte L. Forten Grimké," *Notable American Women*, Vol. II (Cambridge, Mass., 1971), pp. 95–97, and *Lockwood and Forten: Two Black Teachers During the Civil War* (New York: Arno Press, 1969), which includes a reprint of "Life on the Sea Islands."

    15. Loewenberg and Bogin, pp. 222–23.

    16. Ibid., p. 126.

    17. Frances E. W. Harper, *Iola Leroy, or Shadows Uplifted* (New York: AMS Press, 1971), p. 282.

    18. Charles W. Chesnutt, *The Conjure Woman* (Ann Arbor: University of Michigan Press, 1969), p. 100.

    19. Hemenway, p. 242.

    20. See the essay "Looking for Zora," *In Search of Our Mothers' Gardens*, pp. 93–116.

    21. Zora Neale Hurston, *Their Eyes Were Watching God* (Urbana, Ill.: University of Illinois Press, 1978). All references to this novel will be cited parenthetically in the text.

    22. See *In Search of Our Mothers' Gardens*, pp. 305–306.

    23. Ibid., p. 86.

24. Ibid., p. 107. She has also worked extensively to increase critical recognition for Hurston. She wrote the Foreword to Hemenway and edited *I Love Myself When I Am Laughing*, a collection of writings by Hurston (Old Westbury, N.Y.: The Feminist Press, 1979).

25. *In Search of Our Mothers' Gardens*, p. 266.

26. *In Love and Trouble* (New York: Harcourt Brace, 1967), p. 67.

27. Ibid., p. 68.

28. Ibid., p. 70.

29. In Part II of *Mules and Men* (New York: Harper & Row, 1970; reprint of the 1935 edition), titled "Hoodoo," Hurston describes that "apprenticeship."

30. *In Love and Trouble*, pp. 71–72.

31. "Everyday Use," *In Love and Trouble*, p. 57.

32. Ibid.

33. For further discussion, see Trudier Harris, "Folklore in the Fiction of Alice Walker: A Perpetuation of Historical and Literary Traditions," *Black American Literature Forum* 2 (Spring 1977), pp. 3–8.

34. Sojourner Truth, as quoted in Miriam Gurko *The Ladies of Seneca Falls* (New York: Macmillan, 1974), pp. 214–15.

35. Alice Walker, *The Color Purple* (New York: Harcourt Brace Jovanovich, 1982). All page references to this novel will be included parenthetically in the text.

36. *In Search of Our Mothers' Gardens*, p. 273.

37. Ibid., p. 355.

38. Louise Meriwether, *Daddy Was a Number Runner* (New York: Prentice-Hall, 1970), p. 187.

39. *In Search of Our Mothers' Gardens*, pp. 256–57.

40. Ibid., p. 196.

1

Adding Color and Contour to Early American Self-Portraitures: Autobiographical Writings of Afro-American Women

FRANCES SMITH FOSTER

In the early sixties, when scholars began to sound clarion calls to disenthrone the New Critics by rallying the literary troops in favor of a "Historicism Once More," Roy Harvey Pearce was one who argued that

> When we come to try to understand our literature in our history and our history in our literature, . . . we have to be ready to see new forms, new modes, new styles emerging and to realize how all that is new results from a particular confrontation of [one's] culture made by a particular [person] at a particular time.[1]

The historicists' readiness to see new forms and to accept the particular as having increased significance for the general is one of the reasons for the enormous increase in the status and the study of American autobiography. As Robert F. Sayre reminds us:

Autobiographies have been written in almost every part of the country
by presidents and thieves, judges and professors, Indians and immi-
grants (of nearly every nationality), by ex-slaves and slaveowners, by
men and women in practically every line of work, abolitionists to zoo-
keepers, by adolescents and octogenarians, counterfeiters, captives,
muggers, muckrakers, preachers, and everybody else.[2]

Not only is autobiography the most democratic genre in American
literature, it is also one of the oldest and offers the best opportunity
for examining a variety of particular confrontations of culture by particular people in particular settings.

Scholars of ethnic studies and of women's studies have been especially quick to exploit the treasures that the personal narratives'
combination of history and discourse provides. In black studies the
research has focused upon the testimonies of slaves and ex-slaves
concerning their lives in slavery and their determination to be free.
However, the enormous popularity of the slave narrative, both in the
nineteenth century and at the present time, has contributed to a perception of the Afro-American experience prior to the Civil War as a
monolithic oppression, differing in detail, perhaps, for the house and
the field slave, but generally contoured by daily struggle for survival.
The slave narrative becomes for most people the voice of our Afro-
American ancestors. The slave narrative becomes synonymous with
early Afro-American autobiography; and the prototypical autobiographer, then, is the slave.

The study of women's personal narratives has been similarly limited. Focusing upon the restrictions that women encountered in the
nineteenth century, scholars frequently argue that the auction block
and the pedestal are similar in form and function. The personal narratives of many nineteenth-century white women contribute to this
tendency, for white women, especially in the South, compared their
situations to slavery "too often," says Ann Firor Scott, "to be counted
simply as rhetoric."[3]

Although the majority of the slave narratives were written by men,
nineteenth-century black women did write a significant number of
personal narratives. While these are most certainly particular stories
of particular people in particular times, they also present a spectrum
of classes and geographies sufficient to challenge popular notions of
a monolithic slave experience and to remind us that all maidens were
not blond, nor, in fact, did all Afro-Americans live in the South. For
this discussion I have chosen three particularly interesting autobiographical works by free black women of the early nineteenth century:
The Life and Religious Experiences of Jarena Lee, A Coloured Lady (1836),

A Narrative of the Life and Travels of Mrs. Nancy Prince (1853), and *Our Nig; or, Sketches from the Life of a Free Black* (1859).[4]

Each of these personal narratives illustrates the emergence of new forms, modes, and styles from the particular confrontations of nineteenth-century black women in the United States. Jarena Lee writes from the tradition of spiritual autobiography. In the manner of the Puritan and Quaker conversion narratives, hers has three major parts: confession of sin, testimony of conversion, and demonstrations of subsequent commitment to God's work. While the bulk of her narrative concerns her conversion, the work transcends the conventions of spiritual autobiography. Nancy Prince's work belongs to the tradition of travel literature. Not only does her narrative cover the wonderful events of her own life but, as her title promises, it presents detailed accounts of the geography, people, and customs that Prince encountered. *Our Nig*, by Harriet E. Wilson, is, as Henry Louis Gates, Jr., has pointed out,[5] autobiographical fiction. Wilson utilizes the patterns of the sentimental novel for her own purposes. Consideration of these three texts helps us further illuminate the history and the literature of the United States.

The new uses to which Lee, Prince, and Wilson adapt literary conventions suggest a number of possibilities about the relation of history to discourse. By choosing to work within existing narrative traditions, they may be reaffirming social values while forcing a larger definition of their society, exhibiting their "belief not only in individualism as a common cultural value but also in *identity* as a vital personal achievement."[6] Their variations in form may be explained as dramatic assertions that they are individuals, that they are invoking their prerogatives as artists to appropriate literary forms as their needs and desires direct. It is also possible that the differences between their histories and those of their white audiences necessitated formal compromise. The question "how all that is new results from a particular confrontation" is being pursued by many scholars.[7] Although the particular focus of my discussion may supplement such studies, my immediate aim is motivated by theories such as Albert E. Stone's that

> we must not only look more closely at particular texts than some critics in pursuit of an overarching thesis have done, but also compare synchronically works which deal with similar themes, social situations, or strategies of self-construction. In the process we may be able to throw light on cultural contexts which both unite and separate one life-story and another. (p. 19)

In the essay that follows I wish to examine briefly some "strategies of self-construction" employed in the works of Jarena Lee, Nancy

Prince, and Harriet E. Wilson and to compare these constructions with the more well-known characterizations of the period, those of the Heroic Slave and the True Woman.

As a spiritual autobiography, Jarena Lee's work does not focus upon the details of her daily life. We know that she was born in Cape May, New Jersey; left her family at age seven to enter domestic service; and lived and traveled extensively throughout the mid-Atlantic region. She was a member of the Free African Society in Philadelphia until she married the Reverend Joseph Lee and moved to Snow Hill, New Jersey. During her six-year marriage, she devoted herself to supporting her husband's ministry, though she chafed under the restrictions put upon the wife of a minister in a small rural community. Lee does not reveal the number of children that she bore, their names, or the circumstances that allowed only two infants to survive, nor does she discuss in detail her own ill health or the manner of her husband's death. She simply indicates that, when he died, she returned with her babes to Philadelphia, that God provided friends to comfort and to care for them, and that she began her long-delayed ministry. Her interest is clearly in recording "for the satisfaction of such as may follow after me, when I am no more, . . . how the Lord called me to his work, and how he has kept me from falling from grace, as I feared I should" (p. 24).

Nancy Prince begins her travel narrative by identifying herself as a member of a strong but peripatetic family group. "I was born in Newburyport, September the 15th, 1799," she says. "My mother was born in Gloucester, Massachusetts—the daughter of Tobias Wornton, or Backus, so called. He was stolen from Africa" (p. 5). Her mother was thrice widowed, and after learning that her last husband, a sailor, had died in the "English dominions," Prince says, "her grief, poverty, and responsibilities, were too much for her; she never again was the mother that she had been before" (p. 8). Thrown upon her own resources at an early age, Prince worked in various Massachusetts towns, moving wherever she could get better wages, trying to support her mother and younger siblings, residing always with "respectable people" until, at age twenty five, she married and moved to St. Petersburg, Russia. As the wife of the Emperor's palace guard, Prince had entrance to court life where, as she reports, "there was no prejudice against color" (p. 23). During her first years in Russia, Prince traveled often and participated in all the important holiday celebrations, attending funerals and entertainments, visiting tourist attractions, and witnessing floods and political turmoil. But most of her time was devoted to running a boarding house for schoolchildren and establishing a clothing business that eventually employed a journeywoman and apprentices. Ill health forced her to return to the United States, but after the death of her husband she became involved in a number of abolitionist, educational, and charitable endeavors that took her to the West Indies; Key West, Florida; New Orleans; and New England.

Our Nig; or Sketches from the Life of A Free Black, In a Two-Story White House, North is Harriet E. Wilson's story of Frado, the "beautiful mulatto" with the "roguish eyes" and exuberant spirit who after the death of her black father was abandoned by her white mother. Though the letters in the appendix testify to the authenticity of the story, Wilson tells the narrative in the third person and follows many of the conventions of the sentimental novel. Frado serves a long indenture wherein her life is made miserable by the "she-devil" Mrs. Bellmont and her vicious daughter, Mary. The noble son, Jack, and his Aunt Abby protect Frado as best they can, serve as her confidantes, and instruct her in religious matters. When her indenture is over, the years of abuse have left Frado lame and too feeble to earn her own way in the world. Between bouts of illness, she learns to sew and to weave straw bonnets well enough to support herself. At other times she must rely upon public charity. Eventually she marries, but unlike heroines of sentimental novels, Frado does not live happily ever after. Her husband turns out to be a ne'er-do-well who fathers a son but ultimately abandons them both and dies of yellow fever in New Orleans.

Each of these works was published during the antebellum period, an era dominated by reform literature. As Emerson described it: "We are all a little wild here with numberless projects of social reform. Not a reading man but has a draft of a new community in his waistcoat pocket."[8] The two most striking social movements centered around the status of black people and of women. Although they were not writing specifically to argue against slavery or the suppression of women, as black women, Lee, Prince, and Wilson are clearly concerned about and affected by both issues.

Harriet E. Wilson tackles racism in the North—noting in her preface that while she does not intend to palliate southern slavery, it is important to show that "Slavery's shadows" also fall in the North. Like many abolitionist writers, Wilson attacks Christian hypocrisy but she exceeds most reform literature of the time by introducing the most taboo version of miscegenation, the marriage between a white woman and a black man. Mag, a "fallen woman," is rescued from starvation by a black man who prizes her white skin. Though true (until her husband's death) to her marriage vows, Mag does not hesitate to call her children "black devils." Racism destroys childhood innocence as well as sunders family bonds. Her schoolmates often hurl racial insults at Frado and otherwise make her life intolerable. Though Mrs. Bellmont notes that she doesn't "mind the nigger in the child" (p. 26), she shaves Frado's "glossy ringlets," and since "Religion was not meant for niggers" (p. 68), she does not allow her to attend church with the family. When Frado wants to learn a trade, she reveals Wilson's perception of racism as a significant factor in northern life, wondering, "but how should *she*, black, feeble and poor, find anyone to teach her" (p. 124).

Jarena Lee's *Life* confronts both racism and sexism. She writes that having been convinced of her sin and the need to join a congregation, she examined various religious doctrines—those of independent fundamentalist evangelists as well as those professed by Quakers and Roman Catholics. She regularly worshipped with the Episcopal congregation led by Joseph Pilmore, but felt there was "a wall between me and a communion with that people, which was higher than I could possibly see over, and seemed to make this impression on my mind, *this is not the people for you*" (p. 5). St. George's Methodist Church had a large black population, however, and once she discovered that congregation and heard Richard Allen preach, Lee concluded that "this is the people to which my heart unites" (p. 5). Three weeks later she had her long-sought conversion experience and, after a while, through the help of another black minister, William Scott, Lee received sanctification. Although Jarena Lee ministered to all races, she clearly needed the community of blacks. She joined the Free African Society and with Richard Allen eventually withdrew from St. George's and became a part of the African Methodist Episcopal Church. Yet within the black community, Lee experienced further difficulties because of sexual prejudice. Although her congregation accepted her sanctification, it was reluctant to accept her call to the ministry and it took eight years before she won the right to exhort. Even then, she reports numerous incidents in which her ministry was questioned because she was a woman.

Nancy Prince relates similar experiences with racial and sexual prejudice. Twice she was forced to remain aboard storm-wrecked ships in order to escape becoming enslaved the moment she stepped off the deck. Her efforts to solicit funds for her Jamaican school for ex-slaves and her efforts to work with abolitionist societies are especially revealing of the interworkings of whites and blacks, men and women, involved in religious or charitable organizations.

Although all three of these authors in creating their narratives are aware that their lives deviate from the conventions prescribed for blacks and for women—that they be Heroic Slaves or True Women—

they do not present themselves as models or spokespersons for either social group. Instead they assert the right and the necessity for self-definition according to their understandings of God's intentions for them as individuals.

In one obvious way these self-portraits create another image than that of the Heroic Slave. In the slave narratives black women are almost always depicted as victims of sexual abuse or as *tableaux vivants* in a tragic scene which could be called "The Sundered Slave Family." They resemble women like William Wells Brown's sister, whose careful beauty and grace has resulted in her being sold away with four other young women for their master's "own use."[9] They are like the Patsey of another narrative, who "shrank before the lustful eye of her master, and was in danger even of her life at the hands of her mistress."[10] And they share the experience of Frederick Douglass's mother—whose son was tended along with all the other naked children by an old, feeble slavewoman while she was forced to live many miles away.[11] Though she would occasionally make a surreptitious visit to her child, when she died, Douglass said: "Never having enjoyed, to any considerable extent, her soothing presence, her tender watchful care, I received the tidings of her death with much the same emotions I should have probably felt at the death of a stranger" (p. 3). Says one narrator, to say the word *slave* is to call to mind the "tearing of children from their parents" and "female virtue trampled under foot with impunity."[12]

The slave narrator's two-dimensional portraits of victimized black women result, in part, from a genre—that of the personal narrative—which focuses complexity on the protagonist, and most slave narrators were men. Moreover, the anti-slavery context of these narratives required that the testimony emphasize the horrors of slavery and the necessity to free those who remained in bondage. Though ostensibly individual life stories, these narratives created a protagonist who was not an individual but a type. The Heroic Slave narrates a success story. He has endured the most inhumane environment imaginable and, without stooping to revenge, has escaped with his life and his integrity. He is Everyslave, innocent, ignorant, and abused but a human being who needs only free soil in which to blossom into an industrious, literate, and totally moral citizen. Though he proclaims himself a Christian (often citing his religion as the catalyst for his quest), he cannot indulge any inclination to confess struggles against sin or temptation. His is decidedly a temporal and essentially parochial theme—liberation in this life of those physically enslaved in the southern United States.

The Heroic Slave struggles not only against physical brutality and oppression but also against the subjugation of his human spirit. The slave protagonist typically begins his journey with an ignorance of his birth and heritage that is matched only by his naiveté concerning the geography and customs of the free world. He knows only that he lives within an institution that denies his humanity and threatens his very survival and that he is willing to risk his life to save himself. Repeatedly, the Heroic Slave narrator begins in words similar to those of William Wells Brown:

> I was born in Lexington, Ky. The man who stole me as soon as I was born, recorded the births of all the infants which he claimed to be born on his property, in a book which he kept for the purpose . . . . My father's name, as I learned from my mother, was George Higgins. He was a white man . . . . My master owned about forty slaves, twenty-five of whom were field hands. He removed from Kentucky to Missouri when I was quite young . . . . I was a house servant. (pp. 180–81)

Brown links the fact of his birth with questions which include the identity of his father and whether he is chattel or human being.

In contrast, the protagonists exemplified by Jarena Lee, Nancy Prince, and Harriet E. Wilson are free, northern, urban women with very clear and definite knowledge of their heritages and of their roles in society. Says Lee:

> I was born February 11, 1783 at Cape May, state of New Jersey. At the age of seven years I was parted from my parents, and went to live as a servant maid, with a Mr. Sharp, at the distance of about sixty miles from my place of birth. (p. 3)

Brown writes, "I was a house servant," then proceeds to contrast the daily routine of house servants and field hands, thereby assuming not only the identity of a house servant but merging that into the more general classification, slave. Lee clearly separates her intrinsic self from the roles that she assumed. She went to "live as a servant maid" for a person whom she recognized as assuming the role of employer, a person whom she further depersonalizes by identifying him as "*a* Mr. Sharp" (emphasis mine). Brown blurs his individuality and any separation between his identity and his social role by writing that "My master" removed the household and property to another place and by continually referring to white slaveholders and overseers by titles such as "Mr. Cook," "Major Freeland," and "master." Lee, on the other hand, grants titles only to clergy, calling others "a Mrs.

Cook," "an Englishman by the name of Pilmore," "a deist," or simply "an old man."

Like Lee, Nancy Prince shows herself to be a unique individual clearly familiar with the circumstances of her entry into the world. "I was born," she says, "in Newburyport, September the 15, 1799" (p. 5). Like Lee and Frado, but unlike Brown, Douglass, and most slave narrators, she knows very well her parentage. She denies any white man the presumption to mastery or ownership, saying that her grandfather was "stolen" from Africa, and "although a slave, he fought for liberty" at the battle of Bunker Hill. Her grandmother was "an Indian of this country" who "*served as a* domestic" (emphasis mine) (p. 5). Prince even knows that her mother's third husband had been selling baskets at the time he was kidnapped from Africa and she deviates from her genealogical recitation to give a detailed description of his escape from the slave ship. Her assertion that she had "often heard him tell the tale" (p. 6) reveals not only her personal knowledge of antecedents but implies that her family's history as freedom-seeking people was a valued part of her upbringing. Like those of most slave narrators, Prince's family was scattered about, but unlike the slave narrators, she indicates that the family members communicated with one another and, though separated by miles and time, maintained strong family identities.

However, Prince's depiction of herself as she set out for Salem, Massachusetts, "without friend, without guide" corresponds to those of Lee and Wilson as well as the slave narrators in that they are all early separated from family and friends in a solitary quest for a better life. Though they were each leaving a restrictive environment, the women create themselves in the image of pioneer, not fugitive. They contradict the standard paradigm of slave autobiographies in that their movement is not the "*break away* from the imprisoning community" as much as it is "a *break away* in the community, a reenactment of America's secular drama of selfhood."[13] They were to achieve such selfhood not only as black people, but as black women—who could demonstrate strength and independence without endangering their identities as "True Women."

The problem of maintaining this aspect of their identity was significant. If their life stories were to be appreciated by nineteenth-century white audiences, who were generally unsure of the basic humanity of blacks, or by black readers, jealous of their precarious social status, the protagonists must be exemplary in all ways. Women judged themselves and were judged, as Barbara Welter reminds us, by their adherence to four virtues—piety, purity, submissiveness and domesticity. Put them all together and they spelled mother, daughter, sister, wife—woman. Without them no matter whether there was fame, achievement or wealth, all was ashes. With them she was promised happiness and power.[14]

Nina Baym summarizes the predicament of those who did not conform to the True Woman ideal this way:

[Woman] was naturally designed for the home and the private sphere; laws aiming to keep her there were for her own benefit as well as the public good; women who felt legally or culturally restrained were unnatural; women who, for whatever reason, *had* to leave the home were pitiable and of no account.[15]

Although the social and economic realities of black life did not allow strict adherence to the Cult of True Womanhood, black women, at least publicly, aspired to this standard. The earliest and most pervasive image of the female protagonist in Afro-American literature is that of the tragic mulatto, the epitome of True Womanhood. Not only is she pious and pure, but she is also beautiful and more refined than most white women. The most heart-rending passages in the slave narratives concern the alabaster-skinned concubine of "unparalleled beauty" whose natural grace and refinement have only hastened her tragic fate. In the early novels, these gentle creatures are models of domesticity and refinement, winning the devotion and gratitude of their white lovers if not the sanctity of marriage for which they yearn.[16]

The attitudes toward the Black True Woman can be extrapolated from a variety of other sources as well. In 1852 the AME *Christian Recorder* berates women who seek more public positions in the church, saying that "the man, strong in body and mind, is fitted by nature to execute what the weaker sex is incapacitated for, both physically and mentally."[17] Martin Delaney in his *The Condition, Elevation, Emigration and Destiny of the Colored People of the United States* considered it "evidence of the degradation of our race" that some women, "the *first ladies* . . . whose husbands are industrious, able and willing to support them"[18] do not willingly climb upon the pedestal. Bess Beatty sums up nineteenth-century blacks' images and descriptions of the ideal woman as being

a beautiful but frail woman, often frivolous, gossipy, scatterbrained, and at times devious, whose highest mission was caring for her home and children, serving as her husband's helpmate, and maintaining the highest standards of morality.[19]

Wilson's Frado comes closest to this ideal. She is a mulatto, pious, sensitive, and long-suffering, eager to "trust and repose on human arm" and relieved to find a suitor to whom she could look "for comfortable support" (p. 127). However, when her marriage does not provide the protection and support she deserves, Frado does not pine away, but as soon as her "babe could be nourished without his mother," she finds him a nurse and herself a job. Like Frado, Wilson herself demonstrates greater strength and tenacity than the stereotyped True Woman, for she becomes a professional writer to support herself and her child, appealing in her preface to her "colored brethren universally for patronage" and asking their "support and defense" for her efforts to provide for herself.

The lives of Jarena Lee and Nancy Prince vary even more from those of True Women. Their decisions to write their life stories would indicate this even if within their narratives they had not directly argued against the home as the natural sphere for all women. Their narratives establish them as independent women who work not only to support themselves but because it is the right thing for them to do. Fifty-four-year-old Nancy Prince says in her preface, "There are many benevolent societies for the support of Widows, but I am desirous not to avail myself of them, so long as I can support myself by my own endeavors." And Jarena Lee's defiance is immediately apparent when she begins her narrative with the epigram: "And it shall come to pass . . . that I will pour out my Spirit upon all flesh; and your sons and your *daughters* shall prophesy."

Personal histories by women such as Lee, Prince, and Wilson present protagonists who transcend the images of the victimized slave woman and the home-bound True Woman. However, their characterizations are more complex and subtle than a simple reversal of stereotypes might imply. They offer alternatives to the image of the ultra-feminine lady and suggest a more liberal interpretation of femininity and woman's proper sphere. Their characterizations do not go against the cardinal virtues of womanhood: instead they argue for freer interpretations by demonstrating that even when their activities appear "unseemly," they did not abandon piety, purity, submission, and domesticity. In her title Jarena Lee identifies herself as "a Coloured Lady," immediately asserting the compatibility of those terms. Nancy Prince's claim, that her writing is "by divine aid" and is not prompted by a vain desire to appear before the public, is mirrored in writings by other nineteenth-century women—including, for example, Harriet Beecher Stowe—and exhibits a sense of modesty and decorum. Jarena Lee's reluctance to acknowledge her call to ministry was based upon her familiarity with "the proper role" for a woman and it was only with the authority of a heavenly voice commanding her to "Preach to Gospel" that she could approach Richard Allen for his permission. To her readers, Lee justifies her actions by saying, " . . . as unseemly as it may appear nowadays for a woman to preach, it should be remembered that nothing is impossible with God" (p. 14). And unlike male narrators who often accentuate their heroism by their abilities to live virtuously in the midst of evil, both Prince and Lee take great care to assure their readers that they lived with or emulated only "respectable colored families," or "religious people," throughout their lives.

Even the world traveler, Nancy Prince, makes it clear that she did not stray from the paths of virtue. Though she witnessed many of their customs and often socialized with ladies of the court, Prince assures us that she did not partake of such amusements as dancing and gambling because they were not in keeping with her native country's notions of propriety. Moreover, though she is proud of the success of her clothing business, Prince suggests that it did not interfere with her womanly responsibilities, saying

> My time was taken up in domestic affairs; I took two children to board, the third week after commencing housekeeping, and increased their numbers . . . . The Rev. Richard Kennel, was the Protestant pastor. We had service twice every Sabbath, and evening prayer meeting, also a female society, so that I was occupied at all times. (p. 39)

Similarly Jarena Lee adhered to basic definitions of proper female conduct until convinced that God not only sanctioned but sometimes demanded greater demonstrations of submission and piety. Upon being told that woman did not preach, she submitted to convention, married, and bore several children. She supported her husband's ministry though convinced that God had given her permission to preach abroad. When she did begin her own ministry, she confined her activities to those least offensive: visiting the sick, holding prayer meetings, and exhorting only in private homes when she "had liberty to do so." Only when "an altogether supernatural impulse" forced her to interrupt a sermon to testify and the Bishop accepted this as divine sanction, was her apprehension replaced with "a sweet serenity, a holy joy of a peculiar kind," and Lee began to speak publicly. Likewise, she broke up her household and "forsook all to preach the Everlasting Gospel" only when she perceived that God did not want her to be diverted from her calling and therefore provided friends to care for her children.

The narratives of other nineteenth-century black women provide more examples of the complex portraits presented by Lee, Prince, and Wilson. Many, like Jarena Lee, were evangelists who forsook hearth and home to travel about spreading the Gospel. Others, like Nancy Prince, went to the West Indies or Africa, to the rural South and the western frontier, or simply to the neighborhoods of their own cities to teach and to create institutions for the protection and advancement of women, children, and men. Harriet E. Wilson expressed the feelings of some when she wrote that, by the circumstances in which she found herself, "I am forced to some experiment which shall aid me in maintaining myself and child without extinguishing this feeble life." In details, the personal narratives of early Afro-American women vary widely, but in each case they shed new light upon our too dimly perceived history. They offer new forms, new modes, new styles to our rigid definitions of literature. They add contours and color to our picture of America, the proper study of which will enrich our concepts of our history, our literature, and ourselves.

Notes

1. Roy Harvey Pearce, *Historicism Once More* (Princeton: Princeton University Press, 1969), p. 59.

2. Robert F. Sayre, "The Proper Study—Autobiographies in American Studies," *American Quarterly* 29 (1977), p 241.

3. Anne Firor Scott, *The Southern Lady From Pedestal to Politics 1830–1930* (Chicago: The University of Chicago Press, 1970), p. 50.

4. Jarena Lee, *The Life and Religious Experiences of Jarena Lee, a Coloured Lady* (Philadelphia: Printed for the author, 1836); Nancy Prince, *A Narrative of the Life and Travels of Mrs. Nancy Prince*, 2nd ed. rev. (Boston: Published by the author, 1853); Harriet E. Wilson, *Our Nig; or, Sketches from the Life of a Free Black* (1859; rpt. New York: Vintage Books, 1983). Subsequent references to these editions are noted in the text.

5. In his introduction to the 1983 edition, Gates calls the work "a fictional third person autobiography," and catalogs a compelling number of autobiographical parallels between Wilson and her protagonist.

6. Stone specifically notes the significance of such an attitude when repeated in personal narratives by minorities. Albert E. Stone, *Autobiographical Occasions and Original Acts* (Philadelphia: University of Pennsylvania Press, 1982), p. 10. Subsequent references to this volume are found in the text.

7. Of special value to this discussion are the following works: Estelle C.

Jelinek, ed., *Women's Autobiography* (Bloomington: Indiana University Press, 1980); John Sekora and Darwin T. Turner, eds., *The Art of Slave Narrative* (Macomb, Ill.: Western Illinois University Press, 1982); Frances Smith Foster, *Witnessing Slavery* (Westport, Conn.: Greenwood Press, 1979).

8. Reported in James D. Hart, *The Popular Book* (Berkeley: University of California Press, 1963), p. 106.

9. William Wells Brown, *Narrative of William Wells Brown* (1847); rpt. in Gilbert Osofsky, ed., *Puttin' on ole Massa* (New York: Harper & Row, 1969). Subsequent references to this volume are found in the text.

10. Solomon Northrup, *Twelve Years a Slave* (1853); rpt. in Gilbert Osofsky, ed.

11. Frederick Douglass, *Narrative of the Life of Frederick Douglass* (1845); rpt. New York: Doubleday and Company, 1963). Subsequent references to this volume are found in the text.

12. Henry Bibb, *Narrative of the Life and Adventures of Henry Bibb* (1849); rpt. Osofsky, p. 81.

13. Sidonie Smith, *Where I'm Bound* (Westport, Conn.: Greenwood Press, 1974), p. 29.

14. Barbara Welter, *Dimity Convictions* (Athens: Ohio University Press, 1976), p. 21.

15. Nina Baym, "Portrayal of Women in American Literature, 1790–1870, " in Marlene Springer, ed., *What Manner of Woman* (New York: New York University Press, 1977), p. 212.

16. The image of the tragic mulatto continued well into the twentieth century. After the Emancipation, concubinage was replaced in most instances with marriage or the offer of marriage, and the chastity of such heroines was not questioned. For examples, compare the following works: William Wells Brown, *Clotel; or the President's Daughter* (London: Partridge & Oakly, 1853); Frank Webb, *The Garies and their Friends* (London: G. Routledge, 1857); Frances Harper, *Iola Leroy* (Philadelphia: Garrigues Brothers, 1892); Pauline Hopkins, *Contending Forces* (Boston: The Colored Co-Operative Publishing Company, 1900).

17. Daniel A. Payne. *History of the African Methodist Episcopal Church* (1891; rpt. New York: Johnson Reprint Co., 1968), p. 301.

18. Martin Robison Delaney, *The Condition, Elevation, Emigration, and Destiny of the Colored People of the United States* (1852; rpt. New York: Arno Press, 1969), pp. 198–99.

19. Bess Beatty, "Black Perspectives of American Women: The View from Black Newspapers, 1865–1900," *The Maryland Historian* 9 (Fall 1978), p. 47.

2

Green-eyed Monsters
of the Slavocracy:
Jealous Mistresses
in Two Slave Narratives

MINROSE C. GWIN

Historians of the southern experience have observed volatile psychological and sociological connections between the white man's sexual
exploitation of the slave woman and the evolution of the white woman's pedestal.[1] It is not the smallest irony of the slavocracy that its
codes of conduct demanded moral superiority from white women and
sexual availability from black, yet simultaneously expected mistress
and slave woman to live and work in intimate physical proximity. As
Katherine Fishburn points out, southern *mythos* denied women of
both races sexual self-determination: "Whereas the lady was deprived
of her sexuality, the black woman was identified with hers." White
women were characterized by their "delicate constitutions, sexual
purity and moral superiority to men," while southern mythology cast
black women into roles of "subhuman creatures who, by nature, were
strong and sexual."[2]

The virgin/whore dichotomy that was imposed upon white and

This essay expands on the author's discussion of slave narratives in *Black and White
Women of the Old South: The Peculiar Sisterhood in American Literature* (Knoxville: University
of Tennessee Press, 1985).

black southern women deeply affected their images of themselves and of each other. Yet one of the most obvious but seldom asked questions about slavery and the southern racial experience—and certainly one of the least satisfactorily answered—concerns the explosive psychological realities of the relationships between these women of the mid-nineteenth century. Placed as they were in an opposing but a similarly dehumanizing mythology, how did the stereotypical sexual roles and obverse images assigned them by white males affect their relationships with one another? In cases of miscegenation, a white wife might be expected to react with terrible vengeance and intense sexual jealousy toward a coerced slave woman, seeing in her, perhaps, something of a lost female sexuality which she herself had been denied. Powerless against a lustful husband and blind to the harsh realities of chattel slavery, the enraged wife often vented her jealous rage upon the one person whom she *could* control, the black woman. The slave woman thus became a double victim of the two-headed monster of the slavocracy, the lecherous master and the jealous mistress. The white man demeaned and controlled her through what Angela Davis calls "an institutionalized pattern of rape";[3] his enraged wife punished the victim instead of the victimizer.

In the mistress-slave relationship the white woman exerted ultimate power, and that power could transform sexual jealousy into intense cruelty. The abolitionists' slogan that complete power corrupts is nowhere more apparent than in the relationships between these southern women, whose common bonds of suffering and dehumanization might have bound them in mutual compassion. Stephen Butterfield points out that black autobiography is often a "mirror of white deeds";[4] and it is in the slave narratives, not in the white women's journals and reminiscences, that the jealous mistress springs to life in all of her fury and perversity. Particularly in two women's narratives of the 1860s, the jealous mistress becomes a symbol of the narrators' past powerlessness and of the terror and degradation perpetrated under the South's "peculiar institution." Harriet Jacobs's *Incidents in the Life of a Slave Girl* (1861) and Elizabeth Keckley's *Behind the Scenes: Thirty Years a Slave and Four Years in the White House* (1868), perhaps the two best-known women's book-length slave narratives of the nineteenth century, depict former mistresses as cruel, jealous, vindictive women. Yet, in remaking their own lives in language, both Jacobs and Keckley exert upon these white women the control that they as mistresses formerly exerted upon them as slaves. In this sense these narratives become avenues of self-determination and of emotional freedom from the specter of slavery. As Jacobs and Keckley reshape their lives as slaves and reenact the cruelties of their jealous mistresses, they remake and strengthen themselves as ontological beings in a free world where cross-racial female bonds are possible.

The two black women write of their resentments against their mistresses, but not with as much total condemnation as a contemporary reader might expect. As Frances Foster points out, writers of the slave narratives, both men and women, were writing to a white audience.[5] In the antebellum and Civil War periods, the slave narratives were designed first of all to convince a white northern audience that slavery was wrong—not just for the slave but for everyone. Wronged mistresses were depicted as cruel and vindictive, but they were also construed as victims themselves of an institution which allowed sexual degradation of black women and forced an acceptance of the double standard for white women. As Harriet Jacobs writes of her perversely vindictive mistress Mrs. Flint, ". . . I, whom she detested so bitterly, had far more pity for her than [her husband] had, whose duty it was to make her life happy."[6] When the subject matter of the narratives changed during and after Reconstruction, deemphasizing the horror of slavery and concentrating instead on the contributions of blacks,[7] freedwomen such as Kate Drumgoold in 1898 and Annie Burton in 1909 wrote of their former mistresses with affection and emphasized female nurturance in the slave-mistress relationship.

The autobiographical writings of Jacobs and Keckley may thus reflect their relationships to white women in ways limited by diverse purposes of the writings, by the contingencies of genre, and particularly by the need to define and assert selfhood in the face of repression and denial. As a genre, the slave narrative became a means of asserting black humanity and identity. The narratives were, as Foster puts it, "retrospective endeavors which helped narrators define, even create, their own identities."[8] This should be particularly true for the black woman writer, yet out of thousands of slave narratives, written and orally transmitted by blacks,[9] there are fewer than thirty written by black women and published as books during their lifetimes.[10] Although scholars have raised questions about the extent of editorial involvement in many of these volumes, some were undoubtedly written by black women and are products of conscious literary endeavor that the transcribed oral accounts do not reflect. All of these women's books were written or dictated by former slaves who had either escaped or been manumitted.

In this fact we find one reason for their scarcity. Only those who went north, whether as fugitives or freedwomen, could find resources to produce such books. With such notable exceptions as Harriet Tubman, Harriet Jacobs, and Ellen Craft, most slave women were so tied to their children that they found the harrowing journey north impossible. Though theories that slaves lived essentially in a matriarchal society have been disproven in recent years,[11] the black mother did have enormous responsibility for child care, simply because her children were owned by her master and were usually kept with her in their early years. From the 1830s through the war years, the anti-slavery press and the northern public turned avidly to the adventurous slave narratives both as testimonials of the evils of slavery and as exciting, sensational, even titillating reading. When black women did write or tell of their experiences, they were meant to be and often *were* particularly vivid testimonials of sexual exploitation and disruption of family ties, the two greatest evils of slavery for the American Victorian mind. These emphases in the women's narratives set them apart, not because they gave more accounts of sexual coercion and family disruption than the men's narratives did, but because they rendered these accounts from the female viewpoint of the rape victim, the bereft mother, the grieving wife.

This point of view was not without conflicts and problems. Though, as Marion Starling suggests, "the helplessness of the slave woman depicted in the slave narrative might serve as a galvanizing agent, spurring lukewarm sympathies into active anti-slavery ferment,"[12] the black woman wrote in a tradition of sentimental literature in which her experiences and life situations were anomalies. In a number of ways the slave narrative does represent, as Sidonie Smith suggests, "a spiritual transcendence over the brutalizing experience of slavery."[13] Often, however, the black woman found herself in the difficult position of writing to Victorian audiences and attempting to explain how and why she felt it necessary to succumb to the repeated sexual blandishments of white men rather than to remain chaste—in the tradition of the sentimental heroine—though refusal meant rape, death, or severe abuse. Foster shows that the period 1831–1865, which saw the height of popularity and literary achievement of the slave narrative, was characterized by sentimental literature which "emphasized the cultivation of sensibility, the glorification of virtue, the preservation of family life, the revival of religion, and the achievement of a utopian society."[14] The ideals of sensibility and virtue were incompatible with the slave woman's experience. The black woman was indeed measured by the standards of the nineteenth-century Cult of True Womanhood, as Erlene Stetson suggests,[15] but her situation of enslavement prevented her from being able to live up to the Victorian ideal of chastity. Many of her comments about sex in the narratives seem attempts to explain why her experiences did not lend themselves to Victorian behavior and how, as Bell Hooks puts it, "passive submission" to the white man's sexual demands should not be viewed as complicity.[16] If the black woman had any choices at all, often they were merely the lesser of evils.

At fifteen, for example, Harriet Jacobs became the mistress of a white man quite simply to escape the clutches of her lecherous master. Nonetheless, in writing her *Incidents in the Life of a Slave Girl*, she remains apologetic about the affair and attempts to defend her decision to give up her chastity:

> But, O, ye happy women, whose purity has been sheltered from childhood, who have been free to choose the objects of your affection, whose homes are protected by law, do not judge the poor desolate slave girl too severely! (p. 54)

After explaining the hardships of slave girls which made them "prematurely knowing, concerning the evil ways of the world," Jacobs acknowledges that her decision to submit was motivated by the fact that "it seems less degrading to give one's self, than to submit to compulsion. There is something akin to freedom in having a lover who has no control over you, except that which he gains by kindness and attachment" (p. 54). The black woman might be expected to view the southern white female as someone who had choices she did not have and as the embodiment of a respectability nurtured by that freedom of choice.

Writing within this tradition of the sentimental novel, the black woman also adhered to the demands of the period and the genre in which she told her story. Although a detailed analysis of the slave narrative would not be relevant to my argument,[17] depictions of crossracial female relationships were surely influenced by the distinctive structures and purposes of the genre, which changed when the abolitionist impulse no longer motivated the narratives but they rather became tracts for continued black progress in the late nineteenth and early twentieth centuries.[18] Jacobs's portrait of the horrific Mrs. Flint who exudes evil from every pore is obviously tied to the intense antislavery sentiment of the late 1850s, just as Drumgoold's love of her "white mother" in *A Slave Girl's Story* of 1898 stresses Christian endurance and cross-racial female nurture.

In all types of slave narrative the primary purpose was, as Charles Nichols points out, quite simply to show "what it feels to be a slave."[19] Such autobiographical writings lend themselves to an episodic structure and a focus on external details. A peculiar tension arises from the conflicting purposes of the narrative. The narrator may write out of a need to assert an individual identity, to exert her own ordering power over the chaos which has been her life. Yet in this process of self-definition she must also accept the demands of the genre that she become the Everywoman of the slave experience. As Butterfield points out, this tension between communal and individual self is apparent in all slave narratives.[20] It is perhaps most acute in the autobiography of the former slave woman who was subjected to all the labor and punishments of the male slaves but was in addition sometimes subjected to denial of self-determination in sexual choice. Jacobs's gesture of taking a white lover, is, in this sense, a grand show of choice, as she herself emphasizes. In a literary remaking of her life as a slave, the black woman sees herself dually as an individual with a burgeoning sense of self and as a symbol of former powerlessness. Both as black self and as black symbol, she ponders the relationship with the white female other and either accepts or rejects the ideal of mutual female nurturance.

One aspect of the study of women's autobiographies about the slavery experience involves the issue of authenticity and the meaning of the term *autobiography*. Roy Pascal separates autobiography from memoirs, diaries, and reminiscences by its emphasis on self-examination.[21] By this definition few if any of the women's slave narratives may be considered true autobiography. The issue is clouded further by the fact that, as Starling notes, the autobiographer sometimes needed editorial assistance[22] and the extent of that assistance is often a matter of conjecture. One can only accept, as does Nichols,[23] Lydia Maria Child's assertion that her editorial changes of Jacobs's manuscript were made "mainly for purposes of condensation and orderly arrangement."[24] But it has been speculated that abolitionist editors such as Child and the unnamed editor of *Aunt Sally* may have had essential shaping influences upon the narratives. In the early and later years of the narratives, evangelical northern ministers like G. W. Offley molded women's accounts of slave life as *exempla* of Christian endurance and triumph over great suffering.[25]

Despite the many textual questions concerning the autobiographies of black southern women published directly before, during, and well after the Civil War, several book-length reminiscences are purported to have been written by literate freedwomen of the region and relate in first-person accounts these former slaves' experiences with white women in a southern setting. Among those are Jacobs's *Incidents* and Keckley's *Behind the Scenes*, which were both prepared with editorial assistance. Child edited *Incidents*, and James Redpath is believed to have helped Keckley prepare her book. As mentioned, Child writes that her impact was minimal. There is no such statement by Redpath.[26] We can only assume that these are stories of the experiences of articulate black women and should be critically approached as such. Jacobs's narrative was closely tied to the abolitionist movement through the involvement of Child, who edited the *National Anti-Slavery Standard*, a weekly published in New York, and who wrote *Appeal in Favor of that Class of Americans called Africans* which won many to the antislavery cause.[27] Although Keckley's *Behind the Scenes* was published after the war and written mainly to relate her association with the Lincolns, the early chapters about her lurid experiences as a slave woman show the influence of antebellum antislavery writings such as Theodore Weld's *American Slavery As It Is* and the essays, travel books, and journals of Frances Kemble, the Grimké sisters, and Harriet Martineau.

In each of these two autobiographies the white women's sexual jealousy becomes perverse cruelty, and the black women are victimized again and again by their mistresses' displaced rage at their husbands' lechery. In describing these white women as enraged monsters, these two early women writers seem to view their mistresses as specters of slavery itself. Far from adhering to the code of the Cult of True Womanhood, which demanded piety and morality, the white women become evil creatures, nurtured by the institution which allows them and their husbands absolute power over other human beings. It is as if white women perceive the slave woman's stereotypical association with sexuality to mock her mistress's socially imposed purity. Therefore Keckley's and Jacobs's autobiographies portray the white southern woman as defiled not only by her husband's sexual misdeeds but by her own acts of cruelty to the black woman.

Jacobs's Mrs. Flint is particularly cruel and Jacobs's depiction of her evil mistress deeply ironic. Yet this demonic portrait is drawn against a background of the slave girl's early happiness with a mistress who taught her to read and write and who was "so kind . . . that I was always glad to do her bidding" (p. 10). Actually, though, even this kind mistress fails her because, at the white woman's death when Jacobs is twelve, the slave girl is bequeathed to the five-year-old daughter of her former mistress's sister, the ogress Mrs. Flint. Jacobs had hoped to be freed by her kind mistress and feels the provisions of her will a direct personal betrayal. She writes bitterly:

> My mistess had taught me the precepts of God's Word: "Thou shalt love thy neighbor as thyself." "Whatsoever ye would that men should do unto you, do ye even so unto them." But I was her slave, and I suppose she did not recognize me as her neighbor. I would give much to blot out from my memory that one great wrong. As a child, I loved

my mistress; and, looking back on the happy days I spent with her, I
try to think with less bitterness of this act of injustice. (p. 6)

This same "kind" mistress also reneged on a promise to young Linda's
grandmother that, upon her death, the old slave woman should be
freed. Instead, when the estate is settled, Dr. Flint, the old mistress's
brother-in-law, dispatches "Aunt Marthy" to the auction block where,
luckily, a family member buys her for fifty dollars and sets her free.

It is small wonder that Jacobs has a difficult time forgiving her
former mistress's "one great wrong." From the time she is sent to
the Flints, her young life becomes a nightmare punctuated by Dr.
Flint's lechery and his wife's jealousy. To maintain some control over
her life, young Linda, then fifteen, takes a white lover and has two
children whom Mrs. Flint immediately assumes are her husband's
own offspring. When the Flints decide to "break in" her children on
the plantation, Jacobs, realizing that they are being punished because
of her, runs away, hides in the home of a sympathetic white woman,
and then is concealed in a casketlike space of a shed attached to the
roof of her grandmother's house through which she bores a peephole
in order to watch her children as they play. After seven years of this
living death, Jacobs manages to escape to Philadelphia—a physical
and emotional wreck.

Motivated as she was to write her narrative by abolitionist sup-
porters and by her own outrage, Jacobs is scathingly ironic in her
discourse, particularly as it applies to Mrs. Flint. In the actions of her
mistress toward her and toward other black women, Jacobs sees not
only the cruelty perpetrated by the system but also the hypocrisy of
the slavocracy. Jacobs has a strong sense of the moral responsibilities
of women in an immoral society, and her vivid depictions of Mrs.
Flint's immorality are designed to shock those who believed that the
plantation mistress was, as Catherine Clinton puts it, "the conscience
of the slave South."[28] She describes Mrs. Flint as "totally deficient in
energy" but with "nerves so strong, that she could sit in her easy
chair and see a woman whipped, till the blood trickled from every
stroke of the lash" (p. 10). The white woman's Christianity is a sham:
with biting irony Jacobs writes that Mrs. Flint

> was a member of the church; but partaking of the Lord's supper did
> not seem to put her in a Christian frame of mind. If dinner was not
> served at the exact time on that particular Sunday, she would station
> herself in the kitchen, and wait till it was dished, and then spit in all
> the kettles and pans that had been used for cooking. She did this to
> prevent the cook and her children from eking out their meagre fare
> with the remains of the gravy and other scrapings. (pp. 10–11)

Mrs. Flint's sins are cataloged in horrendous detail throughout *Incidents*. Like Prue's fictional mistress in *Uncle Tom's Cabin*, she locks the cook away from a nursing baby for a whole day and night. Jacobs relates an incident in which her mistress makes her walk barefoot on a long errand through the snow. Later in the narrative, Jacobs gives an account of Mrs. Flint's treatment of her aunt, who, although she had many miscarriages, is forced to lie at her mistress's door each night to listen for the white woman's needs. When Aunt Nancy dies, a victim of mistreatment all of her life, Jacobs writes with the deepest irony, "Mrs. Flint took to her bed, quite overcome by the shock." The mistress "now [becomes] very sentimental" and demands that the body of the black woman whose health she has wrecked "by years of incessant, unrequited toil, and broken rest" be buried "at her feet" in the white family plot. Though dissuaded from that wish by a minister who reminds her that the black family might wish to have some say in the matter, "the tender-hearted Mrs. Flint" makes a pretty picture at Aunt Nancy's funeral "with handkerchief at her eyes" (pp. 148–50).

Mrs. Flint's most memorable characteristic, though, is the jealous rage which she directs toward young Harriet, the hapless victim of Dr. Flint's lust. Her mistress's behavior bears brutal testimony to Jacobs's plaint: "I would rather drudge out my life on a cotton plantation, till the grave opened to give me rest, than to live with an unprincipled master and a jealous mistress" (p. 49). Jacobs paints Mrs. Flint's jealousy as a kind of madness brought on by the institution of slavery and sees herself, the beleaguered slave girl, and the scorned white woman as its mutual victims. She feels a kinship for her mistress: "I never wronged her, or wished to wrong her; and one word of kindness from her would have brought me to her feet" (p. 31). Yet that kinship is not reciprocated. Like many southern white women whose husbands were guilty of philandering with slave women, Mrs. Flint is totally blind to the plight of the female slave. "She pitied herself as a martyr," writes Jacobs, "but she was incapable of feeling for the condition of shame and misery in which her unfortunate, helpless slave was placed." Mrs. Flint "would gladly have had me flogged . . . but the doctor never allowed anyone to whip me" (p. 33).

When Jacobs's first child is conceived, Mrs. Flint, thinking it is her husband's offspring, vows to kill the young woman. The jealous Dr. Flint, whose injunction against violence does not extend to his own, throws Harriet down a flight of stairs, shears her hair, and beats her. In her account of Mrs. Flint, Jacobs stresses also the woman's desire to dominate. When she is sent away to the plantation of Dr. Flint's son and has worked there for five years, Jacobs must wait on the table at which the visiting Mrs. Flint is served. "Nothing could please her better than to see me humbled and trampled upon," the black woman writes. "I was just where she would have me—in the power of a hard, unprincipled master. She did not speak to me when she took her seat at table; but her satisfied, triumphant smile, when I handed her plate, was more eloquent than words" (p. 95). When Jacobs runs away, the enraged Mrs. Flint is reported to have said, "The good-for-nothing hussy! When she is caught, she shall stay in jail, in irons, for one six months, and then be sold to a sugar plantation. I shall see her broke in yet" (p. 105). Throughout Jacobs's account, Mrs. Flint is depicted as struggling for control of young Harriet, and later of her children. The white woman equates these blacks to animals to be conquered and tamed. As Jacobs depicts her, Mrs. Flint is at the same time horribly vindictive and pitifully weak. She longs to control her husband's sexual appetites, but cannot. Instead she transfers her rage to Jacobs and her children and attempts, also unsuccessfully, to control them as symbols of the lust which her husband embodies.

Jacobs writes so bitterly and so thoroughly about Mrs. Flint that she seems at times to transform *Incidents* into a vehicle of rage directed toward her former mistress. If the slave narrative is indeed a means of controlling past experiences and asserting personal order upon social indignity, then *Incidents* is surely the artifact created by Jacobs's impulse to control and dominate, in language, those who controlled and dominated her. She imbues her descriptions of Mrs. Flint with terrible irony and bitterness. In so doing, she, as narrator, dominates and manipulates Mrs. Flint. She herself becomes the old slave woman with a dead, cruel mistress about whom she relates an anecdote. When the mistress dies, Jacobs writes, the old slave woman who has borne the brunt of her many beatings and cruelties steals into the room where the dead woman lies. "She gazed a while on her, then raised her hand and dealt two blows on her face, saying, as she did so, 'The devil is got you now!' " (p. 48). Like the old slave, Jacobs flogs her powerless former mistress over and over throughout her narrative. At long last the slave woman controls the plantation mistress, and the vehicle of that domination, language, becomes infinitely more powerful and more resonant than the lash or the chain could ever be.

Unlike Jacobs, Keckley dispenses with her years of bondage in the early part of her autobiography. Yet her focus, like Jacobs's, centers on the brutality of a southern mistress with "a cold jealous heart." Keckley is more reticent than Jacobs about her master's sexual coercion, which resulted in the birth of her only child. But it is easy to read between the lines. Like Jacobs, young Keckley was sent to a new master and mistress when she was in early puberty. When she was eighteen and had grown into "strong, healthy womanhood," her master Mr. Burwell, a Presbyterian minister, and his "helpless" ill-tempered wife moved from Virginia to Hillsboro, North Carolina, taking Keckley, their only slave, with them.

It is at this point that Keckley's tortures begin. Her mistress, Keckley writes, "seemed to be desirous to wreak vengeance on me for something," and "Mr. Bingham, a hard, cruel man, the village schoolmaster" became Mrs. Burwell's "ready tool" (p. 32). At her mistress's behest, Keckley undergoes a series of savage beatings and personal exposure at the hands of the sadistic schoolmaster. In addition, Keckley suffers violent abuse in the Burwell home—in which she has a chair broken over her head. When even the perversely cruel Bingham refuses to whip the black woman again, Mrs. Burwell urges her husband to "punish" her. Mr. Burwell, Keckley writes with grim irony, "who preached the love of Heaven, who glorified the precepts and examples of Christ, who expounded the Holy Scriptures Sabbath after Sabbath from the pulpit," cuts the heavy handle from an oak broom and beats her so brutally that her bloodied condition, she writes, touched even the "cold, jealous heart" of her mistress (p. 37). (Mrs. Burwell's "pity" more likely was motivated by the probability of losing a valuable piece of property, her only maid.)

Up to this point in Keckley's narrative the Burwells' sadism appears motiveless. Keckley writes only that the beatings were to "subdue [her] pride" (p. 38). But their motives, particularly Mrs. Burwell's, crystallize as the black woman admits that the savage actions of owners "were not the only things that brought me suffering and deep mortification" (p. 38). In her half-apologetic account of her own sexual coercion Keckley chooses her words carefully. Her hesitant, tentative story shows above all a continuing psychological enslavement to the white man and to a cardinal rule that the black woman must never reveal the name of the father of her mulatto child. It also paints the minister Burwell as even more of a perverse monster. Not only does he force sex upon the slave woman; he beats her savagely even after his cruel wife begs him to desist. Burwell is a prime example of Davis's and Hooks's theory that sexual domination of female slaves was an avenue to power for the white male and that rape became in the slave South a symbol of white man's total dominance over blacks and over women.[29] Burwell dominates Keckley through sex and through violence; and although the hesitancy in her account of sexual coercion may be partly ascribed to nineteenth-century reticence on such topics, it is also testimony to a prevailing fear of the immense power of the southern white man:

I was regarded as fair-looking for one of my race, and for four years a
white man—I spare the world his name—had base designs upon me.
I do not care to dwell upon this subject for it is one that is fraught with
pain. Suffice it to say, that he persecuted me for four years, and I—I—
became a mother. The child of which he was the father was the only
child that I ever brought into the world. If my poor boy ever suffered
any humilating pangs on account of birth, he could not blame his
mother, for God knows that she did not wish to give him life; he must
blame the edicts of that society which deemed it no crime to undermine
the virtue of girls in my then position.

Among the old letters preserved by my mother I find the following,
written by myself while at Hillsboro'. In this connection I desire to state
that Robert Burwell is now living at Charlotte, North Carolina. (p. 38)

In this account and in the letter which follows it, Keckley mentions
"griefs and misfortunes" which result in family disapproval. From
her specific mention of Burwell, we can infer that he was the father
of her child. Keckley's account of Burwell's sexual aberrations restores, by contrast, a more sympathetic view of her mistress. It is she
who finally falls on her knees and begs her husband to stop beating
Keckley. Faint glimmerings of a sympathetic portrait emerge from
this part of the narrative. In her former mistress Keckley shows us a
white woman warped by her husband's perverse will to sexually dominate a female slave. Her sadism is horribly engendered by his lust
for power.

We wonder how representative Mrs. Flint and Mrs. Burwell are.
An unpublished study of the role of plantation mistresses in the lives
of slaves shows mistresses to have been responsible for only a small
portion of punishments inflicted upon slaves. Yet the study, in which
Elizabeth Craven surveyed nineteenth- and twentieth-century slave
narratives, also shows that many incidents involving the cruelty of a
mistress also concerned a female slave's alleged intimacy with the
master. Clinton, who cites the study in *The Plantation Mistress*, summarizes Craven's findings: "When [male] slaveowners sexually harassed or exploited female slaves, mistresses sometimes directed their
anger, not at their unfaithful husbands, but toward the helpless
slaves."[30] In writing about the white women who transferred their
jealous rages to them, Jacobs and Keckley evoke the autobiographical
process as an avenue toward understanding and order. It is only
through confrontation with the human evil of slavery that the freed
woman can reorder experience, redefine her place in the world, and
assert her human rights. Keckley and Jacobs see their relationships
with their former mistresses as paradigmatic of the essential evil of
slavery—the perversity of that "peculiar institution" which trans-

formed victim into victimizer and severed potential bonds of sisterhood. By recreating Mrs. Flint and Mrs. Burwell and their "cold,
jealous heart[s]," these two black women writers rise in language from
the ashes of their enslavement and create themselves anew—as ontological selves, as nonvictims.

Notes

1. See, for example, John W. Blassingame, *The Slave Community: Plantation
Life in the Antebellum South* (New York: Oxford University Press, 1972); W. J.
Cash, *The Mind of the South* (New York: Knopf, 1941); Catherine Clinton, *The
Plantation Mistress: Woman's World in the Old South* (New York: Pantheon, 1982);
Angela Davis, *Women, Race & Class* (New York: Random House, 1981); Herbert
G. Gutman, *The Black Family in Slavery and Freedom, 1750–1925* (New York:
Pantheon, 1976); Bell Hooks, *"Ain't I a Woman?": Black Women and Feminism*
(Boston: South End, 1981); Anne Firor Scott, *The Southern Lady: From Pedestal
to Politics 1830–1930* (Chicago and London: University of Chicago Press, 1970);
Kenneth Stampp, *The Peculiar Institution: Slavery in the Ante-bellum South* (New
York: Knopf, 1956); C. Vann Woodward, *The Burden of Southern History* (Baton
Rouge: Louisiana State University Press, 1960).
2. Katherine Fishburn, *Women in Popular Culture: A Reference Guide* (Westport, Conn.: Greenwood, 1982), pp. 10–11.
3. Davis, p. 23.
4. Stephen Butterfield, *Black Autobiography in America* (Amherst: University
of Massachusetts Press, 1974), p. 3.
5. Frances Foster, *Witnessing Slavery: The Development of Antebellum Slave
Narratives* (Westport, Conn.: Greenwood, 1979), p. 65.
6. Harriet Jacobs [Linda Brent], *Incidents in the Life of a Slave Girl*, ed. L.
Maria Child (1861; rpt. New York: Harcourt Brace Jovanovich, 1973), p. 31.
Subsequent references will be designated parenthetically.
7. Foster, pp. 60–61.
8. Foster, p. 3.
9. Marion Starling lists more than 6,000. See "The Slave Narrative: Its Place
in American Literary History," Diss. New York University, 1946.
10. For separate bibliographies of women's slave narratives, see Erlene Stetson, "Studying Slavery," in *But Some of Us Are Brave*, ed. Gloria Hull, Patricia
Bell Scott, and Barbara Smith (Old Westbury, N.Y.: The Feminist Press, 1982),
pp. 82–84 (contains several errors); Stetson, "Black Women In and Out of
Print," in *Women in Print—I*, ed. Joan Hartman and Ellen Messer-Davidow
(New York: MLA, 1982), p. 97 (a more selective, but also more accurate listing).
Marion Starling in "The Slave Narrative," Francis Foster in *Witnessing Slavery*,
and Charles Nichols, *Many Thousand Gone*, 2nd ed. (Bloomington: Indiana
University Press, 1969) all list female and male narratives together. For col-
lected excerpts of some women's narratives, see Bert Loewenberg and Ruth
Bogin, *Black Women in Nineteenth-Century American Life* (University Park: Penn-
sylvania State University Press, 1976).

11. See, for example, Blassingame and Gutman.

12. Starling, p. 294.

13. Sidonie Smith, *Where I'm Bound: Patterns of Slavery and Freedom in Black American Autobiography* (Westport, Conn., and London: Greenwood, 1974), p. 10.

14. Foster, p. 64.

15. Stetson, "Studying Slavery," p. 79.

16. Hooks, p. 26.

17. See Starling, Foster, Nichols, and Butterfield.

18. Foster makes these distinctions in *Witnessing Slavery*, p. 150.

19. Nichols, ix.

20. Butterfield, p. 3.

21. Roy Pascal, *Design and Truth in Autobiography* (Cambridge: Harvard University Press, 1960), pp. 3–5.

22. Starling, p. 311.

23. Nichols, xi.

24. Lydia Maria Child, "Introduction," *Incidents*, xi.

25. See, for example, *Narrative of Jane Brown and Her Two Children* (Hartford: Published for G. W. Offley, 1860).

26. Dorothy Porter, "Introduction," in Elizabeth Keckley, *Behind the Scenes or, Thirty Years a Slave, and Four Years in the White House* (1868; rpt. New York: G. W. Carleton, 1968), pp. i–ii. *Behind the Scenes* was initially recalled from the market at the request of Robert Lincoln, who rebuked Keckley for publishing his mother's letters. In 1935 an Associated Press story credited Jane Swisshelm, a Washington reporter, with authorship of the book and denied the existence of Elizabeth Keckley. John Washington, author of *They Knew Lincoln*, soundly refuted this report. The extent of Child's and Redpath's assistance is not known. (Subsequent references to this edition are designated parenthetically.)

27. Walter Tenner, "Introduction," *Incidents*, x.

28. Clinton p. 189.

29. Davis, p. 23; Hooks, p. 27.

30. Clinton, p. 188.

3

Pauline Hopkins: Our Literary Foremother

CLAUDIA TATE

In 1900 Charles Waddell Chesnutt (1858–1932) published his first novel, *The House Behind the Cedars*. This work along with its two predecessors, *The Conjure Woman and Other Tales* (1899) and *The Wife of His Youth and Other Stories of the Color Line* (1899), launched Chesnutt on a writing career that ultimately established him as the first important Afro-American novelist to treat racial prejudice in his fiction. Like most of his black contemporaries, Chesnutt had a single purpose in mind for his writing ambitions, which he defined at the age of twenty-one in a May 29, 1880, journal entry:

> I think I must write a book. . . . If I do write, I shall write for a purpose, a high, holy purpose . . . .I consider the unjust spirit of caste which is so insidious as to pervade a whole nation, and so powerful as to subject a whole race and all connected with it to scorn and social ostracism— I consider this a barrier to the moral progress of the American people; and I would be one of the first to head a determined, organized crusade against it . . . . If I can do anything to further this work, and can see any likelihood of success in it, I would gladly devote my life to it.[1]

With this "high [and] holy purpose"[2] directing the course of his pen, Chesnutt predictably dedicated all of his work to acclimating "the [white] public mind"[3] to accepting the equality of black Americans.

Also in 1900, Pauline Elizabeth Hopkins (1859–1930) published *Contending Forces: A Romance Illustrative of Negro Life North and South*. In addition, she published two more novels, *Winoma: A Tale of Negro Life in the South and Southwest* (1902) and *Of One Blood, or the Hidden Self* (1902/03);[4] a novella, "Topsy Templeton";[5] several short stories;[6] and two plays, "One Scene from the Drama of Early Days" and "Slaves' Escape, or the Underground Railroad."[7] Like her black, literary contemporaries, Hopkins believed that fiction could be used as a vehicle for racial advancement. In fact, she stated in the preface to *Contending Forces* that this belief gave direction to her writing venture:

> In giving this little romance expression in print, I am not actuated by a desire for notoriety or for profit, but to do all that I can in a humble way to raise the stigma of degradation from my race.[8]

She further insisted that black Americans should develop their own literature and, thereby, create and preserve "*the innermost thoughts and feelings of the Negro with all the fire and romance which lie dormant in our history*" (p. 14). The preface's principal argument, however, is not aesthetic but social. It is her appeal to white Americans to extend their love of justice and morality to oppressed black Americans:

> I have presented both sides of the dark picture . . . truthfully and without vituperation, pleading for that justice of heart and mind for my people which the Anglo-Saxon in America never withholds from suffering humanity. (p. 15)

The expression of such an appeal was a conventional practice for nineteenth- and early twentieth-century black writers, who, after all, directed their dramatized arguments for racial justice to an upperclass, white audience.

Despite her prolific writing career, Hopkins has been omitted from the canon of American literature. We might conjecture that her race and gender are somewhat responsible for her omission, in that white male writers, by and large, receive critical attention from white male critics. Furthermore, male critical judgments have categorically established the canon of Afro-American literature and literary criticism. Thus, it is not surprising to find that Ann Allen Shockley's 1972 *Phylon* article, entitled "Pauline Elizabeth Hopkins: A Biographical Excursion into Obscurity," is the only critical piece that gives Hopkins more than a passing nod.[9] In fact, when surveying Hopkins's critical reception, it is much simpler to cite the few works in which she is mentioned than to refer to the many which fail to mention her at all. In this regard, we find Hopkins's work discussed in Vernon Loggins's *The Negro Author: His Development in America* (1931), Hugh Glouster's *Negro Voices in American Fiction* (1948), Robert Bone's *The Negro Novel in America* (1965), and Judith Berzon's *Neither White nor Black: The Mulatto Character in American Fiction* (1978). But these sources only treat *Contending Forces*, thereby further neglecting the full body of Hopkins's published work.

According to Loggins, *Contending Forces* is a complicated work of exaggerated injustice, cruelty, and brutality.[10] He compares Hopkins's novel only to that written by Frances Harper, as if the novels of William Wells Brown, Martin Delaney, Sutton Griggs, or Charles Chesnutt were somehow different in their basic themes, plot structures, and authorial intentions.[11] That Loggins placed Hopkins's work into an artificial context, isolated from her male contemporaries, was not an unusual critical practice. This type of gender segregation was the rule rather than the exception.[12]

Glouster, her next critic, reports that Hopkins was motivated to do all that she could "in a humble way to raise the stigma of degradation from her race."[13] Like Loggins, Glouster focuses on Hopkins's preface in order to explain her motive for writing. Also like Loggins, Glouster seems to subscribe to gender segregation in that he places Hopkins solely in the company of her female contemporaries, Frances Harper and J. McHenry Jones.

Bone, her third critic, mentions Hopkins as an early Negro novelist, who had adopted the stance of strict moral piety in her work in order to promote the social advancement of Afro-Americans.[14] He also contends that she was a subscriber to the myth of Anglo-Saxon superiority[15] and guilty of stereotyping her minor characters.[16] All of these comments are undisputed characteristics of the fiction of Hopkins and her contemporaries, writers who staunchly believed in moral piety and personal industry and who used the tragic mulatto as a vehicle for racial protest.

Finally, Berzon remarks that "Hopkins's ideology is . . . distinctly DuBoisean . . . . Sappho, Hopkins's beautiful golden-haired black heroine, is opposed to industrial education exclusively."[17] Berzon continues to quote Sappho as a means of giving expression to Hopkins's DuBoisean conviction that black Americans must have full political rights in order to ensure their social advancement. Although Berzon makes particular reference to Hopkins's dramatization of the DuBois-Washington controversy,[18] Berzon seems more concerned with using Hopkins's work to mark an appearance of the mulatto character in American literature than with placing her work in the literary tradition of her day.

Pauline Hopkins was an important writer who deserves serious attention because, in being both black and female, she documents the cross section of the literary concerns of two major groups of American writers: turn-of-the-century black writers, who primarily dramatized themes of racial injustice, and mid- to late-nineteenth-century white women writers, some of whom wrote sentimental and domestic novels that acclaimed Christian virtue. In some of these novels, a young girl is deprived of the family assistance she had depended on to sustain her throughout her life. The popular success of white women in depicting their heroines' necessity of making their own way in the world despite injustice provided a ready and fertile context within which black women writers might also place their fair-haired black heroines and dramatize racial protest. For many black women writers embellished the plot line of their white predecessors and contemporaries. They include Amelia Johnson, Sarah Allen, Emma Kelley, Ruth Todd, Marie Burgess Ware, Frances Harper, and J. McHenry Jones. In their work we find that the youth is black and may be male but is more often female. She believes herself to be white, obviously having no knowledge of her African ancestry. This knowledge is withheld so that she can enjoy the privileged life afforded her by her white father. Circumstances lead to his death, and as a result the child and her mother are subjected to the horrors of slavery. Both are abused by cruel slave masters, despite the fact that they are as white and as noble as any one of their former caste and more handsome than most. The child survives and eventually marries well, thereby concluding the tragedy of her plight. This marriage is not only based on love but forms a partnership for continued work in racial advancement and, thus, gives the union a high and noble purpose. But practically every one of these writers has been lost in out-of-print books and periodicals which have long ceased to be available. Their work must be retrieved in order to correct the now longstanding misconception that Phillis Wheatley and Frances Harper were the lone literary women of the eighteenth and nineteenth centuries, who all by themselves brought forth the generation of black women writers of the Harlem Renaissance.

Contending Forces, Hopkins's first and best-known novel, conforms to the basic plot structure I have outlined. The story begins in 1790 on the island of Bermuda, when Charles Montfort decides to move his family to North Carolina to invest in a cotton plantation in order to secure his fortune. All goes as planned until a jealous neighbor, Anson Pollock, suspects that Montfort's beautiful wife, Grace, has black blood. He conspires to kill Montfort, claim Grace as his slave mistress, make her two children—Charles and Jesse—chattel slaves, and steal a portion of Montfort's estate. The conspiracy is successful, and after Montfort's murder, Grace commits suicide in order to escape her fate. Charles is sold to an Englishman who subsequently frees him and takes him to England, while Jesse suffers under the abuse of Pollock, until he manages to escape to New England. He eventually marries the daughter of his black benefactor and fathers a large family in Exeter, Massachusetts. These events comprise the background for the novel's central story, which concerns Jesse's grandchildren, Will and Dora Smith.

The central story is set in Boston. Will Smith is a philosophy student at Harvard College, and Dora assists her mother in running the family-owned rooming house. Among the roomers are Sappho Clark and John Langley. Will falls in love with Sappho, a beautiful, virtually white young woman with a mysterious, southern past. John Langley, who is engaged to Dora, also falls in love with Sappho, but his intentions are not honorable. He plots to force Sappho into becoming his mistress, while planning to marry Dora. Sappho escapes Langley, but in so doing she must abandon her lover Will. She leaves behind a letter for him, explaining Langley's intentions as well as her mysterious and tragic past. Will shares this information with Dora, who immediately breaks off her engagement to Langley. Will then tries to find Sappho, but she has left without a trace. In an effort to heal his broken heart, Will goes abroad to continue his studies after graduating from Harvard. Dora eventually marries her former childhood friend, Dr. Arthur Lewis, who is the head of a large industrial school for Negroes in Louisiana. The newlyweds move to Louisiana, and while Will is paying them a visit, he unexpectedly finds Sappho. They are united in marriage a few weeks later on Easter Sunday. Thus, the virtuous are rewarded with happy marriages, made even more fulfilling because of their commitments to racial progress, while the villainous John Langley dies in a mining accident, after having repented much too late for his "sins."

Hopkins's characters conform, as we would expect, to nineteenth-century conventions in that their inner virtues are reflected in their outward appearances. Dora Smith is described as an "energetic little Yankee girl" (p. 114) with a "delicate brown face" and "smooth bands of dark-brown hair" (p. 80). Will Smith, Hopkins's DuBois-like hero, is "tall and finely formed, with features almost perfectly chiseled, and a complexion the color of an almond shell. His hair is black and curly, with just a tinge of crispness to denote the existence of Negro blood" (p. 90). John Langley, on the other hand, is "shorter in stature and very fair in complexion. His hair is dark and has no indication of Negro blood in its waves; his features are of the Caucasian cut. . . . [But] . . . the strong manhood and honesty of purpose which existed in Will Smith are lacking in John Langley. He was a North Carolinian—descendant of slaves and Southern 'cracker' blood" (p. 90). Hopkins accounted for Langley's ignoble character as an inherent result of his poor ancestry, and in so doing, she further qualified the nineteenth-century notion that the mulatto was a degenerate by making degeneration the result not of miscegenation in and of itself but of poor-quality white blood.

When we turn our attention to the beautiful Sappho Clark, we find that her appearance conforms more readily to that of the mulatto heroine: "Tall and frail, with hair of a golden cast, aquiline nose, rosebud mouth, soft brown eyes veiled by long, dark lashes" (p. 107). Although Sappho is fair enough to pass into the white world and secure herself a rich, handsome, white husband, she chooses instead to unite her plight to that of her black brethren. Her most important role, however, is not that of the "tragic mulatto" but that of Hopkins's spokeswoman for the political rights of black Americans. When her argument is combined with Will's contention that "No Negro college . . . ought to bestow a diploma upon a man who had not been thoroughly grounded in the rudiments of moral and natural philosophy, physiology, and economy" (pp. 167–68), we have their combined social program for the advancement of the Negro. Their program is a fictionalized version of DuBois's position in the DuBois-Washington controversy. Washington, his opponent, argued for industrial education for the Negro and believed that this program could be best accomplished by not antagonizing whites over the black vote. Hopkins dramatized Washington's position through the character of Dora's admirer, Dr. Arthur Lewis. Whereas the real-life controversy was never resolved, Hopkins resolved her fictionalized version quite easily by joining the two programs in marriages at the novel's conclusion. As a consequence, we find that the Lewises promote industrial education for the Negro, while their in-laws, the Smiths, promote liberal, academic education for the Negro and agitate for his political rights as well.

It is not surprising to find that Hopkins, being both black and female, complemented her racial argument with her concern for women's issues. In the chapter entitled "The Sewing Circle," Hopkins characterized a "race woman" by the name of Mrs. Willis who is a proponent for the "evolution of true womanhood in the work of the 'Woman Question' as embodied in marriage and suffrage" (p. 146). Hopkins, through this spokeswoman, contends that women should chart their advance within the domain of marriage and with the assistance of the vote. Mrs. Willis further says that "the advancement of the colored woman should be the new problem in the woman question" (p. 147), and in order to pursue this inquiry she supports "the formation of clubs of colored women banded together for charity, for study, and for every reason under God's glorious heavens that can better the condition of mankind" (p. 147).

The advancement of the black woman was certainly an area of concern at the time of the publication of *Contending Forces*. No doubt the women's clubs which were chartered in the late nineteenth century provided stimulation for the black women's development,[19] although Hopkins had little more than tentative programs to propose, theories to assert, and positions to state. But she did have her spokeswoman, Mrs. Willis, insist that women construct their advancement on virtue and duty within the domain of marriage and with the responsibility of the vote. In addition, Hopkins had Mrs. Willis further reiterate an underlying theme of the entire novel, namely that blacks and women, especially, must be on constant guard to subdue the growth of any passion: "Enthusiasm for any one object or duty may become a passion. I believe that in some degree passion may be beneficial, but we must guard ourselves against a sinful growth of any appetite" (p. 154). Therefore, if we view *Contending Forces* as Hopkins's dramatized expression of a tentative program for the advancement of black Americans in general and black American women in particular, we can surmise that black men and women must be responsible for the course of their own advancement and that duty, virtue, carefully controlled emotions, the institution of marriage, and the vote are the key components for directing social progress and achieving results.

The first serialized installment of Hopkins's second novel—*Winoma: A Tale of Negro Life in the South and Southwest*—appeared in the May 1902 issue of *The Colored American*, and the final installment was published in the October 1902 issue of the same periodical.[20] Like *Contending Forces*, *Winoma* conforms to the basic plot structure I have described. In 1849 an unknown white man joins the Indian tribes around Buffalo, New York, and eventually becomes their chief, taking the name of White Eagle. Buffalo is the last and, therefore, most important stop in the underground railroad, and as a result many fugitive slaves arrive there in pursuit of freedom. One such fugitive is a mulatto slave woman whom White Eagle marries and who dies shortly after the birth of their daughter, Winoma. Another fugitive slave woman also dies shortly thereafter, leaving her small son, Judah, in White Eagle's care. The children grow up as brother and sister, totally unaware of their racial origin; in fact, they believe themselves to be Indians. They spend their days fully enjoying the adventures afforded by the forest, but they also heed the importance of securing a public-school education. In 1855 Warren Maxwell, an Englishman, comes to America in search of the heir to the Carlingford estate. On the first night of Maxwell's arrival, White Eagle is murdered by an unknown assailant. Maxwell learns of his death from Winoma and Judah, to whom he immediately becomes attached, so much so that he plans to take them to England with him. But before they can leave, Maxwell has to complete his search, which will take him to another location. When he returns to make arrangements for their trip, he finds that the children have been claimed as chattel slaves by their mothers' owners under the Fugitive Slave Act of 1850 and subsequently have been taken to Missouri.

Two years later Maxwell, still searching for the missing Carlingford heir, visits Colonel Titus's plantation in Missouri, where he finds Winoma and Judah in bondage. They plan an escape, and while Maxwell is awaiting their arrival, he meets Maybee, a friend, who is on his way to Kansas to join John Brown and his militia. When Winoma and Judah arrive, they are taken to Brown's camp and left in his care. The next night Maxwell is taken prisoner by Thomson, who was White Eagle's murderer. Thomson subsequently tries Maxwell for inciting slave escapes and ultimately sentences him to be hanged. While he awaits his fate, Brown's men discover his whereabouts and he is rescued. The story comes to a quick conclusion when Maxwell learns that White Eagle was the missing Carlingford heir. As a result Winoma and Judah, who are now both young adults, inherit his legacy. By this time, as we might have expected, Maxwell has fallen deeply in love with Winoma and she with him. They return to England, a nation which Hopkins described as being beyond American caste prejudice, and they are married. Judah, who also accompanies them to England, is eventually knighted by the Queen. He grows prosperous and marries a woman from an old English family. Thus, the story concludes with both couples thriving in domestic bliss.

The structure of this novel conforms to basic conventions. But *Winoma* is even more sensational than *Contending Forces* in that there are more incredible coincidences, swashbuckling adventures, and exaggerated heroic descriptions, all held together with a very sentimental love story. Winoma's appearance, as we might expect, conforms to the tragic mulatto mold: "Her wide brow, about which the hair clustered in dark rings, the beautifully chiselled features, the olive complexion with a hint of pink" (p. 31). And her hero, Maxwell, is equally as handsome, though fair: ". . .a slender, well-knit figure with a bright, handsome face, blue eyes and a mobile mouth slightly touched with down on his upper lip" (p. 33). The virtuous pair are rewarded with prosperity and happiness, while the villain suffers a painful death.

Hopkins placed this novel into the genre of the fugitive slave story and identified her protest as that against the arbitrary segregation and subjection of black Americans:

> Many strange tales of romantic happenings in this mixed community of Anglo-Saxons, Indians and Negroes might be told similar to the one I am about to relate, and the world stand aghast and may try to find the dividing line supposed to be a natural barrier between the whites and the dark-skinned race. (p. 29)

Thus, as is the case with *Contending Forces*, the central issue of *Winoma* is its protest against racial injustice, but unlike *Contending Forces*, *Winoma* outlines no program of social reform other than that offered by escape. Whereas escape offered a possible resolution to the slave's dilemma prior to 1864, Hopkins's contemporary scene of 1901 afforded virtually no ostensible reason for her to write an abolitionist novel. Perhaps she wrote the novel as an exercise in nostalgia, intended to arouse sympathy for oppressed black Americans. There was, however, more than sufficient reason to condemn the practices of employment and housing discrimination, separate public accommodations, mob violence, and lynching, as she had done in *Contending Forces*. Whereas her first novel was very sensitive to the racial issues of 1900 and consequently addressed each of them, *Winoma* seems to be essentially an escapist, melodramatic romance in which Hopkins used sentimental love as a means for supporting an appeal for racial justice. Though, granted, Hopkins does dramatize the fact that being black in America means being subjected to racial abuse, she offers little hope to those who cannot escape like Winoma and Jude.

Women's issues, which were central to the argument of *Contending Forces*, have been abandoned entirely in *Winoma*. Although marriage is depicted as woman's ambition in both *Contending Forces* and *Winoma*, in the latter novel a woman's role is seen exclusively as finding a suitable husband and tending to his needs. Love is translated singularly into duty, and duty finds expression only on the domestic front. We do not see women, like Mrs. Willis of *Contending Forces*, who are their husbands' helpmates in the struggle for racial advancement. On the contrary, marriage offers women its own blissful escape in *Winoma*, and marital love is portrayed as the balm which soothes their worldly wounds. When we turn our attention to the subject of the advancement of black women, we find no discussion of this topic at all. Although Hopkins was, nevertheless, a product of the nineteenth century's rising consciousness of women's concerns, it is surprising to find that this issue appears so inconsistently in her work.

The change in argument and setting in *Winoma* may be a signal for

Hopkins's own growing frustration with the effort to improve both the American racial climate and the quality of life for black American women. In 1899, when *Contending Forces* was written, Hopkins's argument concerned the advancement of black Americans in general and black American women in particular. In 1901, when *Winoma* was written, her argument seems to focus on escape. Whereas escape is an incident of plot in *Winoma* and love is, likewise, translated into domestic duty, both the themes of escape and love evolve into even more limited contexts in Hopkins's third novel, *Of One Blood, or the Hidden Self*, published in 1902/03. Here, the effort to escape becomes total and comprehensive, as the story moves beyond the American social scene to a mysterious Atlantis-like region of an underground city in Africa. And love is translated into racial imperatives on one hand and perversion on the other. Thus, instead of finding urgent social problems dramatized in a somewhat realistic fictional setting, we find the remote landscape of science fiction. Although it can be argued that much of this genre provides critical observations and predictions about the real world, in Hopkins's case, however, her science fiction novel seems almost entirely gratuitous. *Of One Blood* is, nonetheless, an extremely intriguing, imaginative, and provocative novel.

The first serialized installment of *Of One Blood, or the Hidden Self* appeared in the November 1902 issue of *The Colored American*, and the conclusion appeared in the September 1903 issue of the same periodical.[21] *Of One Blood* is set in the stimulating climate of early twentieth-century scientific discoveries. William James and Sigmund Freud were advancing theories about the nature of the subconscious, while archaeological finds in Egypt were uncovering modern man's racial and cultural history. In this setting we find Reuel Briggs, a young black medical student who is particularly interested in mysticism and the powers of the subconscious mind. The story begins on one evening when he sees the face of a beautiful woman, whom he cannot seem to forget. A few days later, he attends a Negro concert with his best friend, Aubrey Livingston, and who should appear but the beautiful woman, singing a haunting melody. In this manner her racial identity is uncovered. Soon thereafter, Briggs is called upon to assist the victims of a railroad accident at a local hospital, and who should he find but this same young woman, who is presumed dead but who is actually in a catatonic sleep. Briggs succeeds in restoring her consciousness, although she can remember nothing of her past life. As we would expect, Briggs falls in love with the woman, whose name we learn is Dianthe Lusk. He marries her, but his financial situation is so strained that he decides to postpone its consummation until he can secure his fortune and make a name for himself as a member of an archaeological expedition headed to Meröe, Ethiopia. He leaves her care entrusted to his friend Livingston. But soon after Briggs's departure, Livingston expresses his passionate love for Dianthe, who finds that she is unable to resist the mysterious power he has over her. He plans to take her away, but he must first rid himself of his fiancee, Molly Vance. He conspires to arrange a boating accident in which Molly is drowned. He and Dianthe are presumed dead, although their bodies are never found.

Meanwhile the expedition arrives in Ethiopia, and Briggs is very uneasy because he has not heard from Dianthe. His concern grows to the point that he experiences a clairvoyant trance of the boating accident. As a result, Briggs is brokenhearted, and he becomes seriously ill. When his strength returns, he wanders into a mysterious pyramid in the hope that a man-eating beast may release him from his grief. While exploring the pyramid, he loses consciousness, and when he awakens he finds himself in a mysterious underground city. The populace proclaim him as their long-awaited monarch, King Ergamenes, and he is subsequently betrothed to Queen Candace. Together they are to bring forth a long line of monarchs who will reclaim Ethiopia's former glory. Despite his new life, Briggs cannot forget Dianthe, and while having another trance, he learns that she is still alive.

Meanwhile, Livingston has married Dianthe, who is distraught when she learns that Briggs is not dead, as Livingston has told her. She tries to escape but gets lost in the woods. An old black woman by the name of Aunt Hannah rescues her and immediately recognizes that she is her daughter Mira's child and, therefore, her own granddaughter. Hannah tells Dianthe that Mira was also the mother of Briggs and Livingston; hence, Dianthe learns in the span of a few moments that she, Livingston, and Briggs are all "of one blood" and that she has married not one but both of her brothers. As a result of this knowledge, Dianthe loses her mind and attempts to poison Livingston, but he discovers her plan and makes her drink the poison instead, which she does without regret. When Briggs finally traces the whereabouts of Dianthe and Livingston, he arrives only to find Dianthe dead. Soon afterward, Livingston commits suicide, and Briggs returns to the Hidden City with Aunt Hannah, his grandmother. There he spends the rest of his life with his Queen Candace, doing God's work to prove that "Of one blood has [God made] all races of men" (p. 807).

Like *Contending Forces*, *Of One Blood* has an early twentieth-century setting. No sooner has the story begun than we find the Fisk Jubilee

Singers presenting a concert to a Boston audience, which provides the occasion for Dianthe's introduction. In addition, the startling scientific discoveries in psychology and archaeology of that era provide a launching point for the fantastic events which follow. In fact, the entire intellectual milieu from which the story arises gives Hopkins the opportunity to display the breadth of her knowledge in the arts and the sciences, as if she were using her own writing in a self-conscious attempt to prove that the inherent intellectual capacity of black Americans was equal to that of their Anglo-Saxon counterparts. Moreover, the archaeological expedition is the means by which Hopkins underscores her contention that the biblical references to Ethiopia as a former world power could have been, indeed, factual rather than mythic. In this regard, she spends considerable effort describing Ethiopia's past glory, in addition to arguing her underlying point that there is no scientific basis for the arbitrary separation of the races. Hopkins further contends that knowledge is a serious impediment to racial prejudice, and although readers of today may detect the naiveté of such a position, Hopkins and her contemporaries firmly believed that knowledge would eliminate social injustice of all kinds and improve the quality of human life.

Although most Afro-Americans came from West Africa and not East Africa, this geographical oversight does not offset Hopkins's basic argument that "Afro-Americans are," as she wrote, "a branch of the wonderful and mysterious Ethiopians who had a prehistoric existence of magnificence, the full record of which is lost in obscurity" (p. 342). Hopkins did not appear to be fundamentally concerned with providing a genealogical tree for modern-day American blacks but with presenting broad notions of cultural and racial origins for them specifically and for mankind in general. In this regard, the ambition to retrieve Ethiopia's lost record of glory provides the impetus for the unfolding story and forms the foundation for Hopkins's racial argument.

Hopkins focused most of her attention on dramatizing the racial argument in *Of One Blood*, and as a consequence little emphasis falls on women's issues. There are, however, references to two issues which are related topically to women. The first concerns Queen Candace's physical appearance, and the second concerns Hopkins's mandate that passion must be subjected to reason. Turning our attention first to Candace, we find that, although her name seems peculiarly inappropriate for an Ethiopian queen, her physical portrayal marks a very early appearance of the "brown" heroine in Afro-American fiction. Instead of the conventional olive-skinned heroine, Queen Candace, though she resembles Dianthe, has a "warm bronze complexion; thick black eyebrows and great black eyes" (p. 495). Interestingly enough, she is the means by which pigment is reintroduced into the royal line, inasmuch as Ergamenes (alias Reuel) lost that trait as a result of American miscegenation. Hence, pigment becomes a positive physical attribute measured in terms of feminine beauty more than sixty years prior to the coinage of the slogan "Black is Beautiful." The second issue which finds repeated expression is Hopkins's admonition for restraining passion with reason and for not equating passion to love. This theme consistently appears in all of Hopkins's work, as well as in that of her female contemporaries. Its repeated expression measures the extent of their concern that women avoid being viewed merely as passionate creatures but be seen instead as rational human beings capable of serious thought. Hopkins also makes repeated references to marriage as the proper social domain for both men and women. In this regard, marriage is characterized as the distinctly harmonious setting in which good works abound, and Omnipotence directs good works, in her novels, toward the elimination of caste prejudice and the elevation of racial pride.

Of One Blood brings Hopkins's major themes, which were dramatized in her earliest play to this her last novel, full circle. In each work we find that she habitually insisted that black men and women be responsible for the course of their own advancement and that duty, virtue, carefully controlled emotions, and the institution of marriage are the key components for directing social progress. Her excessively episodic and melodramatic techniques resulted in her failure to meet twentieth-century critical standards; nevertheless, she was a serious writer, who wrote three novels at the turn of the century. This fact, alone, demands that we retrieve her work from obscurity.

Notes

1. Darwin Turner, "Introduction," *The House Behind the Cedars* (New York: Collier-MacMillan, 1969), p. viii.
2. Ibid.
3. Ibid.
4. Both *Winoma* and *Of One Blood* were serialized in *The Colored American Magazine* (Boston: The Colored Cooperative Publishing Company).
5. Published in *New Era Magazine* (Washington, D.C.: New Era Company, 1916).
6. "The Mystery Within Us," *The Colored American*, 1:1 (May 1900), pp. 14–

18; "Talma Gordon," *The Colored American*, 1:5 (October 1900), pp. 271–90; "George Washington, a Christmas Story," *The Colored American* 2:2 (December 1900), pp. 95–104; "A Dash for Liberty," *The Colored American*, 3:4 (August 1901), pp. 243–47; "Bro'r Abr'm Jimson's Wedding, A Christmas Story," *The Colored American* 4:1 (December 1901), pp. 103–112; "As the Lord Lives," *The Colored American* 6:11 (November 1903), pp. 795–801.

7. Ann Allen Shockley, "Pauline Elizabeth Hopkins: A Biographical Excursion into Obscurity," *Phylon* 33:1 (Spring 1972), p. 23. "Slaves' Escape" was later renamed "Peculiar Sam, or the Underground Railroad." There are no records to indicate whether "One Scene" had been produced. There is, however, reference in the *Boston Herald* regarding the performance of the "Slaves' Escape" by the Hopkins's Colored Troubadours at the Oakland Garden in Boston on July 5, 1880.

8. Pauline E. Hopkins, *Contending Forces: A Romance Illustrative of Negro Life North and South* (Carbondale: Southern Illinois University Press, 1978), p. 13; and Pauline E. Hopkins, *Contending Forces* (Boston: The Colored Cooperative Publishing Company, 1899). All future references will appear parenthetically in the text with respect to the most recent edition.

9. Shockley, pp. 22–26.

10. Vernon Loggins, *The Negro Author: His Development in America to 1900* (New York: Columbia University Press, 1931), p. 326.

11. Brown's *Clotel* (1853); Delaney's *Blake or the Huts of America* (1859); Griggs's *Imperium in Imperio* (1899), *The Hindered Hand* (1901), *Overshadowed* (1901), and *Unfettered, a Novel* (1902); and Chesnutt's *The House Behind the Cedars* (1900), *The Marrow of Tradition* (1901), and *The Colonel's Dream* (1905).

12. See Elaine Showalter, *A Literature of Their Own* (Princeton: Princeton University Press, 1977), p. 61.

13. Hugh M. Glouster, *Negro Voices in American Fiction* (Chapel Hill: University of North Carolina Press, 1948), p. 33.

14. Robert A. Bone, *The Negro Novel in America*, rev. ed. (New Haven, Conn.: Yale University Press, 1965), p. 14. His comment is obviously based on Hopkins's own assessment of her intentions, as she expressed them in the preface to *Contending Forces*.

15. Ibid., p. 19.

16. Ibid., p. 26.

17. Judith R. Berzon, *Neither White nor Black: The Mulatto Character in American Fiction* (New York: New York University Press, 1978), p. 202.

18. Ibid.

19. See Emma L. Fields, "The Women's Clubs Movement in the United States 1877–1900." M.A. Thesis, Howard University, 1948.

20. Published in *The Colored American* (May 1902–October 1902).

21. Published in *The Colored American* (November 1902–November 1903). Future references will appear parenthetically in the text.

4

Out of the Woods and into the World: A Study of Interracial Friendships between Women in American Novels

ELIZABETH SCHULTZ

Anyone who has taken an American literature survey course knows that classical American novels do not end in the same way as classical American melodramas. A middle-class prince and princess do not go off into the sunrise of a new society to live happily ever after. Instead, these novels, written by white males, conclude with a male, usually white, going off alone into the wilderness. He carries with him, however, the memory of a dark-skinned companion, for in these novels the friendship between white man and dark man nurtures and sustains them against the vicissitudes of the social, natural, and cosmic worlds. One thinks, of course, of Natty Bumppo and Chingachgook of *The Last of the Mohicans*, Ishmael and Queequeg of *Moby-Dick*, Huck and Jim of *The Adventures of Huckleberry Finn*, Ike McCaslin and Sam Fathers of "The Bear," Jed Tewksbury and the Afro-American swami of *A Place to Come to*, Henderson and Dafu of *Henderson the Rain King*, Randall Patrick McMurphy and Chief Bromden of *One Flew over the Cuckoo's Nest*. The relationship between the two men is idyllic; as

Leslie Fiedler has suggested, it is "a *Pagan* Paradise Regained that Americans have dreamed in the forests of the New World, a natural Eden lost when Christianity intervened—which means when woman intervened."[1] The relationship reflects perhaps the white male's yearning to restore himself to wholeness—if he perceives his dark–skinned brother symbolically or stereotypically as representing intuitive or emotional powers which contrast with his rational powers. Or perhaps the relationship reflects his yearning—and his guilt—to restore his society to wholeness—if, indifferent to sexism, he perceives the loss of the democratic dream as resulting from racism. This proliferation of interracial male friendships in American fiction created by white males—there are no such friendships in fiction created by Afro-American males or by women—is comprehensible if considered as embodying myths central to American culture. But apprised of the paucity of examples of interracial friendships between women in American fiction, we are initially astonished.

Diane K. Lewis points to the fundamental reason for the failure and the scarcity of most friendships between black and white women in American society, a reason realistically reflected in novels by American women, a reason reflected in the reluctance black women have shown to establish black feminist organizations and to affiliate with national feminist organizations:

> White women have not only been given deference. They have also had some access to power and authority. While they themselves lacked authority in the dominant society, they have had a route to power through their kinship and marital ties with men (e.g., fathers, husbands, and sons) who do exercise authority in the public sphere. Moreover, white women, as members of the dominant group, formerly held both considerable authority and power vis-à-vis the subordinate racial group.
>
> The variance in deference and access to power and authority between black and white women have proven to be critical factors underlying the black woman's perception of common group interest with black men and distrust of white women.[2]

Most novels written by American men and women, white as well as black, describe white women as functioning from a position of power in their relationships with black women. In *Uncle Tom's Cabin*, for example, Stowe presents us with a variety of white women—the vicious Marie St. Clare, the self-righteous Miss Ophelia, the condescending and kindly Little Eva, Mrs. Shelby, and Rachel Halliday—all of whom "exercise authority in the public sphere." The black woman generally responds in one of two ways. Again using Stowe's novel as a paradigm, we see that like Eliza Harris, Aunt Chloe, and Mammy, she may respond with gratitude, or like Topsy, Rosa, Dinah, and Cassy, she may respond with deception and defiance. In most American novels the relationship between white women and women of color follows this paradigm of mistress and servant, victimizer and victim, with only an occasional reversal which converts the historical victim to victimizer, the historical victimizer to victim. Novels written by American men almost consistently adhere to this pattern in describing interracial relationships between women.[3] The effect of limiting the relationships between women to a power struggle in these novels is to reduce the women to single-dimensional stereotypes or elevate them to symbols; the effect is to deny them their individuality and their humanity, to make them merely racial and cultural reflections.

To my knowledge, there is no novel by a white American male that veers from this pattern. To my knowledge, among novels written by black American males only James Baldwin's *Another Country* (1963) and Al Young's *Who Is Angelina?* (1975) suggest the possibility of a nurturing, fulfilling, sustaining, interracial relationship between two women. In Baldwin's novel, however, the relationship between a black and a white woman depends upon their relationship to men. Although Baldwin represents these women as individuals, he does not focus on their particular friendship. His focus being the interaction between the male and female characters and between the male characters, he makes the basis of the women's friendship a concern for the well-being of the men in their lives.

Who Is Angelina? seems to stand alone among novels written by men, white or black, which examine the possibility of friendship between black and white women. *Who Is Angelina?*, as its title suggests, tells the story of one woman's search for her identity. Assisting in her search is Margo Tanaka, a southern white woman, who "in many unofficial ways, was blacker in expressing herself than Angelina was or would ever become. Margo had soul, and soul, like blood, went way beyond pop ideas of sisterhood and brotherhood."[4] The color of one's soul—one's capacity for compassion, generosity, humor, wonder—is the basis for the friendship between the two women. Time and society are, however, the context for their friendship, and consequently their relationship is not static. Young forces Angelina to consider Margo in relation to race:

> All this time she'd been knowing Margo, all this time they'd been hanging out together, leaning on one another, and they still had to go

through these changes. The American Racial Problem. Wouldn't they
be better off talking about men or menstrual periods and letting old
blood feuds run their course?[5]

Their conversation rouses anger in the black woman and guilt in the
white woman. But Young lets the moment pass as they both are jarred
beyond "The American Racial Problem" by the death of one of Angelina's neighbors, jarred beyond their private egos. Thus although
he fails to explore fully the racial and sexual implications of the "Problem," Young's allusion to race in the context of the two women's
friendship in a culture which has made myth of interracial male friendships gives his novel the seal of reality and reason for hope.

Novels written by women, perhaps predictably, reflect a wider
spectrum of possible relationships between women. Unlike their male
counterparts in the fiction of white male writers, black and white
women friends in novels by American women are not mythicized.
Nor are they sequestered from society; these friendships are formed
and maintained, not on ocean, river, or prairie, but in kitchen, office,
and classroom.[6] As do the interracial friendships in fiction by white
men, the interracial friendships in the fiction of both black and white
women challenge American racism. In addition, two remarkable
works by black women challenge the double whammy of racism and
sexism. The friendships created by black women novelists differ, however, significantly from those created by white women novelists.

In depicting interracial friendships between two women, several
white women novelists confront the historical pattern based on
power. For example, Ellen Glasgow describes the relationship between white Dorinda Oakley and her black servant, Fluvanna, in her
novel *Barren Ground*:

> Gradually, as the years passed [Dorinda's] human associations nar-
> rowed down to Fluvanna's companionship . . . . The best years of her
> youth, while her beauty resisted hard work and sun and wind, were
> shared only with the coloured woman with whom she lived. She had
> prophesied long ago that Fluvanna would be a comfort to her, and the
> prophecy was completely fulfilled. The affection between the two
> women had outgrown the slender tie of mistress and maid, and had
> become as strong and elastic as the bond that holds relatives together.
> They knew each other's daily lives; they shared the one absorbing in-
> terest in the farm; they trusted each other without discretion and with-
> out reserve. Fluvanna respected and adored her mistress; and Dorinda,
> with an inherited feeling of condescension, was sincerely attached to
> her servant . . . . Sometimes on winter nights when the snow was fall-
> ing or the rain blowing in gusts beyond the window, the two women

would sit for an hour, when work was over, in front of the log fire in Dorinda's room which had once been her mother's chamber. Then they would talk sympathetically of the cows and the hens, and occasionally they would speak of Fluvanna's love affairs and of Dorinda's years in the city.[7]

The strength of this relationship, unusual in its having been created in 1925 by a southern white woman, is undermined, however, by an "inherited feeling of condescension." Although Glasgow seems temporarily to have transcended racism in describing the closeness of Dorinda and Fluvanna, she then reinforces it by resorting to the stereotype of the cheerful, lazy darkie and to the power paradigm of mistress over maid. For example, we read: "In return for Fluvanna's sunny sympathy and her cheerful alacrity, which never faltered, Dorinda had discreetly overlooked an occasional slackening of industry."[8]

Acknowledging the historical power struggle between white mistress and black maid, Carson McCullers and Anita Clay Kornfield in their novels *A Member of the Wedding* (1946) and *In a Bluebird's Eye* (1975) attempt to demolish it as the primary basis for establishing a relationship. As did Twain in *The Adventures of Huckleberry Finn* with his description of Huck and Jim, McCullers and Kornfield describe a white youngster, at odds with family and society, discovering in an older black person a sympathetic sounding board for a developing conscience and consciousness. Given the discrepancy in age, experience, and position between the white girl and the black woman in McCullers's and Kornfield's novels, it is perhaps difficult to postulate a friendship between them. However, if Berenice and Lola occasionally come down to Frankie's and Honor's age by playing at cards or fantasy, they are also, as is Jim, spiritual mentors, and the young Caucasians must reach up to their level. A mutual trust and respect evolves between the girl and the woman as it does between the man and the boy in the course of these novels.

Both Berenice and Lola border on being conventional Mammy figures—all-loving and long-suffering; however, McCullers and Kornfield clearly indicate that they are individuals with distinguishing features of their own and women who have known the agonies and ecstasies of sexual love, knowledge of which they pass on to the young girls. The relationships between the white girl and the black woman are set in the security of kitchens, wombs where discussion and contemplation, laughter and love can occur without interruption. Danger awaits in the rooms, houses, streets, and woods beyond the kitchen. It would thus seem that McCullers and Kornfield have created a situation analogous to that world of the river and the raft which in *Huck*

Finn stands in opposition to the shore and society. However, the effect of making sexual love, with its burden of grief, anger, fear, and loneliness, a subject for discussion in the kitchen is to demythicize the women; the blues permeate the kitchens of McCullers and Kornfield and bind Berenice and Frankie, Lola and Honor. The Duke and the Dauphin may disrupt the harmony of Twain's raft, but death destroys the security of the kitchens. At the conclusion of *The Member of the Wedding*, the precocious little boy, John Henry West, who had been a part of the kitchen community, dies, and at the conclusion of *In a Bluebird's Eye*, Lola herself is dead, shot, ironically, as a black panther while attempting to follow Honor's plan for her escape—a plan resembling Tom Sawyer's "evasion" plan for Jim.

At the conclusion of these novels by white women, the young girls are older and wiser. Frankie with a new name and a girl friend her own age and race and Honor with a new commitment to her family both make preparations to move to new houses in new communities. In contrast to Huck, who prepares to light out for the territory, seeking to recreate the idyllic life of the raft, Frankie and Honor will continue their lives in a violent, racist society. As a result of their friendships with Berenice and Lola, their lives may be enriched by compassion and knowledge; yet the relationships between the black women and the white girls have faded just as did Huck's relationship with Jim.

In their novels—*The Shadow Knows* (1975) and *Listening to Billie* (1978)—Diane Johnson and Alice Adams go further than do McCullers and Kornfield in exploring the difficulties and possibilities of interracial friendship between women. Both insist on their white protagonists' examination of the stereotypes generated by a racist society and their own subsequent position of power. Ensnared in society by various relationships, these adult women attempt to understand themselves particularly through their associations with black women. The fluid society of California provides them with the social milieu in which to know themselves and to shape their lives.

In a world in which she and her children are plagued by random threats and acts of violence, N. Hexam of Johnson's novel takes comfort primarily in her friendship with Evalin Wilson, the black woman who lives with her, caring for her children while she attends graduate school. Impoverished (a recent condition for N.) and deserted by their husbands, these women share a common desperation. Of their relationship, N. remarks: "We do our best here, Ev and I. We are allies, and love a lot of the same things—men and children and pretty clothes. We have to expect reverses sometimes, I guess."[9] Yet N. recognizes that her uncertainties pale by comparison with the realities of Ev's situation; she recognizes that if she detects signs of violence in her life, Ev experiences it; if she knows impermanence, Ev is intimately acquainted with death; she recognizes that the difference in their perceptions is the difference in their races.

However, N.'s affection for Ev and her realistic recognition of the injustices and brutality of her life are balanced by her fear and hatred of Osella, the black woman who cared for her children during her marriage. She acknowledges her racist attitude toward Osella:

> I didn't understand her at all, or didn't try. She was an alien to me, so dark and fat. It was harder for me that Osella was fat than that she was black, although the reverse was true for her, I think she would have said. Her fatness seemed ordinary to her, and to me wondrous. She was like someone reflected in a fun house mirror to inhuman width . . . . She is the color of chamois, "high yaller," with the mild brown eyes of the grain-fed. I notice that whenever I describe Osella or think of her, it is in metaphors of things not people, or of fat animals. It is as if I did not consider her human, this fellow woman with whom I shared my children and my home.[10]

When Ev is murdered, N. confronts not only the fact of death, but also the possibility that, if Osella is the murderer, her act committed out of envy, hatred, and revenge, she herself has roused her to these passions. In the conclusion of *The Shadow Knows*, however, Osella is transformed into a monstrous sex symbol at the hands of a black entrepreneur, more victim than victimizer, and the generally powerless N., realizing that she uses her historical power as a white woman, bargains with this man to prevent Osella's continued harassment of her and her children. Although Johnson's novel on the one hand projects stereotypical representations of black women—Ev, Nubian, beautiful, and battered; Osella, Amazonian, ferocious, and mysterious—on the other hand, Johnson undercuts these stereotypes by shifting their static dimensions—Ev, never subservient, is strengthened by female friendship; Osella is weakened by her female sexuality. In addition, by projecting these stereotypes through her protagonist's eyes, Johnson suggests that they are the fabrication of personal psychological need. So long as N. endorses such stereotypes in the interest of attempting to guarantee her own fragile security, so long will they and the incomprehensible chaos in which she lives endure.

Alice Adams's *Listening to Billie* (1978) establishes a tenuous relationship between Eliza Hamilton Quarles, a white divorcee, sometime secretary, and poet, and Miriam, an eighteen-year-old black file clerk with aspirations to move upward. Eliza's interest in civil rights and voter registration is rejected by Miriam, and Miriam's violent experiences in the ghetto are repulsive to Eliza, but in the tense office situation in which they both work, they are able to discuss trivialities and to laugh. Eliza's feeling for Miriam, which is so protective she thinks of adopting her, must be understood as related to her long-standing idealization of Billie Holiday. Having heard Billie in a night-club at the very moment when she—Eliza—was on the brink of ma-turity, Eliza retains a memory of her performance, her presence, and her songs which pervades her life. The beautiful black singer, whom, intuitively, Eliza knows to have suffered, struggled, and survived, seems to provide the clues which Eliza needs to understand her own life; and Billie seems to be reincarnated in Miriam. But Eliza wonders: "Do I really need an eighteen-year-old black daughter?"[11] and when she is told, " 'You're really nutty about black women. Why don't you try living with one?',"[12] Eliza realizes that she prefers living alone. She listens to Billie less and writes her own poetry more. Miriam simply disappears. Adams seems to imply that patronizing and ideal-izing can form the basis neither for a sound relationship nor for a sound self. Free of the burden of racist stereotypes, Eliza is also free to be herself.

In these novels written by white women, several characteristics shape an interracial friendship. The central character, always a white woman, steps out of her historical position of power to form a friend-ship with a black woman. Her action challenges America's racist so-ciety with its pernicious stereotypes. However, like the interracial friendships between men created by white novelists, the interracial friendships between women created by white women novelists do not actually survive their novel's conclusions. Often the dark-skinned character, who has been a significant agent in the white character's growth, does not himself or herself survive. Thus, as in novels by white men, the friendships in these novels by white women may temporarily sustain both white and black, but, finally, the white char-acter prevails, the black character's life a mere memory.

The brief encounter between white Gertie Nevels and an unnamed black woman in Harriet Arnow's *The Dollmaker* (1954) poignantly ex-presses both the possibility for and the impossibility of interracial friendship. Both women are uprooted, taking their children on a train from the known and rural South to the unknown and urban North. Poor and among strangers, disoriented by their swiftly shifting sit-uation, they should be friends, Arnow suggests. Their racial differ-ences seem insignificant. In the dimly lit limbo of the train, they discover that they share each other's values: love of children and hope for a better life for them, delight in creativity—good soil and well-made objects—and in beauty—song and health; above all they share a self-respect. In a 600-page novel, this is a fleeting meeting, occurring early in the work, finished in two pages. Off the train, the two women never see one another again, and although we can assume that the black woman's expectation for "paradise on earth" is to be eroded as tragically as is Gertie's, we can appreciate the veracity of Arnow's portrayal of their relationship.

The friendship which develops between white Lydia Mansfield and black Renee Peverell-Watson in a more recent novel—Gail Godwin's *A Mother and Two Daughters* (1982)—is also based on shared conditions and values though reflecting a different class. Each woman living independently with a child is determined to chart her own destiny; each is proud of her family, financially well endowed, attractive, and educated, with Godwin reversing the historical power pattern by establishing Renee as Lydia's professor. They discuss children and sex, ideas and goals together; they are "best friends." Although Godwin projects the possibility of an interracial friendship in which racial power plays and stereotypes have no place, she implies finally that, when race does become an issue, the friendship wanes. In the novel's last chapter, we learn that Renee's and Lydia's children marry; however, at the great celebration of this marriage which is attended by all Lydia's family and friends, Renee is conspicuously absent, having determined to become a civil rights lawyer in order to defend herself and her people.

The similarities between women of different races, such as both Arnow and Godwin describe, may demolish racial hierarchies; yet American society has not encouraged interracial friendships. Thus that white women novelists suggest that interracial friendships between women are tenuous at best is perhaps not surprising. Adams's and Johnson's characters do indeed begin to examine the causes of racism in our society, but it seems that not until more white women openly face the racism in themselves can interracial friendships endure.

Women characters in novels by black women come to appreciate one another as individuals, as women, as members of different races or the relationship dissolves. In these novels, the backgrounds and experiences of the women may differ, but their ages and interests are similar. When what Angelina calls "The American Racial Problem" becomes of concern to both friends, it is discussed by them with its social, psychological, and historical scars and wounds acknowledged. Some friendships survive the stress of such discussion with the conclusion of these novels presenting all women with the difficult challenge as well as with the hope of friendship.

Repeatedly in the novels of black women, however, interracial friendships are interrupted by a racial power play on the part of the white woman. Thus Selina Boyce of Paule Marshall's *Brown Girl, Brownstones* (1959), from the time she is a youngster, is described as relishing her visits with the bedridden old white woman, formerly maid in the once elegant brownstone where she is now merely a boarder since Selina's mother's purchase of the house. Selina enjoys the tales Miss Mary tells of a life serene and lovely, and she is appalled at her mother's abhorrence of the filthy old woman. Not until she herself is degraded and demoralized by a white woman can she understand her mother's reaction. As a college student and an accomplished dancer, she becomes the friend of two white women; they discuss classes, parents, boys, futures together. Together they make "a startling trio—Selina, in the black leotard, resembling somewhat a cavalier; Rachel a fabulous sprite and Margaret, her hair catching each passing light, a full blown Wagnerian heroine";[13] together they dance "as if guided by a single will, as if, indeed, they were simply reflections of each other."[14] But confronted with the dehumanizing racial judgments of her friend's mother, Selina feels the sense of reflected similarity shattered; she sees racial reality instead in the mirror:

> . . . when she looked up and saw her reflection in those pale eyes, she knew that the woman saw one thing above all else. Those eyes were a well-lighted mirror in which, for the first time Selina truly saw—with a sharp and shattering clarity—the full meaning of her black skin.[15]

And seeing herself clearly for the first time in the white world, she flees.

The implication of *Tar Baby* (1981), the only one of her novels in which Toni Morrison describes white and black people in sustained interrelationship, is that racial power plays cannot go unchallenged. If the white and black women in *Tar Baby* move toward a friendship in the novel's conclusion, it is because they have confronted head-on the stereotypes and emotions generated by racism. Morrison's plot emanates from the historical power relationship: Margaret Street, young and white, uncultured and lower class, marries an elderly, wealthy businessman and is set over Ondine, the middle-class black housekeeper, who has long maintained order in Mr. Street's estate. Margaret, insecure and lonely in the upper-class world into which she married, believed in the possibility of friendship with Ondine. As she says toward the novel's conclusion: " 'We could have been friends, Ondine. Like at first when I used to come in your kitchen and eat your food and we laughed all the time. Didn't we, Ondine? Didn't we use to laugh and laugh?' "[16] Although we may sympathize

with her situation, Margaret's sense of instant friendship, in its pre-
sumptuousness, represents a psychological abuse paralleling her
physical abuse of her only son. Both actions reflect the terrible transformation of loneliness and insecurity into manifestations of power.
Both actions reflect the way in which a sexist and racist society may
result in a white woman's abusing those weaker than she: a black
woman and a child.

Ondine, by keeping secret her knowledge of Margaret's horrible
deeds, reverses the position of power. As Margaret realizes, the black
woman has been able to hold moral authority over her: " ' . . . you
felt good hating me didn't you? I could be the mean white lady and
you could be the good colored one.' "[17] Through their final conversations, Morrison implies that only after such knowledge as they reveal they have of themselves and each other can there be the possibility of friendship:

> "You have to forgive me . . . Ondine. You have to."
> "You forgive you. Don't ask for more."
> "You know what, Ondine? You know what? I want to be a wonderful,
> wonderful old lady." Margaret laughed a rusty little bark that came
> from a place seldom used. "Ondine? Let's be wonderful old ladies. You
> and me."
> "Huh," said Ondine, but she smiled a little.
> "We're both childless now, Ondine. And we're both stuck here. We
> should be friends. It's not too late."
> Ondine looked out of the window and did not answer.
> "Is it too late, Ondine?"
> "Almost," she said. "Almost."[18]

At the conclusion of *Tar Baby*, the two women are both middle-aged,
both bereft of children, both vulnerable as they confront the terrors
of the known past and the terrors of the unknown future. For them
there can be no flight. Like Brer Rabbit and the Tar Baby, they are
entangled in one another's lives; yet Morrison suggests that knowledge and forgiveness can redeem them, can change bondage to friendship, " 'Almost' " to "Certainly."

In McCullers's and Kornfield's novels, sex is discussed between the
white girls and black women, differentiating the friendships in these
novels by white women from similar friendships in novels by white
men. Sex in these novels, however, can be objectified and generalized
in a blues song, for no competition exists between girl and woman;
sex's historical role in reinforcing the peculiar intensity of American
racism is ignored. In novels by black women the difficulties of a black
and a white woman's achieving friendship are exacerbated by sexual

competition and by the sexual dimension of American racism; they are not ignored. Black Sally Hemings in Barbara Chase-Riboud's novel of the same name (1979) and white Martha Jefferson are the same age, share the same man although one loves him as wife, the other as daughter. In Paris where Sally's life-long affair with Thomas Jefferson begins, Martha becomes for her "a refuge from the masculine world of the ministry and from my powerful lover . . . . I turned to Martha. She was my link with home, with my mother, perhaps the other women. She returned my affection that summer with a warmth we were never to recapture again."[19] The summer friendship between the two women deteriorates, however, when Martha discerns the nature of Sally's bondage to her father. In the final confrontation between them, Sally is triumphant. Not only does she appear only slightly aged, but she also knows and cherishes the truth; vindictive and defensive, Martha deludes herself by continual denial of the fact of her father's and Sally's love for each other. Yet if Sally can think of her victory over Martha—"If the power had been hers, . . . the endurance was mine"—she can also feel the loss of their potential friendship:

> My mistress. Had her life been so much different from mine? Or as happy, for that matter? Slave or free, white or black, women are women and they were indentured to husbands, fathers, brothers, children, in sickness and in health, in death and life, to pain and pregnancy, work exhaustion, grinding solitude, and waiting.[20]

The relationship between Meridian Hill and Lynne Rabinowitz in Alice Walker's *Meridian* (1976) begins because of their mutual commitment to the Civil Rights Movement, intensifies because of their mutual commitment to black movement worker Truman Held, and becomes a friendship because they are able to transcend the racist and sexist stereotypes imposed upon them. Their recognition of themselves and of each other as anguished, erring, struggling human beings comes slowly. That this recognition occurs with racial and sexual stereotypes confronted and demolished so that love does credibly prevail is testimony to the power of Walker's artistry.

From the perspective of conventional American norms, both Meridian and Lynne would be called deviants, Meridian for her mysticism, Lynne for her intellectualism, both for their courage in attempting to alter entrenched social patterns. Yet, both women are victimized by the patterns they attempt to alter. Both allow themselves to be abused by Truman. Meridian allows him to take his sexual pleasure, and Lynne allows him to put her on a pedestal, each therefore playing out traditional roles for black and white women. Each, realizing Truman's failure to love, immerses herself in her love of a small child. When the children die, Walker seems to imply that the child in each woman also dies, and each must turn to loving herself, skin color and all. Each must also turn to loving the other woman.

Meridian has always carried with her an image of black women as adventurers: they were, to her mind, "always imitating Harriet Tubman—escaping to become something unheard of. Outrageous."[21] By comparison, she categorizes white women as "frivolous, helpless creatures, lazy and without ingenuity," and in line with her grandmother's opinions, "1. She had never known a white woman she liked after the age of twelve. 2. White women were useless except as baby machines which would continue to produce little white people who would grow up to oppress her. 3. Without servants all of them would live in pigsties."[22] But before Meridian can overcome her antipathy toward white women, she must acknowledge and nurture the outrageous in herself. Developing the courage to chastise Truman for his abuse of both herself and Lynne, she does. Developing the courage to forgive them both, she does. And finally developing the courage—or call it love—to sacrifice her life for a vision of social change, Meridian becomes, in Walker's terms, absolutely outrageous. Lynne, ill at ease on her pedestal, descends by reaction. First she becomes the fallen woman, i.e., a white whore who will sleep with any black man; then, she becomes convinced of her own inferiority as a pale-face unable to compete with Meridian, with "the voluptuous . . . bodies" of black women, "heaving, pulsating, fecund"[23] whom Truman makes the subject of his paintings. Following the brutal death of hers and Truman's six-year-old daughter, Lynne, grieving, sends for Meridian. Together in the chapter entitled "Two Women" they spend their days:

> Meridian would sometimes, in the afternoons, read poems to Lynne by Margaret Walker, and Lynne, in return, would attempt to cornrow Meridian's patchy short hair, they hungered after more intricate and enduring patterns. Sometimes they talked, intimately, like sisters, and when they did not they allowed the television to fill the silences.[24]

Together they do find a more intricate and enduring pattern; as they watch a young black man's face on television, a common vision of hope for the South, for the United States, for humanity comes to them:

> Still, the face got to them. It was the kind of face they had seen only in the South. A face in which the fever of suffering had left an immense

warmth, and the heat of pain had lighted a candle behind the eyes. It sought to understand, to encompass everything, and the struggle to live honorably and understand everything at the same time, to allow for every inconsistency in nature, every weird possibility and personality, had given it a weary serenity that was so entrenched and stable it could be mistaken for stupidity. It made them want to love. It made them want to weep. It made them want to cry out to the young man to run away, or at least to warn him about how deeply he would be hurt. It made them homesick.[25]

In the following chapter, entitled "Lynne," Lynne reaches a sense of her own selfhood; her final conversations with Meridian make clear that she has come to accept her own origins, her white skin, and her Jewish heritage:

"Black folks aren't so special," she said. "I hate to admit it, but they're not."

"Maybe," said Meridian, as if she had been wide awake all along, "the time for being special has passed. Jews are fighting for Israel with one hand stuck in a crack in the Wailing Wall. Look at it this way, black folks and Jews held out as long as they could." Meridian rubbed her eyes.

"Good God, this is depressing," said Lynne. "It's even more depressing than knowing I want Truman back."

"That *is* depressing," said Meridian.

" . . . No, Truman isn't much, but he's *instructional*," said Lynne. "Besides," she continued, "nobody's perfect."

"Except white women," said Meridian, and winked.

"Yes," said Lynne, "but their time will come."[26]

As Barbara Christian has commented, Meridian and Lynne do indeed become sisters in these final scenes, united in an awareness of their own and of Truman's imperfections, united in their forgiveness of him, united in their humor and their hopes.[27]

In *The Black Woman* (1970), Toni Cade asks, "How relevant are the truths, the experiences, the findings of White women to Black women? I don't know that our priorities are the same, that our concerns and methods are the same."[28] With the growth of the black middle class and of black women's involvement in the feminist movement,[29] certain black women novelists have recognized, like white novelists Arnow, Adams, Johnson, and Godwin, that friendship may indeed be based on shared priorities. Although neither Allison Mills's *Francisco* (1974) nor Ann Allen Shockley's *Loving Her* (1974) protests racism or explores the racial dimension of the interracial friendship, each of these novels reflects the destructive potential of sexism to a friendship.

The basis for the friendship between the black narrator and "chris," her white friend, in Mills's novel is a shared class; in Shockley's novel the basis for the friendship between black Renay and white Terry is a sexual love. Mills's story concerns a young black woman who travels with the jet set; her friends are French, Swedish, American; poets, designers, filmmakers; hers and chris's interests are their clothes and boyfriends. The relationship between the two women is casual and assured although the conclusion of Mills's novel suggests that her heroine must emancipate herself from the values which her friendship with chris reinforces if she is to find her own integrity. Shockley's story focuses on the problems of a lesbian relationship in a homophobic society. Black Renay, wife of a brutal and deceptive man, mother of a beautiful daughter, and a talented musician, turns with joy from the violence and limitations of her marriage to the sanctity and beauty of a life with white Terry, rich, respected, a well-known writer. The difficulties that arise between them reflect the struggles of two lovers, and although Shockley protests vigorously the anti-lesbianism of Afro-American culture, the love that the two women have for each other is devoid of racial overtones. At the conclusion of *Loving Her*, Renay and Terry are settled in Terry's luxurious woodland retreat, their secluded existence known only to two gay white men and an elderly white woman, intelligent and liberal; only in this story of a friendship turned to love between a white and a black woman does an interracial relationship in a novel by a black woman take on some of the idealized qualities of the relationship between a white man and a dark-skinned man. However, the wedded bliss which Twain implies Huck and Jim have achieved on their raft is interrupted by violence and betrayal ten chapters before the novel's conclusion whereas Shockley implies at the end of her novel that the perfect world which Renay and Terry have won will be sustained.

Alice Childress posits another idealized friendship between a black and a white woman in *A Short Walk* (1979). The friendship between black Cora Green and white May Palmas happens simply and spontaneously because of the proximity of their apartments and because of the respect each has for the other. Cora says, "May is my first close friend-girl of any race—my closest friend since Papa died. Like him, she also knows how to look at matters and trace meanings and feelings down to the core."[30] Married to a Filipino and consequently ostracized by her mother, May is familiar with the pain caused by racial prejudice and counts on love, as she tells Cora, to conquer all. However as no racial tension exists between the two women, race is not a subject for discussion between them. Always supportive of each other, May sees Cora through her decision against abortion and through childbirth, and Cora sees May through suicide and loneliness when her husband is jailed. They struggle together against their common poverty, and they take a common delight in food and music. Through the repeated exchange of gifts, Childress suggests that their friendship is ritualistically sealed forever. Although Childress confronts racist and sexist dilemmas in describing Cora's relationship with other characters in *A Short Walk*, the friendship between Cora and May, which continues until the end of Cora's life, in its lack of conflict and growth, might seem an unrealizable model. Yet in her representation of May's apartment as a meeting place for the countries and races of the world and of Cora's parties as a center for people from all walks of life, all classes, and all sexual preferences, Childress seems to be emphatically suggesting that it is possible for human beings to accept their national, sexual, individual, and racial differences and to live together with peace and pleasure. The central theme of Childress's novel seems to be expressed in Cora's explanation of the basis of her friendship with May, " ' . . . she's my friend. I love her for good and sufficient reason. It's not ever easy, but I try to accept people just as they come wrapped . . . . I treat white folks according to how they act, not by how they look.' "[31]

Like the novels written by white males which describe an interracial male friendship, the majority of those written by white and black women describing an interracial female friendship oppose American racism. Only *Who Is Angelina?*, *Tar Baby*, *Meridian*, *Francisco*, *Loving Her*, and *A Short Walk*, all novels by black Americans, suggest that a friendship between a black and a white woman can last through time. Only *Tar Baby* and *Meridian* establish the open confrontation of racial stereotypes as the necessary basis for an interracial friendship. Perceived stereotypically, the women in *Tar Baby* and *Meridian* do not respond stereotypically; they make apparent that when the effects of racism and sexism can be identified and acknowledged, then forgiveness is possible, then hope is possible, for then change is possible. For this hope we must applaud two proud black women, two great artists: Alice Walker and Toni Morrison. Unafraid to explore the psychological wilderness of racism, sexism, and humanity, they have created in their fiction models of interracial friendships that endure, not in memory, but in reality; not in fantasy, but in our common lives.

In discussing the necessity of including both black and white women writers in our American literature curriculum, Mary Helen

Washington answers Toni Cade's earlier question by insisting upon the priorities of shared experience:

> I will never again divide a course outline and curriculum along racial lines so that the controlling purpose is to compare the responses of white women and black women, . . . I do not want to see black women in opposition to white women as though that division is primary, universal, absolute, immutable, or even relevant. It makes students think that integration is like having so many crayons of each color in your crayon box . . . . [The literature of black women] cannot be dismissed by such token language as "the literature of the oppressed." These are American lives, these are American sons and daughters, this is the literature of America.[32]

Yet Washington's assertions, like the friendships in *Francisco* and *Loving Her*, *Who Is Angelina?* and *A Short Walk* might seem merely sanguine. Audre Lorde, however, reminds us in her "Open Letter to Mary Daly" that black and white women must struggle, openly and painfully, as Ondine and Margaret, Meridian and Lynne have done, to appreciate the differences as well as the similarities in our common lives:

> The history of white women who are unable to hear black women's words, or to maintain dialogue with us is long and discouraging. But for me to assume that you will not hear me represents not only history, but an old pattern of relating, sometimes protective and sometimes dysfunctional, which we, as women shaping our future, are in the process of shattering. I hope. I believe in your good faith toward all women, in your vision of a future within which we can all flourish, and in your commitment to the hard and often painful work necessary to effect change. In this spirit I invite you to a joint clarification of some of the differences which lie between us as a black and a white woman.[33]

Notes

1. Leslie Fiedler, *Return of the Vanishing American* (New York: Stein and Day, 1969), pp. 115–16.

2. Diane K. Lewis, "A Response to Inequality: Black Women, Racism, and Sexism in *Issues in Feminism: A First Course in Women's Studies*, ed. Sheila Ruth (Boston: Houghton Mifflin Co., 1980), p. 530.

3. Examples of novels, in addition to *Uncle Tom's Cabin*, that reinforce the

historical, racist pattern of placing white women in positions of power over black women are as follows: by white men—William Faulkner's *The Sound and the Fury* (1929), Robert Penn Warren's *Meet Me in the Green Glen* (1971); by black men—Langston Hughes's *Not Without Laughter* (1930), Calvin Hernton's *Scarecrow* (1974); by white women—Margaret Mitchell's *Gone with the Wind* (1936), Willa Cather's *Sapphira and the Slave Girl* (1940); by black women— Sara Wright's *This Child's Gonna Live* (1969), Toni Morrison's *The Bluest Eye* (1970).

4. Al Young, *Who Is Angelina?* (New York: Holt, Rinehart & Winston, 1975), p. 26.

5. Ibid., pp. 261–62.

6. Writing about fiction written by white women in the nineteenth century, Nina Baym asserts that

They told stories about the emergent self negotiating amidst social possibilities, attempting to assert and maintain a territory within a social space full of warring claims. The process was fatiguing and frustrating, but none of these authors proposed the Huck Finn solution of abandoning "sivilization" because none of them could imagine the concept of self apart from society. If critics ever permit the woman's novel to join the main body of "American literature," then all our theories about American fiction, from Richard Chase's "romance" to Richard Poirer's "world elsewhere" to Carolyn Heilbrun's "masculine wilderness" will have to be radically revised.

In *Woman's Fiction: A Guide to Novels by and about Women in America, 1820–1870* (Ithaca: Cornell University Press, 1978), pp. 36–37.

7. Ellen Glasgow, *Barren Ground* (Garden City: Grosset & Dunlap, 1925), pp. 339–40.

8. Ibid., p. 455.

9. Diane Johnson, *The Shadow Knows* (New York: Pocket Books, 1976), p. 14.

10. Ibid., p. 43.

11. Alice Adams, *Listening to Billie* (New York: Alfred A. Knopf, 1978), p. 47.

12. Ibid., p. 175.

13. Paule Marshall, *Brown Girl, Brownstones* (New York: Avon Books, 1970), p. 233.

14. Ibid., pp. 231–32.

15. Ibid., pp. 238–39.

16. Toni Morrison, *Tar Baby* (New York: Alfred A. Knopf, 1981), p. 240.

17. Ibid.

18. Ibid., p. 241.

19. Barbara Chase-Riboud, *Sally Hemings* (New York: Avon Books, 1980), p. 132.

20. Ibid., p. 381.

21. Alice Walker, *Meridian* (New York: Harcourt, Brace, Jovanovich, 1976), p. 105.

22. Ibid., pp. 104–106.

23. Ibid., p. 170.

24. Ibid., p. 176.
25. Ibid., pp. 176–77.
26. Ibid., 185.
27. Barbara Christian, *Black Women Novelists: The Development of a Tradition, 1892–1976* (Westport, Conn.: Greenwood Press, 1980), pp. 231–32.
28. Toni Cade, *The Black Woman* (New York: New American Library, 1970), p. 9.
29. Diane K. Lewis discusses the growing participation of black women in the wider society, pp. 544–45.
30. Alice Childress, *A Short Walk* (New York: Coward, McCann & Geoghegan, Inc., 1979), p. 158.
31. Ibid., p. 294.
32. Mary Helen Washington,"How Racial Differences Helped Us Discover Our Sameness," *Ms.* (September 1981), p. 76.
33. Audre Lorde, "An Open Letter to Mary Daly," in *This Bridge Called My Back: Writings by Radical Women of Color*, ed. Cherríe Moraga and Gloria Anzaldúa (Watertown, Mass.: Persephone Press, 1981), p. 94.

5

The Neglected Dimension of Jessie Redmon Fauset

DEBORAH E. MCDOWELL

Jessie Fauset's novels are generally read as novels of manners of the black middle class, the refined intelligentsia, written to emphasize that, except for the biological accident of color, blacks are no different from whites and should therefore enjoy all the rights and privileges that whites enjoy. Robert Bone, for example, whose work on the black novel has influenced a number of critics, groups Fauset with the writers he classifies as "the Rear Guard" or "those who lagged behind," seeking a "middle ground between the established traditions of the Negro novel and the radical innovations of the Harlem School," or those black writers who "turned to the folk for their major characters and a low-life milieu for their principal setting."[1] Unlike the Harlem School, the members of the Rear Guard drew their source material from the Negro middle class in their efforts "to orient Negro art toward white opinion," and "to apprise educated whites of the existence of respectable Negroes."[2] Bone charges that Fauset is the foremost member of the Rear Guard, maintaining that her emphasis on the black middle class results in novels that are "uniformly sophomoric, trivial, and dull."[3] Other critics have followed Bone's misguided lead in their cavalier dismissal of Fauset's work on the basis of the characters she chose to depict. David Littlejohn likewise makes short shrift of her work, likening her novels to "vapidly genteel lace curtain romances," none of which "rises above the stuffy, tiny-minded circu-

This essay originally appeared in *Afro-Americans in New York Life and History* 5 (July 1981), pp. 33–49.

lating—library norm."[4] Finally, Addison Gayle accuses Fauset of sacrificing racial uniqueness and individuality for "American standardization," and surrendering "black cultural artifacts in an attempt to become American . . . ."[5] Bone, Littlejohn, and Gayle, in three of the most popular and simultaneously distorted, partisan and inaccurate critical works on Afro-American literature, have consigned Fauset's work to a very narrow groove and have failed to probe beneath its surface realities. In their disproportionate emphasis on her literary traditionalism, for example, they draw hasty and not totally accurate conclusions about her fictional intentions. To be sure, she was traditional to some extent, both in form and content, but as Gary de Cordova Wintz rightly observes, "in spite of her conservative, almost Victorian literary habits," Fauset "introduced several subjects into her novels that were hardly typical drawing room conversation topics in the mid-1920s. Promiscuity, exploitative sexual affairs, miscegenation, even incest appear in her novels. In fact prim and proper Jessie Fauset included a far greater range of sexual activity than did most of DuBois's debauched tenth.[6]

When attention is given Fauset's introduction of these challenging themes, it becomes possible to regard her "novels of manners" less as an indication of her literary "backwardness" and more as a self-conscious artistic stratagem pressed to the service of her central fictional preoccupations. Since many of Fauset's concerns were unpalatable to the average reader of her day and hence unmarketable in the publishing arena, the convention of the novel of manners can be seen as protective mimicry,[7] a kind of deflecting mask for her more challenging concerns.[8] Fauset uses classic fairy tale patterns and nursery rhymes in a similar fashion; however, although these stratagems are consciously employed, they are often clumsily executed.

In addition to the protective coloration which the conventional medium afforded, the novel of manners suited Fauset's works in that the tradition "is primarily concerned with social conventions as they impinge upon character."[9] Both social convention and character—particularly the black female character—jointly form the nucleus of Fauset's literary concerns. The protagonists of all of her novels are black women, and she makes clear in each novel that social conventions have not sided well with them but, rather, have been antagonistic.

Without polemicizing, Fauset examines that antagonism, criticizing the American society which has institutionalized prejudice, safeguarded it by law and public attitude, and in general, denied the freedom of development, the right to well-being, and the pursuit of happiness to the black woman. In short, Fauset explores the black woman's struggle for democratic ideals in a society whose sexist conventions assiduously work to thwart that struggle. Critics have usually ignored this important theme[10] which even a cursory reading of her novels reveals. This concern with exploring female consciousness and exposing the unduly limited possibilities for female development is, in a loose sense, feminist in impulse, placing Fauset squarely among the early black feminists in Afro-American literary history.[11] It is this neglected dimension of Fauset's work—her examination of the myriad shadings of sexism and how they impinge upon female development—that is the focus of this discussion. A curious problem in Fauset's treatment of feminist issues, however, is her patent ambivalence. She is alternately forthright and cagey, alternately "radical" and conservative on the "woman question." On the one hand, she appeals for women's right to challenge socially sanctioned modes of feminine behavior, but on the other, she frequently retreats to the safety of traditional attitudes about women in traditional roles. At best, then, we can grant that Fauset was a quiet rebel, a pioneer black literary feminist, and that her characters were harbingers of the movement for women's liberation from the constrictions of cultural conditioning. For the sake of brevity, I will focus on the strains of feminism in one of Fauset's early short stories, "The Sleeper Wakes" (1920), and in her first novel, *There is Confusion* (1924). In both pieces her tendency toward an oblique and ambivalent treatment of feminism is apparent. To demonstrate the extent to which Fauset questioned conventional views of women, it is necessary to quote extensively from the texts of these two works.

"The Sleeper Wakes"[12] is crucial to an understanding of Fauset's concern with female psychology and socially-conditioned female role patterns. In this story Fauset sets the pattern that she will return to, in varying degrees, in each of her novels. She positions her major character in the adolescent stage—a stage of becoming, of maturing—to demonstrate that her possibilities for development and attainment of freedom, well-being, and happiness are sorely limited in range. These limited possibilities are due both to how she perceives herself, based on socialization, as well as to how society perceives her. This early protagonist, like those to follow, aspires to "grow up" and marry, an orthodox female vocation, but she has extremely romantic notions not only about marriage, but also about life and human relationships in general. To dramatize her character's romanticism, Fauset uses patterns and imagery from classic fairy tales.[13]

It is apparent even as early as 1920 that Fauset was aware of how folk literature—particularly fairy tales—serves to initiate the acculturation of children to traditional social roles, expectations, and behaviors, based on their sex. Marcia Lieberman has cogently explored this concept in " 'Some Day My Prince Will Come': Female Acculturation Through the Fairy Tale," where she outlines the fairy tale patterns and demonstrates how they condition women to limited roles and expectations. Lieberman points out that central to the fairy tale is a beautiful girl who is finally rewarded by marriage to a handsome prince. "The beautiful girl does not have to do anything to merit being chosen; she does not have to show pluck, resourcefulness, or wit; she is chosen because she is beautiful."[14] Lieberman adds, "Since the heroines are chosen for their beauty . . . [and] not for anything they do . . . they seem to exist passively until they are seen by the hero, or described to him. They wait, are chosen, and are rewarded through marriage which is associated with getting rich" (386). Lieberman concludes that "since girls are chosen for their beauty, it is easy for a child to infer that beauty leads to wealth, that being chosen means getting rich" (386). Thus "the system of rewards in fairy tales . . . equates these three factors: being beautiful, being chosen, and getting rich" (387). These fairy tale patterns clearly operate in "The Sleeper Wakes," which Fauset modeled on the classic tale, "Sleeping Beauty," for Amy, the protagonist, exists in a state of suspended animation, passively waiting for her prince to come. Unlike the classic Sleeping Beauty, however, Amy's "prince" does not bring her a "happily-ever-after" existence, but only the temporary illusion of happiness. Fauset inverts the classical ending to demonstrate that women's traditional attitudes and expectations about marriage are romantic and impractical. Moreover, the corresponding marital role-playing dictated by convention keeps women in stasis preventing their development of independence and autonomy.

When the story opens, Amy, a mulatto foster child, is growing up with the Boldins, a black family of modest means. She is youth personified, associated predominantly with the color pink, a symbol of innocence and femininity. We first see her in a dress shop, arrayed in a pink blouse, about to try on an apricot-colored dress. Her face is a "perfect ivory pink," highlighted by her "smooth, young forehead. All this made one look for softness and ingenuousness."[15] Amy's physical appearance mirrors her perceptions. She sees life through the proverbial "rose-colored" lens, living totally in the realm of fantasy, fed by fairy tales, "the only reading that had ever made any impression on her," and movies of poor, beautiful girls who married "tremendous rich" men who gave them everything. Mr. Boldin's warning to Amy that "pretty girl pictures are not always true to life" (169) does nothing to shake her persistent belief that "something wonderful" will happen to her, a belief that demonstrates a passive ("female") rather than active orientation. Following her talk with Mr. Boldin, Amy goes upstairs to her room for her flight into fantasy. She "lit one gas jet and pulled down the shades. Then she stuffed tissue paper in the key hole and under the doors, and lit the remaining gas-jets. The light thus thrown on the mirror of the ugly oak dresser was perfect . . . . In the mirror she apostrophized . . . the beautiful, glowing vision of herself" (170). The passage is important for exposing Amy's tendency to refract the harsh light of reality (suggested by the "ugly oak dresser") through her romantic imagination (suggested by the light from the gas jets). Amy believes that this image of herself reflected in the mirror will bring her happiness. "She had nothing but her beautiful face—and she did so want to be happy" (170). Deciding that her home environment with the Boldins is stifling, Amy runs away to New York, "Altogether happy in the expectation of something wonderful, which she knew some day must happen" (170).

At the end of her second year in New York, Amy meets Zora Harrison; their developing friendship is a study in contrasts, a technique Fauset uses in each novel. The developing protagonist is foiled by more sophisticated characters who introduce her to alternative ways of thinking and behaving. While Amy is soft and pliable, Zora is hard and callous. Amy's "blonde, golden beauty" contrasts with Zora's dark beauty. Amy is passive and naive, Zora, active and worldly. In other words, while Amy is content to be more acted upon than acting, Zora actively goes after what she wants in life with a selfish and hardened determination. She first encourages Amy to marry the wealthy Stuart James Wynne (his name has a regal sound) and then to divorce him should she become dissatisfied. A retired and wealthy stockbroker of fifty-five, Wynne is instantly attracted to Amy. She "seemed to him everything a girl should be—she was so unspoiled, so untouched" (173). He proposes marriage and Amy accepts, thinking that he is her prince, her "dream come true" (173).

In her marriage Amy is nothing but an adornment, a doll for Wynne's amusement. (It is obvious that Fauset is also adapting Ibsen's *A Doll's House* to the special problems of a black woman.) She "was like a well-cared for, sleek, housepet, delicately nurtured, velvety, content to let her days pass by."[16] Their relationship is founded on inequality, analogous to that of vassal and lord, child and parent. Her sole activities are reading to Wynne and affecting her " 'spoiled child air,' as he used to call it. It was the way he liked her best" (268). Amy is perfectly content to act as a spoiled child, fearful of upsetting her placid, "doll house" existence, ruffled only by Wynne's coarse insults to their black servants. Although Amy is passing for white, she intensely identifies with the servants and finally begins to wonder how Wynne would react should he discover that she is black. She confidently assures herself that her beauty has an unshakable hold on him. "She fell to thinking that all the wonderful happenings in her sheltered, pampered life had come to her through her beauty . . . . She was right; it was her chiefest [sic] asset" (228). Amy's assurance and security are soon shattered, however, for in a violent argument between Wynne and one of the servants, Amy confesses her blackness. To her chagrin, her beauty is not a stay against her husband's consuming racial prejudice, for he wants to divorce her immediately after she reveals her heritage.

Amy moves to New York and is supported by Wynne's alimony payments, but her financial ease does nothing to assuage her feelings of emptiness and loneliness. "She missed Wynne definitely, chiefly as a guiding influence for she had rarely planned even her own amusements. Her dependence on him had been absolute."[17] Amy's solitude precipitates a period of introspection during which she reviews her past and slowly rejects her lifelong assumption that her beauty was her pass to a world of infinite possibilities. Admitting to herself that "amazingly [her] beauty availed her nothing" (267), she begins to make plans for her future as a woman single and alone. She contemplates going to Paris to try her hand at dress designing.

One afternoon while she works on a design, Wynne comes to visit. In his characteristic manner, he commands that she come back to live with him, attempting to entice her with jewels as he had before. Amy mistakes his gesture for a marriage proposal but he quickly explains that he merely wants a mistress. Taken aback by his proposition, Amy expresses her anger which unleashes a flood of insults from Wynne. " 'You sold yourself to me once,' " he argues, " 'haven't I reason to suppose you are waiting for a higher bidder?' At these words something in her died forever, her youth, her illusions, her happy, happy blindness" (271). Thus Amy, the sleeper, wakes to the harsh reality of a "prince" transformed into a consummate racist and sexist. Having discovered that Amy is black, Wynne—consistent with the white male's history of sexual exploitation of black women—regards remarriage to her as unthinkable. His attack reveals Fauset's understanding of a sexist society that often makes a marriage a form of prostitution, a vulgar financial arrangement that rewards women for being creatures of artifice and ornamentation and forces them to assume degrading forms of behavior.

With Wynne's insults Amy wakes from her romantic illusions about men and marriage, and to a realization of her own resources kept in dormancy by the dictates of convention. Whereas she had stifled the talent that would earn her a livelihood while relying instead on the supposed advantage of her beauty, Amy vows never more "to take advantage of her appearance to earn a living" (273). She then releases her servants, refuses any more alimony from Wynne, and begins work as a dress designer to pay back all money received from Wynne to this point. When she has paid the sum in full, she feels "free, free! she had paid back her sorry debt with labor, money and anguish. From now on she could do as she pleased" (273). Amy's freedom from monetary debt parallels her psychological freedom from her former slavish conformity to society's most invidious assumptions about blacks and women. Consistent with that nascent freedom, she makes plans to visit the Boldins, finally recognizing that they represent the regenerative virtues and riches of the black experience which she had rejected in pursuit of what was only a figment of happiness. More importantly, however, she makes plans to establish her own business, the returns on which will be not only financial solvency, but also the beginning of the self-reliance and autonomy that is impervious to society's assault. Fauset has thus inverted the classical fairy tale ending. "Happily-ever-after" is not marriage to a handsome, wealthy prince but realization and acceptance of the virtues of the black cultural experience as well as a realization and rejection of conventional social relationships that are injurious to the growth of selfhood.

Early in her career, then, Fauset is challenging sexual stereotypes and criticizing the conditions that give rise to them.[18] In tracing Amy's growth from a fantasy-orientation to a realistic one, Fauset challenges some of society's most cherished sexist beliefs that women have bought wholesale, beliefs that have insured their marginality in society. Amy's story is a criticism of women who rely preeminently on beauty, which requires nothing of them, save for sitting and looking pretty. In so doing, they reinforce and perpetuate conventional stereotypes of women as passive sexual objects. Moreover, Fauset criticizes a society that encourages women to dissemble, to assume, uncritically, insulting and degrading forms of behavior in exchange for the so-called privilege of marriage. For all women who feign childishness and frivolity, who repress their talent and intelligence out of deference to an ideal of woman which men have largely created and maintained, Fauset has a message. These masquerades, she makes clear, are performed at great price. Stereotyped sexual roles, by their very nature, deny human complexity and stifle growth, completeness of being, a state toward which Fauset aims all of her women characters. Inasmuch as this role-playing is, more often than not, a prerequisite to marriage, as well as a requirement during marriage, Fauset questions an institution that demands that women remain locked in growth-retarding roles. Therefore, at least in its more conventional forms, marriage can work to limit women's possibilities for self-realization and autonomy, a position that Fauset curiously repudiates in her first novel, *There Is Confusion*.

There Is Confusion chronicles the development of the protagonist, Joanna Marshall, tracing primarily her ambition to become a stage success as a singer-dancer and the trials she encounters in the process. In form, the novel is quite appropriately titled, for the reader experiences "confusion" indeed in trying to unravel and then keep separate three slenderly-related plot lines, complicated further by too large a canvas of under-developed characters. In addition to weak characterization, the novel suffers from excessive sentimentality of dialogue and image.

The multiple stylistic weaknesses of *There Is Confusion*, however, are somewhat compensated for by its strengths in content. As usual, critics have missed the essential point of the novel, reading it as a formulaic apology for the black middle class and a plea for acceptance by whites.[19] These critics ignore Fauset's continued exploration of the circumscribing effects of sexism on women.

Throughout the novel Joanna is described as self-assured, cool, practical, egotistical, and independent. It seems evident from the beginning of the novel that she has neither desire nor intention to accept or conform to conventional images of women, an option encouraged by the general run of the Marshall household where Joanna's mother "insists on each child's [girls and boys] learning to do housework."[20] The female-related fixation with physical beauty and the cosmetics that are so-called beauty aids is equally unappealing to Joanna. Rather, "she had the variety of honesty which made her hesitate and even dislike to do or adopt anything artificial, no matter how much it might improve her general appearance. No hair straighteners, nor even curling kits for her" (20). Even dolls that have traditionally oriented female children toward roles as wives and mothers fail to appeal to Joanna. Her dolls were usually in her sister Sylvia's care while Joanna was "reading the life of some exemplary female," "notable women of color" (72). Reading of these important women inspires in Joanna a "fixity of purpose." "The phrase 'when I grow up, I'm going to be' was constantly on her lips" (21). " 'I'll be great,' " she vows, " 'I'm not sure how. I can't be like those wonderful women, Harriet [Tubman] and Sojourner [Truth], but at least I won't be ordinary' " (14). With these allusions to Harriet Tubman and Sojourner Truth, both women's rights activists and abolitionists who "won their way to fame and freedom through their own efforts" (14), Fauset introduces possibilities for women that lie outside the traditional home and hearth.

Although Joanna is inspired by the notable examples of her female ancestors, she is initially unaware that racist and sexist practices, deeply entrenched in the social structure, work to frustrate her ambitions. Her father's success as a caterer has instilled in her the American success ethic, and she mistakenly believes that any ambition is realizable if one is diligent and industrious. The success ethic doesn't work for all, Joanna soon discovers, for when she isn't plagued by occupational barriers because of her race, she is because of her sex. Her perennial struggles finally convince her that "it was women who had the real difficulties to overcome, disabilities of sex and of tradition" (234). Although her talent is apparent, the big theatrical trusts refuse to try her; "one had even said frankly: " 'We'll try a colored man in a white company, but we won't have any colored women' " (275). Fauset is suggesting that sexual discrimination, more so than racial, is responsible for Joanna's occupational difficulties.

Joanna's ambitions, her fixity of purpose, are in sharp contrast to those of her boyfriend Peter Bye, who aspires to be a doctor, but whose awareness of racial prejudice paralyzes him and renders him temporarily incapable of fighting to reach his goals. Thus Joanna's and Peter's turbulent relationship, her struggle to help him overcome his inertia, form the second plot of the novel. From the beginning, Joanna places her relationship with Peter second to her career ambitions. Although "she had a very real, very ardent feeling for Peter . . . it was still small, if one may speak of a feeling by size. Her love for him was a new experience, a fresh interest in her already crowded life, but it had not pushed aside the other interests. At nineteen she looked at love as a man of forty might—as 'a thing apart' " (103).

Marriage, likewise, holds little attraction for Joanna. When Peter attempts to persuade her that love and marriage are a woman's natural occupations, she counters, " 'You know perfectly well that for a woman love usually means a household of children, the getting of a thousand meals, picking up laundry, no time for herself, for meditation, for reading or –' " (95).

Joanna's verbal sparring with Peter, her strong and critical objections to love and marriage, are extraordinary and antithetical to those of other young women her age who are predominantly shallow, unambitious, and consumed with thoughts of marriage. Peter is "pleasantly struck" by their "apparent lack of aspiration . . . . They seemed to be pretty well satisfied with being girls. A few were able to live at home, many sewed, a number of others taught. There was no talk of art, of fame, or preparation for the future among them" (107). One, Arabelle Morton, explains to Peter, " 'Well, of course we want to get

married, and we're not spoiling our chances by being high-
brows . . . .' " (107).

Like Arabelle, Maggie Ellersley has been conditioned to repress any
ambition and intelligence for fear of threatening potential mates. Maggie's aspiration for social respectability via marriage constitutes still
another plot line. Fauset sets Maggie and Joanna up as antitheses to
dramatize differing perceptions of self between women and corresponding behavior patterns and expectations. The poor daughter of
a working class woman, Maggie is drawn to Joanna and her family
because of their financial success and their status as "Old Philadelphians." Although she works competently as a bookkeeper for Joanna's father and trains at night to be a cosmetologist, her initiative,
unlike Joanna's, is born out of the need to supplement her mother's
meager income as a laundress rather than of personal ambition to
pursue a career and become financially independent. Maggie sees
marriage to a prosperous and respectable man as "one avenue of
escape" from her "dreary existence." Men "were stronger than
women, they made money" to support women. Joanna's brother,
Phillip, conforms to Maggie's ideal, but Joanna breaks them up because she considers Maggie's social status "beneath" Phillip's.

Her plans to establish a relationship with Phillip foiled, in desperation Maggie begins seeing an older man, Henderson Neal, a boarder
in her mother's house. Fauset provides an ironic twist to Maggie's
story, for unknown to her, he is a gambler, exactly opposite to her
wishes for a socially respectable man. Neal persuades Maggie that
" 'a delicate little girl like you's got no business having to worry her
pretty head about taking care of herself . . . . There's many a man
would be willing to take that job off your hands' " (84).

Although she doesn't love Neal, Maggie marries him, rationalizing
that at least the marriage "represented to her security, a home for
herself and her mother, freedom from all the little nagging worries
that beset the woman who fights her own way through the world"
(90). She later discovers that "marriage did not in reality prove as
interesting and picturesque as she in common with most girls had
conceived it to be. But marriage was marriage, and she must make
the best of it" (118). When Maggie learns that Neal is a gambler, she
divorces him and begins to support herself. The reality of confronting
the day-to-day exigencies of living, however, does not abate Maggie's
still-thriving romantic desire to marry a respectable man. This time
she sets her sights on Peter, who is a penniless medical student, but
who "boasted a long, a bonafide ancestry" (204). "She saw herself
suddenly transformed in this inhospitable snobbish city from Maggie
Neal, alone and déclassé, into Mrs. Peter Bye, a model of respect-

ability. That he had no money, no accepted means of making a livelihood she understood would mean nothing. He was a Bye and she
as his wife could go anywhere . . . . And afterwards when he got his
degree!'' (169–70). Maggie's romantic reasoning is typically "female";
her strategies to win Peter's affections are equally consistent with
traditional female behavior patterns. On one occasion, as Peter is
leaving her apartment, she begins, " 'You're sure you won't have me
fix a cup of cocoa for you before you go? You poor, neglected boy!
Two buttons off that overcoat. Bring it in the next time you come and
I'll put them on for you. I'll find some that will match up here on
South Street.' He said he could attend to it himself but she told him
no, that wasn't a man's job" (143).

Maggie's overwhelming attention is especially noticeable compared
to Joanna's chronic inattention, and because he is conditioned as a
traditional male, Peter temporarily welcomes Maggie's domesticity.
He boasts to Joanna that Maggie does not resent doing "women's
work," that she freely waits on him. Joanna's adamant refusal to
submit to woman's work, as well as her stringent demands on Peter,
create tensions that steadily mount until they break their engagement.
Maggie's fawning passivity, her dependency, provides temporary relief from Joanna's exacting demands. He becomes engaged to Maggie
who promises to "be as unlike Joanna as possible" (171). Maggie has
"a very charming, flattering air of deference, of dependence when
she was out. It was singularly pleasing and yet puzzling to Peter.
Joanna now was just as likely to cross the street as not, without waiting
for a guiding hand, a protecting arm. If she had once visited a locality
she knew quite as much about getting away from it as her escort. But
Maggie was helpless, dependent" (190).

Like Amy in "The Sleeper Wakes," Maggie has capitulated to social
pressures to play dependent roles and to forego self-actualization and
self-sufficiency in exchange for marriage and its spurious rewards.
Peter is soon bored of that dependency and wants to be free of Maggie,
but she pleads, " 'Oh, Peter, can't you see I want to be safe like other
women, with a home and protection' " (193).

Joanna's reaction to her breakup with Peter is diametrically opposed
to Maggie's. Although Joanna is initially disappointed and reveals a
side of her character never before seen, her remorse is shortlived, for
she has begun to realize some stage success. She therefore channels
the energy of her agony over Peter into her work:

> Without it what would she have done? What did girls do while they
> waited for their young men? Heavens, how awful to be sitting around
> listlessly from day to day, waiting, waiting! Anything was better than

that, even pounding a typewriter in a box office. It was this lack of interest in and purpose on the part of girls which brought about so many hasty marriages which terminated in—no, not poverty—mediocrity. Joanna hated the word; with her visual mind she saw it embodied in broken chairs, cold gravy, dingy linen, sticky children (p. 146).

Joanna finally decides, however, that her work is unable to fill what she describes as a gnawing sense of emptiness, a feeling that her life is a "ghastly skeleton" that the "garish trappings of her art" cannot clothe:

It has not occurred to her that [her art] would be the only thing in her life . . . . She had expected her singing, her dancing—her success in a word—to be the mere integument of her life, the big handsome extra wrap to cover her more ordinary dress—the essential, delightful commonplaces of living, the kernel of life, home, children, an adoring husband (p. 274).

While Joanna is changing to a more traditional orientation, Maggie reverts to one somewhat less conventional. Narrowly missing death at the hands of her ex-husband, she takes stock of her life while she is recovering. She begins to examine and then criticize her blind acceptance of the middle-class fixation with "proper" marriage, social mobility and respectability. She decides, rather, that respectability, in its truest sense, is neither passed on from generation to generation nor conferred on a woman by a man in marriage. She decides, moreover, that her dependent personality is not conducive to developing a healthy relationship with a man. Described throughout as a yellow calla lilly—suggesting fragility and pliability—Maggie begins to contemplate the virtues of independence. She says to herself, " 'If I ever get well again I shall be what I want without depending on anybody' " (256).

Maggie seizes the outbreak of World War I as an opportunity to test her budding self-sufficiency. She goes to France to help nurse wounded soldiers, and, while there, makes plans to inaugurate a chain of beauty shops once she returns to America.[21] "She would stand on her two feet, Maggie Ellersley, serene, independent, self-reliant" (261–262). In another of Fauset's embarrassing fictional coincidences, Maggie and her first love, Phillip, are reunited in a hospital ward, where she is assigned to nurse him. They eventually marry and she nurses him until his death. The consciousness with which Maggie enters their marriage is substantially altered from her earlier days, however. Although vestiges of her domestic sentimentalism surface in her treatment of Phillip, it is evident that Maggie is a much stronger, more self-reliant individual with more realistic perceptions of marriage.

Fauset continues to tie up the loose ends of her narrative by re-uniting Joanna and Peter, who also marry. Their marriage, however, means an end to Joanna's career. Unlike the Joanna who dominated throughout the novel with her stubborn independence and indiffer-ence to marriage, she now becomes absorbed in the traditional role as wife and mother, abandoning altogether her earlier passion for a career:

> She was still ambitious, only the field of her ambition lay without her-self. It was Peter now whom she wished to see succeed. If his success depended ever so little on his achievement of a sense of responsibility, then she meant to develop that sense. To this end, she consulted him, she took his advice, she asked him to arrange about the few recitals which she undertook. In a thousand little ways she deferred to him, and showed him that as a matter of course he was the arbiter of her own and her child's destiny, the *fon set origo* of authority (p. 292).

Thus, Joanna unconvincingly settles for biological rather than artistic creativity and, true to the feminine ideal, sacrifices her own career and further development, and defers completely to her husband.

By having Joanna and Maggie trade places in a sense, Fauset is suggesting that each represents the extreme of independence and dependency, extremes that need to be tempered. This position is not unreasonable in and of itself, but it is Fauset's final statement on her joint protagonists that creates problems. In her depictions of Maggie and Joanna, Fauset must be finally seen as a traditionalist regarding women's roles. Both characters, to varying degrees, accede to male-determined roles for women. Joanna's accession is most dramatic, for she has to resolve the classic female conflict between marriage and a career, an either-or proposition historically forced on women by men. Although Fauset herself combined a marriage and a career, she dem-onstrates in her characterization of Joanna that the two roles may be incompatible.[22] Given Joanna's mindset throughout the novel, Fau-set's ending seems forced and inconsistent, not growing organically out of the novel, but rather, "tacked on" to it.[23] Notwithstanding the novel's focus on characters who must all grow and alter their per-spectives in some way, Joanna's growth from stubbornly independent careerist to dependent, self-abnegating wife rings false. What ac-counts for Fauset's retreat to a traditional value system after clearly promising the opposite? A brief look at the peculiar network of social, economic, and literary circumstances under which she composed can help to answer that question.

Fauset admitted to an interviewer that she began earnestly to write fiction to counteract T.S. Stribling's novel *Birthright* that had failed, in her estimation, to depict blacks authentically. She, along with Nella Larsen and Walter White, reasoned, "Here is an audience waiting to hear the truth about us. Let we who are better qualified to present that truth than any white writer, try to do so."[24] Thus Fauset's mission was reconstructive, in a word.

Concomitant with wanting to tell the truth about blacks, Fauset also set out to tell the truth about women, who had been similarly the victims of literary misrepresentation, a reflection of dominant social attitudes. Fauset's mission was necessarily fraught with uncertainty, ambivalence, and fear, for not only was she challenging prominent literary images of women, but she was also challenging traditional expectations of women in the social sphere. She was writing at a time when social definitions of womanhood were in flux. There was a tremendous ferment of ideas concerning sexuality, sex roles, marriage and family, observable in social and political thinking and in literary culture. Fauset was unsure of what road to take. She herself had defied the cult of domesticity by remaining unmarried for an unusually long time and by insisting upon maintaining an active career when she did marry. To transfer that personal, democratic style of life into her writing was not easy. From various ranks within society she invited reprisals for exploring concerns outside the realm of the traditional, reprisals that she, a fledgling writer, would ironically fear and defer to in subtle ways. A perpetual source of fear was the major publishing firms that Fauset continually battled and that stifled her freedom of expression and directness by prescribing and proscribing her literary province. "White readers just don't expect Negroes to be like this," wrote the first publisher to see and reject the manuscript of *There Is Confusion*.[25] Censorship and rejected manuscripts were what she came to expect, and thus, Fauset had to develop strategies to offset rejection, strategies that frequently took the form of indirectness. As Tillie Olsen points out, fear of reprisal is a looming obstacle to the woman writer's coming into her own authentic voice. "Fear—the need to please, to be safe—in the literary realm too. Founded fear. Power is still in the hands of men. Power of validation, publication, approval, reputation . . . ."[26]

Fauset's awareness that the publishing and critical arenas were essentially male preserves may well have pressured her into deflecting her dissenting statements through "safe" literary mediums if not falsifying them altogether. Thus, the indirectness of "The Sleeper Wakes" and the curious and unconvincing resolution of *There Is Confusion* are not without explanation.[27]

Fauset's oblique and ambivalent treatment of women's roles in "The Sleeper Wakes" and in *There Is Confusion*, respectively, is less apparent in her next three novels, *Plum Bun* (1929), *The Chinaberry Tree* (1931), and *Comedy: American Style* (1933). She continues her exploration of women's roles, their lives' possibilities, and her criticism of social conventions that work to restrict those possibilities by keeping women's sights riveted on men, marriage and motherhood. These domestic and biological facets, Fauset suggests, while important, are just one dimension of a woman's total being, one aspect of her boundless capacities and possibilities. Seen in this light, then, fairy tale illusions about life give way to mature realities, and women, instead of waiting for their imaginary princes, aggressively take charge of their lives and move toward achieving authentic selfhood.

The idea of Fauset, a black woman,[28] daring to write—even timidly so—about women taking charge of their own lives and declaring themselves independent of social conventions, was far more progressive than critics have either observed or admitted. Although what Fauset attempted in her depictions of black women was not uniformly commensurate with what she achieved, she has to be credited with both presenting an alternative view of womanhood and a facet of black life which publishers, critics, and audiences stubbornly discouraged if not vehemently opposed. Despite that discouragement and opposition, Fauset persisted in her attempt to correct the distorted but established images of black life and culture and to portray women and blacks with more complexity and authenticity than was popular at the time. In so doing, she was simultaneously challenging established assumptions about the nature and function of Afro-American literature. Those who persist, then, in regarding her as a prim and proper Victorian writer, an eddy in a revolutionary literary current, would do well to read Fauset's work more carefully, to give it a more fair and complete appraisal, one that takes into account the important and complex relationship between circumstances and artistic creation. Then her fiction might finally be accorded the recognition and attention that it deserves and Fauset, her rightful place in the Afro-American literary tradition.

Notes

1. *The Negro Novel in America* (1958; rpt. New Haven: Yale University Press, 1972), pp. 97, 65.

2. *Ibid.*, p. 97.

3. *Ibid.*, p. 101.

4. *Black on White: A Critical Survey of Writing by American Negroes* (NewYork: The Viking Press, 1966), pp. 50–51. See also Hiroko Sato, "Under the Harlem Shadows: A Study of Jessie Fauset and Nella Larsen," in *The Harlem Renaissance Remembered*, ed. Arna Bontempts (New York: Dodd-Mead, 1972), pp. 63–89.

5. *The Way of the New World: The Black Novel in America* (New York: Anchor-Doubleday, 1976), p. 115.

6. "Black Writers in 'Nigger Heaven': The Harlem Renaissance," Diss., Kansas State University 1974, p. 236. Amritjit Singh makes a similar point in *The Novels of the Harlem Renaissance* (University Park: The Pennsylvania State University Press, 1976), p. 74. Singh says that Fauset's subject matter "alternates between the safe formulas of a genteel fictionist and the exploration of challenging themes such as incest and self-hatred."

7. When Fauset began to write, during the Harlem Renaissance, publishers clamoured for books about blacks which depicted them primarily as primitive-exotics, as free, sexually uninhibited creatures. (See Carl Van Vechten's *Nigger Heaven* and Claude McKay's *Home to Harlem* for representative examples of the fiction of the day.) Thus Fauset's choice of subject matter was very coolly received. She criticized publishers for not being "better sport[s]" regarding the portrayal of black characters in literature. Most, she argued, "have an *idée fixe*. They, even more than the public . . . persist in considering only certain types of Negroes interesting and if an author presents a variant they fear that the public either won't believe in it or won't stand for it." "The Negro in Art: How Shall He be Portrayed," *The Crisis*, 32 (June, 1926), 72. Zora Neale Hurston would write later that "publishers and producers are cool to the idea" of literature "about the higher emotions and love life of upper-class Negroes and the minorities in general . . . . It is assumed that all non–Anglo-Saxons are uncomplicated stereotypes. Everybody knows all about them. They are lay figures mounted in the museum where all may take them in at a glance. They are made of bent wires without insides at all. So how could anybody write a book about the non-existent?" "What White Publishers Won't Print," rpt. in *I Love Myself When I Am Laughing*, ed. Alice Walker (New York: The Feminist Press, 1979), pp. 169–173.

8. I borrow this concept of the "deflecting mask" in women writers from Annis Pratt, "The New Feminist Criticism," *College English*, 32 (1971), pp. 872–878.

9. James W. Tuttleton, *The Novel of Manners in America* (New York: Norton, 1974), p. 12.

10. While there aren't any published writings on this aspect of Fauset's work, a few doctoral dissertations make mention of it without going into great depth. See, for example, Martha Hursey Brown, "Images of Black Women: Family Roles in Harlem Renaissance Literature," Diss., Carnegie-Mellon University 1976; Beatrice Horn Royster, "The Ironic Vision of Four Black Women Novelists: A Study of the Novels of Jessie Fauset, Nella Larsen, Zora Neale Hurston and Ann Petry," Diss., Emory University 1975; and Carolyn Sylvander, "Jessie Fauset, Black American Writer: Her Relationships, Biographical and Literary, With Black Writers, 1910–1935," Diss., University of Wisconsin-Madison, 1976.

11. Among the early black feminist writers was Frances E. W. Harper, poet,

novelist, and abolitionist. For a discussion of early black literary feminists see Gloria T. Hull, "Black Women Poets from Wheatley to Walker," in *Sturdy Black Bridges: Visions of Black Women in Literature,* ed., Roseann P. Bell, et al. (New York: Anchor-Doubleday, 1979), pp. 169–186. It is important to note that Fauset came to adulthood and began her literary career during an era of intense black feminist activity. Ida B. Wells-Barnett, Mary Church Terrell, Nannie Burroughs, to name a few, all devoted their energies to women's rights as well as the rights of blacks. For a discussion of these women's activities see the essays in *The Afro-American Woman: Struggle and Images,* ed. Sharon Harley and Rosalyn Terborg-Penn (Port Washington, New York: Kennikat Press, 1978).

12. "The Sleeper Wakes," was published in three installments in *The Crisis,* 20 (August, 1920), pp. 168–172, (September, 1920), pp. 226–229, and (October, 1920), pp. 267–274.

13. Because of her work with the children's magazine *The Brownies' Book,* it is reasonable to assume that Fauset would be familiar with fairy tales, nursery rhymes, and children's literature as a whole. Thus it should come as no surprise that she uses a fairy tale motif as a structuring principle in "The Sleeper Wakes." The magazine was designed especially to give black children a sense of their heritage and thereby instill in them pride in race and hope for the future. Fauset edited the magazine from January, 1920 to December, 1921. For a discussion of Fauset's work with the magazine, see Elinor Sinnette, "The Brownies' Book: A Pioneer Publication for Children," *Freedomways* (Winter, 1965), pp. 133–142.

14. *College English,* 34 (1972), p. 386. Subsequent references to Lieberman's article will be indicated by page numbers in parentheses in the text. For other discussions of folk tales as purveyors of cultural norms, see Karen E. Rowe, "Feminism and Fairy Tales," *Women's Studies* 6 (1979), pp. 237–257 and William Bascom, "Four Functions of Folklore," in *The Study of Folklore,* ed. Allen Dundes (Englewood Cliffs, New Jersey: Prentice-Hall, 1965), pp. 279–298.

15. "The Sleeper Wakes," *The Crisis,* 20 (August, 1920), p. 168. Subsequent references to this installment will be indicated by page numbers in parentheses in the text.

16. "The Sleeper Wakes," *The Crisis,* 20 (September, 1920), p. 227. Subsequent references to this second installment will be indicated by page numbers in parentheses in the text.

17. "The Sleeper Wakes," *The Crisis,* 20 (October, 1920) p. 268. Subsequent references to this third installment will be indicated by page numbers in parentheses in the text.

18. The ending of "The Sleeper Wakes" patently refutes the popular charge that Fauset wants to deny her blackness, for by having Amy return to the Boldins, Fauset reveals pride in her race. Not only in this story but in two of her works—*Plum Bun* (1929) and *Comedy: American Style* (1933)—she demonstrates the pernicious effects of racial passing, seeing in black people a unique strength and vitality.

19. See Wallace Thurman, "Negro Artists and the Negro," *New Republic,* 52 (31 August 1927), pp. 37–39 and Arthur P. Davis's *From the Dark Tower: Afro-American Writers, 1900–1960* (Washington, D.C.: Howard University Press, 1974), p. 92. Those who insist on this reading of *There Is Confusion* are not reading the novel closely. Not only in this novel but also in her letters Fauset's sympathies regarding blacks are clear. In a letter that Fauset wrote to W. E.

B. DuBois, for example, she says, "It is worthwhile to teach our colored men and women race pride, self-sufficiency (the right kind) and the necessity of living our lives as nearly as possible, absolutely, instead of comparing them always with white standards." Herbert Aptheker, ed., *The Correspondence of W. E. B. DuBois, I: Selections 1877–1934* (Amherst: University of Massachusetts Press, 1973), p. 95.

20. *There Is Confusion* (1924; rpt. New York: AMS Press, 1974), p. 2. Subsequent references to the novel will be indicated by page numbers in parentheses in the text.

21. It could be argued, however, that in volunteering her services as a nurse, Maggie is conforming to women's social conditioning to nurture and to serve, conditioning that finds expression in the number of capacities in which women volunteer their services to the public. For a discussion of women and volunteerism, see Doris B. Gold's article by the same title in *Women in Sexist Society*, ed. Vivian Gornick and Barbara K. Moran (New York: Basic Books-Signet, 1971), pp. 533–544.

22. In her examination of nineteenth-century British women writers, Patricia Beer notes that their work "reveals a network of discrepancies concerning what the novelists thought in real life and the views they set forth or implied in their novels; between what they accepted for themselves and what they accepted for their heroines." *Reader, I Married Him* (London: Macmillan Press, 1974), p. 1. See also Elaine Showalter's *A Literature of Their Own* (New Jersey: Princeton University Press, 1977). Showalter argues similarly that women writers have had "to overcome deep-seated guilt about authorship," finding it "necessary to justify their work by recourse to some external stimulus or ideology." In novels of nineteenth-century British women writers, for example, the heroine's aspiration for a full, independent life are undermined, punished, or replaced by marriage" (p. 22). These dynamics noted by Beer and Showalter might have affected Fauset as well.

23. When *There Is Confusion* is compared to "The Sleeper Wakes," the novel's resolution is especially curious. Published in *The Crisis* during her own tenure as literary editor, the story is more direct in its criticism of culture-bound stereotypes of femininity. Perhaps Fauset's more direct stance in the story is explained by her position on the magazine's staff where her work would not be censored. An established publishing firm like Boni and Liveright, the first publisher of *There Is Confusion*, would on the other hand, be likely to have edited out material that challenged the status quo.

24. Marion Starkey, "Jessie Fauset," *Southern Workman* (May, 1932), pp. 218–219.

25. *Ibid.*, p. 219.

26. *Silences* (New York: Delacorte Press, 1978), p. 257.

27. For a discussion of this tendency among women writers to be oblique and ambivalent see Annis Pratt's essay, "The New Feminist Criticisms: Exploring the History of the New Space," in *Beyond Intellectual Sexism: A New Woman, A New Reality*, ed. Joan Roberts (New York: David McKay), pp. 175–195, in which she discusses what she calls the "drowning theory." Her study of a number of plots of novels written by women reveal a consistent pattern "in which sexist norms are criticized in the middle of the action but the critical hero gets it in the end . . . . Feminist consciousness is raised but society has its way in the end . . . ." According to Pratt, her notion of the "drowning theory" derives from a phenomenon in black culture: "You have a little black

church back in the marsh and you're going to sing 'Go Down Moses.' Well, it's right to sing 'Go Down Moses' because the white folks will think you're being religious when you're really singing 'get me out of here.' Every now and then, though, the members of the congregation want to break loose and sing 'Oh Freedom,' with its chorus of 'Before I'll be a slave/I'll be buried in my grave/and go home to my lord/and be free.' Whenever they sing that, they've got this big old black pot in the vestibule, and as they sing they pound the pot. That way, no white folks are going to hear. The drowning effect, this banging on the pot to drown out what they are actually saying about feminism, came in with the first woman's novel and hasn't gone out yet. Many women novelists have even succeeded in hiding the covert or implicit feminism in their books from themselves, as well as from the white man who holds the publishing purse strings. As a result we get explicit cultural norms superimposed upon an authentic creative mind in the form of all kinds of feints, ploys, masks, and disguises embedded in the plot structure and characterization. This way, the woman novelist gets away with the unacceptable portrayal of women as human beings" (183).

28. The idea of Fauset's attempting to earn a partial livelihood by writing was indeed anomalous during the 1920s. Carolyn Sylvander, in the dissertation already cited, reports that "attitudes toward black women working as professionals in 1905 were conservative," as represented by Mrs. R. D. Sprague in "What Role is the Educated Negro Woman to Play in the Uplifting of Her Race?" Says Sylvander, Mrs. Sprague maintained that "the educated Negro woman will find that her greatest field for effective work is in the home." Sylvander notes that, "while not every Black or every Black woman at the time would of course agree with Mrs. Sprague, it is clear that the attitudinal climate supported her view for women, but in an exaggerated way for Black women, and that Jessie Fauset was breaking habits of expectation not only in pursuing a college degree but in attaining financial and personal independence in the professional working world" (61).

6

Ann Petry's Demythologizing of American Culture and Afro-American Character

BERNARD W. BELL

The novels of Ann Petry have been overshadowed and her talent misrepresented by their frequent comparison to the fiction and achievement of Richard Wright and Chester Himes. Robert Bone, for example, claims that *The Street* (1946), her first novel, suffers by comparison to Wright's *Native Son* because "it is an attempt to interpret slum life in terms of *Negro* experience, when a larger frame of reference is required."[1] In contrast, he considers *Country Place* (1947), her second novel, "one of the finest . . . of the period" because it is "a manifestation not so much of assimilation as of versatility."[2] He does not mention *The Narrows* (1953), the best of her three novels, in either edition of his *The Negro Novel in America*. Neither does critic Addison Gayle, Jr., who discusses only *The Street* in his more recent book, *The Way of the New World*.[3] For Gayle, Petry is similar to Himes in that she develops characters with some status and education, and to Wright in that "both were interested in the effects of environment upon the psychological makeup of characters."[4] Unlike Wright, however, Gayle concludes, "Miss Petry is more interested in the effects of the environment upon her characters than she is in the characters themselves."[5] Whether valid or not, these critical views do not adequately express the complexity and distinctiveness of Ann Petry's aesthetic vision and achievement.

Ann Petry actually moves beyond the naturalistic vision of Wright and Himes in her realistic delineation of cultural myths, especially those of the American Dream, the city and small town, and black character. In exploring the black community's place in time and space, its relationship to the American past and future, she effectively debunks the myths of urban success and progress, of rural innocence and virtue, and of pathological black women and men. Embodying the values and beliefs of a community, *myths*, as we are using the term here, are stories people in a particular society tell to organize, explain, and understand the realities and metaphysics of their world. "Myths are not rational," writes James O. Robertson in *American Myth, American Reality*, "at least in the sense that they are not controlled by what we believe to be logic. They are sometimes based on faith, on belief rather than reason, on ideals rather than realities."[6] Thus myths are a kind of behavioral charter that leads to both negative and positive responses.

Since the "truth" about America and Americans is found in both American myths and American realities, Petry dispassionately explores both in her novels. Like realist writers from Sinclair Lewis and Theodore Dreiser to Zora Hurston and Richard Wright, she realizes, moreover, that not all Americans participate in the same myths or use them in the same ways. Race, color, class, sex, and region are the major realities that determine the degree and manner of participation of individuals and communities in our national myths. While, for example, myths of the Founding Fathers like Benjamin Franklin, who is the colonial paradigm of the successful self-made man, are available to all Americans, black Americans rarely refer to them. "On the other hand," as Robertson states, "many black Americans use the stories and myths of Abraham Lincoln more frequently than other Americans."[7] Despite turn-of-the century attacks on small-town life such as Sinclair Lewis's *Main Street*, the rural vision of the city is characterized mainly by sin, crime, and violence. At the same time, however, younger Americans, especially blacks, dream of the city as a place of opportunity, wealth, and progress. The truth, as Petry reveals in her novels, is actually more complex and paradoxical. So, too, is the socialized ambivalence, the pride and shame of one's identity, and double-consciousness, the struggle to reconcile one's dual heritage, of black American character.

The setting and themes of Ann Petry's novels are a natural outgrowth of her intimacy with the black inner-city life of New York and the white small-town life of New England. Born in 1911 in Old Saybrook, Connecticut, Ann Petry grew up in a predominantly white environment and, in the family tradition, graduated in 1934 with a degree in Pharmacy from the University of Connecticut. After working in the family drugstores in Old Saybrook and the nearby town of Lyme, she married in 1938 and moved to New York to work and pursue her childhood interests in writing. From 1938 to 1944 she worked as a journalist for two Harlem newspapers: *Amsterdam News* and *People's Voice*. In 1943 her short stories began appearing in *The Crisis* and *Phylon*. The early chapters of *The Street* won her the Houghton Mifflin Literary Fellowship in 1945. In 1948 she returned to Connecticut to raise her family and continue writing. Her publications include four children's books, a collection of short stories, and three novels: *The Street*, *Country Place*, and *The Narrows*.

The Street is a conventional novel of economic determinism in which the environment is the dominant force against which the characters must struggle to survive. The novel opens symbolically with the November wind and cold and dirt and filth of 116th Street overpowering the hurried Harlem pedestrians, including the apartment-hunting protagonist, Lutie Johnson; it closes with Lutie leaving the city by train after killing the man who assaults her, the snow falling symbolically, "gently obscuring the grime and garbage and the ugliness" of the street. As the plot progresses episodically, we apprehend the street in the same sociological manner as the protagonist:

> It was a bad street . . . . It wasn't just this street that she was afraid of or that was bad. It was any street where people were packed together like sardines in a can.
>
> And it wasn't just this city. It was any city where they set up a line and say black folks stay on this side and white folks on this side, so that the black folks were crammed on top of each other— jammed and packed and forced into the smallest possible space until they were completely cut off from light and air.
>
> It was any place where the women had to work to support the families because the men couldn't get jobs and the men got bored and pulled out and the kids were left without proper homes because there was nobody around to put a heart into it. Yes. It was any place where people were so damn poor they didn't have time to do anything but work, and their bodies were the only source of relief from the pressure under which they lived; and where the crowding together made the young girls wise beyond their years.[8]

Poverty and race are inextricably linked to the "Dirty, dark, filthy traps" in which the characters live and die. It was "Streets like 116th Street or being colored, or a combination of both with all it implied" that drove the protagonist's father to drink and the mother to her early grave. It was the same combination of circumstances that

> had evidently made the Mrs. Hedges who sat in the street-floor window

turn to running a fairly well-kept whorehouse . . . and the superin-
tendent of the building—well, the street had pushed him into basements
away from light and air until he was being eaten up by some horrible
obsession; and still other streets had turned Min, the woman who lived
with him, into a drab drudge so spineless and so limp she was like a
soggy dishrag. (p. 40)

Lutie Johnson was determined that none of these things would happen to her "because she would fight back and never stop fighting
back." But her will to succeed is ineffectual against the relentless
economic and racist forces that Ann Petry saw as the direct cause of
streets like the one on which the protagonist lived. Far from being
an accident, we learn through the narrator's probing into Lutie's
mind, "They were the North's mob . . . the method the big cities used
to keep Negroes in their place" (p. 200).

Unlike Wright's and Himes's protagonists, Lutie Johnson is neither
psychologically tormented nor driven by a fear of white people. Raised
by her tale-telling, Puritan-minded grandmother, she is a respectable, married woman, driven by a hunger for the material trappings
of middle-class success for herself and her family; she longs for a
better life and a place to be somebody. She seeks to satisfy this hunger
by naively subscribing to the Protestant ethic and the American Dream
as expressed by the Chandlers, the wealthy white New England family for whom she worked for two years as a live-in maid, and as
embodied in Benjamin Franklin, with whom she compares herself.
Ignoring her own social reality—a working-class black woman with
an eight-year-old son to support; separated from her unfaithful, un-
employed husband; living in Harlem during World War II; struggling
to maintain her moral principles and to share equally in the wealth
of the nation—she fantasizes "that if Ben Franklin could live on a little
bit of money and could prosper, then so could she" (p. 44). After a
year with the Chandlers she finds herself influenced by their material
values and belief in the American Dream. They promoted the "belief
that anybody could be rich if he wanted to and worked hard enough
and figured it out carefully enough . . . . These people had wanted
only one thing—more and more money—so they got it" (p. 32).

The irony is that Lutie sees, yet fails to act on, the price that the
Chandlers pay in spiritual and personal alienation for their material
success. In blind pursuit of the American Dream, Lutie loses her
family and her hope for happiness, but not her self-respect. When
she fails to get the singing job she had counted on to move off 116th
Street and up the ladder of success, social reality begins to displace
her dream world. "The trouble was with her," she concludes. "She

had built up a fantastic structure made from the soft, nebulous, cloudy stuff of dream. There hadn't been a solid, practical brick in it, not even a foundation. She had built it up of air and vapor and moved right in. So of course it had collapsed. It had never existed anywhere but in her mind" (p. 191).

Although some critics see the sensationalism of the denouement as a weakness, it is inconsistent neither with the naturalism of Dreiser and Wright nor with Petry's use of symbols of confinement and contrasting images of the white world and black world to give structural and thematic coherence to the novel.[9] The wide, quiet, tree-lined, sunny main street of Lyme, Connecticut, where the Chandlers live in gracious luxury is contrasted with the drab, violent, overcrowded streets where Lutie's economic, racial and sexual circumstances trap her. "From the time she was born, she had been hemmed into an ever-narrowing space until now she was very nearly walled in and the wall had been built up brick by brick by eager white hands" (pp. 200–201). The white world had a different set of values from those her grandmother had taught her. It was a strange world in which money was more important than people and young, black women were considered potential whores. Her grandmother had warned her so often about the lust of white men for black women that she found them repulsive. Thus, when Boots Smith, a black musician, attempts to persuade her to exchange sexual favors with Junto, the Jewish owner of the major clubs and whorehouses in the black community, for the two hundred dollars she needed to help keep her boy out of reform school, all she can think is: "Junto has a brick in his hand. Just one brick. The final one needed to complete the wall that had been building up around her for years, and when that last brick was shoved in place, she would be completely walled in" (p. 262). Angrily responding to Boots's actual and threatened violence, she beats his head into a bloody pulp with an iron candlestick, realizing afterwards that "a lifetime of pent-up resentment went into the blows" (p. 266).

Although the story is told by a disembodied third-person, omniscient narrator, Petry allows Lutie's consciousness to dominate the narrative and scrupulously avoids moralizing. The action and setting are subordinated to Lutie's impression of their impact on black women and the black family, thus encouraging our sympathy for her and other black women, who incredulously have no contact with the black church. Except for the denouement, the author-narrator explores the social evils of segregated communities, white and black, with restraint and objectivity. But it is clear that neither Petry nor her protagonist simplistically blame black men for the broken homes, poverty, and hopelessness that characterize too many urban black communities.

The cause of these social problems is not black men like her alcoholic father and adulterous husband, nor black women like Mrs. Hedges, the whorehouse madam, but white people like Junto and the Chandlers, whose prosperity is based on the economic exploitation of blacks. If it is impossible to escape the corruption and despair of the black inner city, it is equally impossible, as the Chandlers reveal, to escape the degeneration and despair of small white towns.

In *Country Place* Petry moves beyond economic and racial determinism to explore the realities beneath the myths of rural, small-town communities. In contrast to traditional stories and images of the beneficence, continuity, integrity, and homogeneity of values in small, rural American communities, her narrative reveals the hypocrisy, violence, prejudice, and stagnation of a small, post–World War II, New England town. *Country Place* is a first-person, retrospective narrative with the town druggist, George Fraser, as the on-the-scene chronicler of events. In the opening five pages, the friendly, sixty-five-year-old narrator immediately establishes his reliability ("I am neither a pessimist nor an optimist"), the setting ("a quiet place, a country place, which sets at the mouth of the Connecticut River, at the exact spot where the river empties itself into Long Island Sound"), and the major theme: " . . . wheresoever men dwell there is always a vein of violence running under the surface quiet."[10] Confessing his own petty prejudice against women, he is nevertheless sympathetic toward the townspeople, especially his friend Mrs. Gramby, and intimately knowledgeable about them and the "untoward events" that occurred during and after a storm the previous year when Johnnie Roane, the protagonist, returned home from the war.

The predominantly white characters of Lennox, Connecticut, are trapped by time, prejudice, and their own illusions. Refusing to sell land on Main Street to the Catholic church, ostracizing the Jewish lawyer Rosenthal, and impugning the moral character of the black maid Neola and her admirer, the Portuguese gardener Portulacca, who are only sketchily delineated, the townspeople belie the myth of the beneficent small town. Glory Roane, the protagonist's wife, and Lillian Mearns, her mother and daughter-in-law to the wealthy Mrs. Gramby, are shallow, covetous women, fighting futilely against time with diets and hair dye while cheating on their husbands and dreaming of inheriting the Gramby house and fortune. Mearns Gramby, the frustrated, middle-aged heir of the wealthiest family in town, is trapped by his mother's illusion of him as "the last of a long and honorable and distinguished family" (p. 84) and by his addiction to vitamin pills and his marriage to a middle-aged, acquisitive bigot.

Only two major characters manage to transcend the moral and social stagnation of the town. The first is Johnnie Roane, who has outgrown the town while serving in the Army and who returns there from the war only because of the love and memory of his wife Glory. When, at the height of the storm that dramatizes the realities beneath the town's surface serenity, he discovers her infidelity to Lennox's middle-aged Lothario, Ed Barrell, Johnnie breaks free from his idealized past to pursue his dream of becoming a painter in New York. The second is Mrs. Gramby, who embodies the virtues of New England Puritanism. She moves beyond the narrow-minded bigotry of her townspeople and the nostalgia of her personal dreams for her son to become the instrument for social change in the town. In death she, herself, becomes that instrument, for she wills land on the main street of town to the Catholic Church; leaves her house, its contents, and money for its maintenance to her black maid, Portuguese gardener, and cook; and provides six thousand dollars to subsidize Johnnie's pursuit of his dream to become an artist. Marred by the melodramatic conclusion of the reading of the will following Mrs. Gramby's and Ed Barrell's fatal heart attacks, *Country Place* is nevertheless an artistically impressive, realistic treatment of small-town life in New England in which time and place are more important thematically than color and class.

In *The Narrows* Petry moves even further beyond economic determinism as she continues to explore the impact of time and place on the shaping of character. The setting is the black community in Monmouth, Connecticut, another small, typically provincial, white New England town, during the era of Senator Joseph McCarthy's witch hunt for Communists in the State Department. The red neon signs on Dumble Street tell the story of its change; we learn through septuagenarian Abigail Crunch's reverie that

> It was now, despite its spurious early-morning beauty, a street so famous, or so infamous, that the people who lived in Monmouth rarely ever referred to it, or the streets near it, by name; it had become an area, a section, known variously as The Narrows, Eye of the Needle, The Bottom, Little Harlem, Dark Town, Niggertown— because Negroes had replaced those other earlier immigrants, the Irish, the Italians and the Poles.[11]

Petry's fine craftsmanship is immediately apparent in the compelling manner that the structure, style and theme of the narrative fuse as Abbie reflects on what in addition to the hate in the world has brutalized her adopted son Lincoln (Link) Williams, the protagonist. "In Link's case—well, if they hadn't lived on Dumble Street, if the Major had lived longer, if Link had been their own child instead of an adopted child, if she hadn't forgotten about him when he was eight, simply forgotten his existence, if she hadn't had to figure so closely with the little money that she had . . . and eke it out with the small sums she earned by sewing, embroidering, making jelly. If" (pp. 13–14).

The theme, simply stated, is that our lives are shaped as much by chance as they are by time and place. "On how peculiar, and accidental, a foundation rests all of one's attitudes toward a people," Abbie thinks. "Frances hears the word Irish and thinks of a cathedral and the quiet of it, the flickering light of the votive candles, the magnificence of the altar, and I see Irishwomen, strong in their faith, holding a family together. Accident? Coincidence? It all depended on what happened in the past. We carry it around with us. We're never rid of it" (pp. 235–36). This theme is developed in the main plot—the love affair between Link, a black orphan and Dartmouth graduate, and Camilio Williams, the internationally known heiress to the wealth and power of Monmouth's most prominent white family, the Treadways—and the several tributary subplots. The movement of the main plot is more psychological than chronological, for its pace is frequently interrupted by digressions and flashbacks some eighteen years to Link's childhood. The meeting of the couple in The Narrows, their falling in love, the discovery that she is rich and married, his rejection of her for betraying his trust and using him as a black stud, her revenge by claiming he attempted to rape her and thus appealing to traditional color and class prejudice are all influenced by chance and the historical past. The weight of their personal histories and the history of American racism and New England hypocrisy are too heavy a burden for Link and Camilio's love to survive. For breaking the American tribal taboo, Link is murdered by Camilio's mother and husband.

Link, as his name suggests, is the major connection between the past and the present, the white world and the black, the rich and the poor; and it is his consciousness that dominates the third-person point of view that shifts from character to character. Adopted when he was eight by Abbie and Major Crunch and having grown up in Monmouth, Link, at twenty-six, has lost faith in himself and other people. Most of the plot unfolds in his and Abbie's minds. His interior monologues, reverie, and flashbacks and those of the other characters weave a gossamer, impressionistic pattern of events that suggest why he is content to be a bartender at the Last Chance although he was a star athlete and Phi Beta Kappa student at Dartmouth, where he majored in history. Abbie's urge to whiteness and New England respectability confused and frightened him when he was young, making him feel ashamed of his color and "as though he were carrying The Race around with him all the time." These feelings were reinforced in school, where he was cast as Sambo in a minstrel show. But Bill Hod, the influential black owner of the most popular bar and whorehouse in town, and Weak Knees, his cook, who became his surrogate parents when Abbie forgot he existed for three months, taught him the positive aspects of blackness and to fight back if he is attacked.

Because Abbie and Bill had betrayed his love and trust—Abbie by rejecting him during her depression over her husband's death and Bill by severely beating him after finding him in a whorehouse—his belief in his ability to control his life and his desire to conquer the world were destroyed. Although his love for Camilio revives his belief in himself and others, he again feels betrayed when he discovers that she has lied to him about who and what she is. Kidnapped at the end of the novel by Camilio's mother and husband, Link remembers the sensational front-page pictures of a drunk Camilio and an escaped black convict under headlines that inflamed historical color and class prejudices by emphasizing that The Narrows bred crime and criminals: "So it was Jubine Lautrec's Harlot and The Convict by Anonymous that got me in this black Packard. That is one-quarter of the explanation. The other three-quarters reaches back to that Dutch man of Warre that landed in Jamestown in 1619" (p. 399).

The frequency, length and occasional remoteness to the events at hand of the digressions and flashbacks give complexity to the characters but annoyingly impede the progress of the plot and emotionally and psychologically distance the reader from the tragedy of the central character. This is most apparent in the denouement when Link is kidnapped and murdered. Equally passive but more strikingly individualized are Abbie and some of the minor characters. Abbie, a black New England Puritan, is an old widow who is driven by an ambivalence about black people and an obsession with aristocratic values; Major, her dead husband, was a robust, sensitive mountain of a man who used to tell stories about the legendary members of his family, whom he affectionately called "swamp niggers"; Jubine, the "recording angel" of Monmouth, is a man with a deep compassion for "the poor peons" like himself, a man "who spent a lifetime photographing a river, and thus recorded the life of man in the twentieth century"; Malcolm Powther, a black Judas, is a pompous, worshipful servant to rich white people, whose values he embraces, and to his sensual, promiscuous wife, whom he fears will leave him for another man; and Peter Bullock, the unprincipled owner and publisher of the *Monmouth Chronicle*, which has been transformed over the years from an antislavery newspaper into an anti-black tool of the white ruling class, is a slave to custom, to a house, to a car, to ulcers, and to the major advertisers in his paper, especially the Treadwell family. Petry's use of symbolic characters like Cesar the Writing Man, the wandering poet who scribbles biblical verses on the sidewalk in Monmouth, is also dramatically effective. Early in the novel Cesar gives philosophical resonance to the characters, plot, and theme when he writes the following passage from Ecclesiastes 1:10 in front of the cafe where Camilio and Link rendezvous: "Is there anything whereof it may be said, See this is new? It hath been already of old time, which was before us" (p. 91).

Petry, like Himes and Wright, is adept at character delineation, but her protagonists are cut from a different cloth than those of her major contemporaries. Rather than sharing the pathology of a Bigger Thomas or Bob Jones or Lee Gordon, Lutie Johnson and Link Williams are intelligent, commonplace, middle-class aspiring blacks, who, despite the socialized ambivalence resulting from racism and economic exploitation, are not consumed by fear and hatred and rage. Petry's vision of black personality is not only different from that of Himes and Wright, but it is also more faithful to the complexities and varieties of black women, whether they are big-city characters like Mrs. Hedges in *The Street* or small-town characters like Abbie Crunch in *The Narrows*. Ann Petry thus moves beyond the naturalistic vision of Himes and Wright to a demythologizing of American culture and Afro-American character.

Notes

1. *The Negro Novel in America*, rev. ed. (New Haven: Yale University Press, 1965), p. 180.
2. Ibid.
3. (Garden City: Anchor Press, 1975), pp. 192–97.
4. Ibid., p. 192.
5. Ibid.
6. (New York: Hill and Wang, 1980), p. xv.
7. Ibid., p. 18.
8. Ann Petry, *The Street* (rpt. New York: Pyramid Books, 1961), p. 130. Subsequent references to this novel will be included parenthetically in the text.
9. See Noel Schraufnagel, *From Apology to Protest: The Black American Novel* (Deland: Everett/Edwards, Inc., 1973), p. 42; and Bone, *The Negro Novel*, p. 185.

10. Ann Petry, *Country Place* (rpt. Chatham: The Chatham Bookseller, 1971), pp. 1, 3, and 4. Subsequent references to this novel will be included parenthetically in the text.

11. Ann Petry, *The Narrows* (Boston: Houghton Mifflin, 1953), p. 5. Subsequent references to this novel will be included parenthetically in the text.

7

"Pattern against the Sky": Deism and Motherhood in Ann Petry's The Street

MARJORIE PRYSE

In an essay titled "Ann Petry: The Novelist as Social Critic," Theodore Gross points to Lutie Johnson's references to Benjamin Franklin in the novel *The Street* as being central to her characterization. Gross reminds us that "at the outset of the book, Lutie expresses an idealistic attitude that is in the traditional American manner." After she buys six hard rolls for herself and her son Bub, she thinks

> of Ben Franklin and his loaf of bread. And grinned thinking, You and Ben Franklin. You ought to take one out and start eating it as you walk along 116th Street. Only you ought to remember while you eat that you're in Harlem and he was in Philadelphia a pretty long number of years ago. Yet she couldn't get rid of the feeling of self-confidence and she went on thinking that if Ben Franklin could live on a little bit of money and could prosper, then so could she.[1]

Bernard Bell takes Gross's observation a step further by noting that although black Americans rarely refer to "myths of the Founding Fathers like Benjamin Franklin, who is the colonial paradigm of the successful self-made man," Lutie Johnson does so,

> naively subscribing to the Protestant ethic and the American Dream as expressed by the Chandlers, the wealthy white New England family

for whom she worked for two years as a live-in maid, and as embodied in Benjamin Franklin, with whom she compares herself.

In depicting the collapse of the American dream for Lutie Johnson, Bell accurately concludes, Petry "thus demythologizes both American culture and Afro-American character."[2]

The precise nature of the social criticism Petry offers in *The Street* relies on the reader's recognition of Lutie's references to Franklin and, even more, on our ability to place these references within the context of American idealism, expressed by Franklin—and others—whom we consider our "Founding Fathers." Once we have taken note of Lutie's specific references to Franklin, we find the early chapters of the novel larded with related allusions. For example, one of the members of the Chandler family, within Lutie's hearing, advises the others to " 'Outsmart the next guy. Think up something before anyone else does. Retire at forty' "(p. 43)—as Franklin himself was able to do. And later, after Lutie leaves the Chandlers and moves in with her father (she learns that her husband Jim has moved in another woman in her absence), she forces herself to study shorthand and typing at night after working all day in a steam laundry to support herself and her son. "Every time it seemed as though she couldn't possibly summon the energy to go on with the course, she would remind herself of all the people who had got somewhere in spite of the odds against them. She would think of the Chandlers and their young friends— 'It's the richest damn country in the world' " (p. 55).

Although Lutie Johnson may seem initially naive in taking Franklin for her model—even when she learns at the Chandlers' house that white people view black women as whores (p. 45), she fails to recognize the stigma of her race and sex and her consequent disqualifications for achieving her particular version of the American dream— by means of dramatic irony as a narrative technique Petry makes sure that the reader understands the limitations society places on Lutie even if she herself does not. The novel's strength lies in Petry's narrative control. For even though we know much more than Lutie does—the effect here is to place every reader, whether white or black, in the position of white society looking in on the world of the street— and even though we are not surprised when Lutie fails to raise herself and her son, we are still surprised, even shocked, at the extent of her fall by the novel's end. When Lutie murders the black band leader and pimp, Boots Smith, who has tried to seduce her, and abandons her son to reform school, we are disappointed and depressed—like some of Petry's early reviewers and critics[3]—even though we knew, both from our own knowledge of our society as well as by means of

Petry's use of dramatic irony—that the model of the self-made man that Benjamin Franklin represents does not, was never intended to, include women or black men. Therefore the origins of Lutie Johnson's narrative fate as well as of her naive faith lie with Franklin and everything he has come to represent about our colonial American origins.

Petry uses dramatic irony to hide from Lutie Johnson the truth that she reveals to the reader early in the novel: that the white bar owner Junto stands behind Lutie's failure to raise herself out of the street. It is Junto who wants Lutie Johnson for himself. Therefore Boots Smith cannot pay Lutie for singing in his band; therefore her son Bub falls under the influence of the atavistic super, Jones, and gets arrested for stealing mail out of post boxes; and therefore, when Lutie discovers that she is expected to pay with her body for a loan to keep her son out of reform school, she effectively strikes back at Junto as she kills Smith with a candlestick.

But the name *Junto* is also a direct allusion to the first significant men's club in American colonial history, the name Franklin gave his secret group of friends.[4] Formed ostensibly for moral and intellectual improvement, Franklin's Junto actually served its members as a central sphere of social and political influence. As Franklin himself implies in his *Autobiography*, and as his biographers reveal, the secret organization helped Franklin solicit trade at his printing shop, it enabled him to put together the capital he needed to dissolve his partnership and become sole proprietor of that shop, and it became, as one of his commentators described it, "an instrument to help him and his associates to rise in the community."[5] In Petry's novel as well, Junto's influence operates in secret, and there is a "club" which appears to be the nameless forces of the street but which in reality includes Boots Smith and the apparently omniscient Mrs. Hedges in league with Junto. In naming her powerful white man Junto, Petry thereby places her references to Benjamin Franklin and Lutie's idealism within the context of the deism which formed the intellectual and philosophical foundations both of Franklin's club and of our country's founding, as *The Declaration of Independence* makes particularly clear.

In light of the novel's references both to Franklin and to his Junto, we can more clearly place Petry's portrait of Mrs. Hedges. Mrs. Hedges, whom Petry invests from the beginning with an omniscience that rivals only that of the narrator's, comes to possess the attributes of a deity. Resembling in particular the deist's god, Mrs. Hedges sets herself apart from events on the street—her "world," which she has even named (p. 251)—even though she sits in her open window, whatever the weather, and watches them. Mrs. Hedges represents for Lutie the street's impersonal and indifferent omniscience. She thinks, "living here is like living in a tent with everything that goes on inside it open to the world because the flap won't close. And the flap couldn't close because Mrs. Hedges sat at her street-floor window firmly holding it open to see what went on inside"(p. 68).

Mrs. Hedges's curiosity is impassive and arbitrary, like that of the watchmaker or the benign policeman whom eighteenth-century colonial and European thinkers envisaged as the First Cause who created the world, then stepped back to let it operate according to its own "laws."[6] Like that First Cause, Mrs. Hedges served as the inspiration and conceptual genius which helped Junto transform himself from gatherer of garbage and junk others have discarded to landlord and proprietor of Lutie's apartment house, various establishments of prostitution (the one Mrs. Hedges runs and the fancier brothel at Sugar Hill), the Junto Bar and Grill, and the Casino where Boots Smith's band plays. And like that impersonal deity, she chooses or chooses not to intervene in the lives of Petry's characters.

She becomes as well, for them, the source of knowledge. Lutie discovers that it is impossible to walk past Mrs. Hedges's window without being seen (p. 84), and when Jones, the building's super, walks past, "he was filled with a vast uneasiness, for he was certain that she could read his thoughts" (p. 89). When Lutie wonders why all the women on the street are separated from their husbands, she thinks, "Certainly Mrs. Hedges should be able to explain it" (p. 76). When Min, the aging woman who lives with Jones, decides to visit a hoodoo doctor, she goes to Mrs. Hedges for a recommendation. After Jones tries to get Mrs. Hedges arrested for running a house of prostitution, he discovers that she is locked into power with the white police. And Mrs. Hedges, appearing to read Jones's thoughts and thereby knowing that he is interested in Lutie, warns him away: " 'There ain't no point in you gettin' het up over her. She's marked down for somebody else' " (p. 90). The language of the warning—that Lutie has been "marked down"—suggests Mrs. Hedges's larger than human knowledge of her fate. All of these details contribute to Petry's portrait of Mrs. Hedges as godlike.

Even in her physical description Petry sets Mrs. Hedges apart from the other characters. From the first time Lutie Johnson turns toward the entrance of the apartment building on 116th Street she notices the "enormous bulk of a woman . . . silhouetted against the light," and the single feature about Mrs. Hedges which impresses itself on Lutie is her eyes. "They were as still and as malignant as the eyes of a snake" (pp. 5–6). Later, when Lutie enters Mrs. Hedges's apartment after the woman rescues her from Jones's attempted rape, Petry describes her, in Lutie's eyes, as "a mountain of a woman" who had "the appearance of a creature that had strayed from some other planet" (p. 237). While she makes Lutie tea, Lutie thinks that "she should have been concocting some witch's brew" (p. 239). Again it is the woman's eyes that strike Lutie: "her eyes were like stones that had been polished. There was no emotion, no feeling in them, nothing visible but shiny, smooth surface" (p. 239). Petry describes the "uncontrollable revulsion in the faces of the white people" who once had looked at the young Mrs. Hedges. "They stared amazed at her enormous size, at the blackness of her skin" and viewed her as "a monstrosity" (p. 241). Petry explains that the woman's coldness results in part from her physical appearance. For after the apartment-house fire which scarred her body and charred her scalp—her blackness further blackened—Mrs. Hedges (who never married) knew that she would never be able to buy, much less attract, a lover.

Yet for all of Mrs. Hedges's power, she is not finally omniscient, and although she reminds us of the deists' god, she is no deity. She fails to detect Jones's scheme to entrap Bub, and she does not see the white policemen when they take Bub away. She doesn't seem to know Boots Smith. And even after Bub's arrest, she limits her interest to what she can see from her window, "urging the contestants on" in the "desperate battle" which the young boys on the street seem to be perpetually enacting (p. 416). Her presence in the novel, however, points to larger forces and gives those forces a tangible, physical agent.

The larger forces in the novel are white people—whom Petry embodies in the Chandlers, the Connecticut family who hire Lutie as live-in domestic; in Junto himself, who looms largely responsible for the street; and in other white representatives—the white reporter who turns a thin man who tries to steal a loaf of bread into a "burly Negro" (p. 198); the white nightclub agent, Mr. Crosse, who promises Lutie a "scholarship" to singing school if she is "nice" to him (pp. 318–22); the white schoolteacher, Miss Rinner, who thinks teaching black kids is like "being in a jungle" (p. 333); and the white lawyer who is willing to charge Lutie two hundred dollars instead of telling her she doesn't need him to keep her son out of reform school (p. 392).

The attitude of hostility and indifference which pervades Petry's description of the landscape—both natural and urban—also connects the forces behind the street with white people. Early in the novel, when Lutie comes home from work to the street for the first time, she finds herself staring at—or being watched by—an advertisement on the subway. In the advertisement she sees a blond girl leaning against a white porcelain sink in a "miracle of a kitchen" accented by "red geraniums in yellow pots" (p. 28). The advertisement leads her to recall the Chandlers' kitchen in Lyme—and the main street of that town. The contrast between that street and the one she now lives on is unmistakable. The Chandlers' street was wide and lined with elm trees whose branches met overhead. "In summer the sun could just filter through the leaves, so that by the time its rays reached the street, it made a pattern like the lace on expensive nightgowns . . . . In winter the bare branches of the trees made a pattern against the sky that was equally beautiful in snow or rain or cold, clear sunlight" (p. 29). The pattern like lace which is beautiful no matter what the weather stands "against the sky"—as if there is a connection between the two. But the sky Lutie sees on her street is different. And the pattern is different.

The white people on the downtown streets stare at Lutie "with open hostility in their eyes" (p. 70), and Lutie concludes that "it all added up to the same thing"—white people (p. 206). It all adds up to white people in the novel because white people, following the lead of Benjamin Franklin, Thomas Jefferson, and John Adams—the committee which submitted the Declaration of Independence to the Continental Congress in 1776—gave the country its deistic foundation. We know, from the manuscript version of the Declaration, that the document Jefferson and his committee submitted was radically different from the one the Congress ratified in one significant respect. Jefferson, in drafting his document using the conventional antislavery political rhetoric of the eighteenth century, in which the colonists become the enslaved and George III the unredeemable tyrant, built his list of colonists' grievances against the king to climax with a long statement condemning the Negro slave trade, blaming the king for refusing to put an end to it, and darkly warning against possible slave insurrections like the very revolution of the colonists themselves. We also know that a "political compromise" with congressional representatives from South Carolina and Georgia led the Congress to delete the specific references to Negro slaves and to replace it with the vague "He has excited domestic insurrections amongst us."[7]

The existence of the draft manuscript of the Declaration of Independence, with its consideration of Negro slavery as a separate issue from the statement that "all men are created equal," is not something about which schoolchildren in this country routinely learn. The discovery that had the founding fathers seen fit to address the question of slavery in 1776, American history might have taken a different course with respect to our treatment of black Americans, is currently reserved for scholars.

Yet in the process by which the Continental Congress saw fit to drop the condemnation of Negro slavery from the Declaration, we can see the process by which Negro slaves were not considered by other men as "created equal"—they became a case for special consideration; and in their exclusion from the document by means of political compromise, we see the indifference that the Declaration builds into our system. In all fairness, historians have observed that the founding fathers thought that slavery would die out on its own anyway—that they couldn't have foreseen Eli Whitney's invention of the cotton gin in 1792 that would make the slave trade economically practical for the South. Nevertheless, the deism of the document finally makes no provision for the humanitarian treatment of the slaves.

In a novel that points to Benjamin Franklin as its protagonist's model and which explains the failure of the American dream for black people in terms of colonial allegory, it seems no accident that when Petry describes her landscapes in *The Street* she uses language that evokes a deistic universe. Early in the novel Lutie agrees to go for a drive with Boots Smith, whom she has just met in the Junto. Petry gives us a "full moon—pale and remote," writes that the "streets had a cold, deserted look" and that "the sky . . . , too, had a faraway look. The buildings loomed darkly against it" (p. 157). The cold distance of the sky, against which the buildings of Harlem loom "darkly," becomes associated with the invisible control white people have exerted over the black world. Behind the wheel of his car, Boots loses his identity as a black man and "plunged forward into the cold, white night," as if "he was a powerful being who could conquer the world." To Lutie, his driving seems "like playing God"; and his engine "roaring in the night" brought the people sleeping in the "white farmhouses . . . half-awake—disturbed, uneasy" (p. 157). In this scene, the indifference of white people toward the plight of the black people on the street seems relegated to the landscape—but Petry makes it clear that Lutie and Boots are dealing with a more active deism, "a world that took pains to make them feel that they didn't belong, that they were inferior." Because of the "delicate balance" of the world white people moved in, "there was nothing left for them but that business of feeling superior to black people." If that was taken away, Petry writes, "even for the split second of one car going ahead of another, it left them with nothing" (p. 158).

The apparently invisible and naturalistic forces behind the street, then, become closely linked with the political attitudes of the white people who founded, then proceeded to run, the country. When Lutie looks out from her apartment window early in the novel she sees not the laws of a street in league with Junto, but rather simply a world let run to chaos: "The rubbish had crept through the broken places in the fences until all of it mingled in a disorderly pattern that looked from their top-floor window like a huge junkpile instead of a series of small back yards" (p. 73). But by the novel's end, Lutie has rejected Franklin's myth of the self-made man and "slowly she began to reach for some conclusion, some philosophy with which to rebuild her shattered hopes" (p. 307). She realizes that "streets like the one she lived on were no accident. They were the North's lynch mobs . . . the method the big cities used to keep Negroes in their place . . . . From the time she was born, she had been hemmed into an ever-narrowing space, until now she was very nearly walled in and the wall had been built up brick by brick by eager white hands" (pp. 323–24). She comes to see a different "pattern against the sky."

The "laws" of the street, which white people have set in motion and allowed to run their course, hem Lutie and the others, particularly the women, into that "ever-narrowing space." The novel depicts, among such "laws," the following: if the women work, the children go to reform school; women become prostitutes when their men leave; women who move in with men must try not to be "put out"; men prey on women; and there is no justice. Unlike Bub Johnson's fantasy, in which, when he is working to steal from mailboxes for Jones, he is really trying to help the "cops catch the crooks" (p. 350), the most powerful "law" on the street is that there is no justice for its inhabitants. Neither is there room for human love in such a world gone wrong, cast away from its moorings: therefore Lutie's husband Jim learns a "pretended indifference" (p. 34) when she decides to take the job as live-in maid for the Chandlers; and therefore Boots Smith weighs Lutie Johnson against all the indignities he has suffered in his life and decides she isn't worth the risk.

In Addison Gayle's view, "*The Street* backs away from a denouement." Gayle praises the novel for delineating the nature of American racism, yet considers Lutie "lacking in power to substantially alter the course of her life."[8] Yet despite the despair of Lutie's life and the futility with which she at first tries to fight for her son, then flees, as Boots's murderer, *The Street* does set up alternative forces which provide its thematic denouement. When we begin to recognize these forces, the novel itself becomes much less bleak—whatever the future holds for Lutie Johnson. Ironically, in light of the forces the novel proposes to counter the "laws" of the street in a world created by white gods, Petry presents Lutie as simply making the wrong choices, following the wrong models; but finally, the power she needs in order to counter the white world already exists, on the street itself.

The first of these alternative forces is represented by Granny. Granny never appears as a character in the novel but she exists as a memory in Lutie's mind. We learn that Lutie's mother died when she was seven and that her grandmother raised her (p. 80). Perhaps if Ann Petry had been able to read recent novels by Paule Marshall, Alice Walker, Toni Morrison, and Toni Cade Bambara,[9] she might have been more aware of the fictional potential of Granny in her novel—for Lutie's Granny (like her fictional predecessor, Janie's grandmother in Zora Neale Hurston's *Their Eyes Were Watching God*) seems to have given Lutie at least some of the right advice and knowledge she needs to counteract the street. Lutie remembers Granny's "tales about things that people sensed before they actually happened. Tales that had been handed down and down and down until, if you tried to trace them back, you'd end up God knows where—probably Africa" (pp. 15–16). Lutie tries to silence what Granny might have said by telling herself she doesn't believe in "instinctive, immediate fear"—even though she knows that Granny would have summed up the super, Jones, as " 'Nothin' but evil, child. Some folks so full of it you can feel it comin' at you—oozin' right out of their skins' " (p. 20). And even though Lutie's grandmother taught her never to let " 'no white man put his hands on you' " (p. 45), Lutie chooses as her model a white man, Benjamin Franklin.

The second alternative force is represented by Mrs. Hedges. Mrs. Hedges is capable of using her power to ward off the evil on the street: she intervenes when Bub is overpowered by the other boys, and she saves Lutie from being raped by Jones. She is also, in her relation to Mary and her other "girls," a mother of sorts. As the "madam" of a whorehouse, where she gives homeless young women a home in exchange for their prostitution, she is a false madonna. Yet she gives Min, Jones's live-in woman, just the right information when Min, oppressed by Jones, tries to do something, herself, to ward off the forces of the street. When Min comes to Mrs. Hedges with her version of Paradise—not being "put out" of Jones's apartment—and asks whether Mrs. Hedges knows of a good root doctor, Mrs. Hedges sends her to see Prophet David. The scene in which Min receives the information and leaves Mrs. Hedges's apartment is significant. Mrs. Hedges tells Min that she doesn't "hold with" root doctors herself, " 'because I always figured that as far as my own business is concerned I was well able to do anything any root doctor could do' " (p. 120). As we have seen, in terms of the power Mrs. Hedges possesses on the street, she certainly could work hoodoo—but chooses not to. And when Min leaves, she sees Mrs. Hedges "brooding over the street like she thought if she stopped looking at it for as much as a minute, the whole thing would collapse" (p. 121). In this image, the deity becomes an inverted goddess, "brooding" over a world she hasn't made, but over which she has mysterious power.

The Prophet David, himself, represents the third and most promising alternative force in *The Street*. When Min is on her way to the Prophet's house, she thinks, "the preacher at the church she went to would certainly disapprove, because in his eyes her dealing with a root doctor was as good as saying that the powers of darkness were stronger than the powers of the church" (p. 122). When Min sees him, Petry writes that "the whiteness of the turban accentuated the darkness of his skin" (p. 129). In contrasting the powers of physical and metaphysical darkness with the "whiteness" of his turban, Min arrives at the first of several important moments of clarity. "It was like Mrs. Hedges and that bandanna she wore all the time . . . . And staring at the Prophet's turban she got the sudden jolting thought that perhaps Mrs. Hedges wore that bandanna all the time because she was bald" (p. 132). In the presence of the Prophet, Min—generally described as a passive, slow-witted creature—begins to see through even Mrs. Hedges herself. The "powers of darkness," however they might be viewed by the white world or the minister of Min's church who scorns root doctors, prove superior to all the doctors and ministers Min has seen in her life. For unlike them, the Prophet gives Min "all of his attention," listens to her in a "quiet way," and "when she came out from behind the white curtains the satisfaction from his attentive listening, the triumph of actually possessing the means of controlling Jones, made her face glow" (p. 137).

The root doctor, representing the strongest evidence of a lingering cultural cohesion among the black community, acts as a potential force against the street's "laws" and the white world. For although the men (and Lutie Johnson) go to the Junto to escape their fears and loneliness, Min sees only women at the Prophet's. The women she sees there want to solve human problems: they are there to keep their husbands in bed nights, or to ward off the specters of white people in their lives. And they all emerge from the Prophet's satisfied and confident. It is important that Mrs. Hedges, who doesn't "hold with" root doctors, is surprised at the renewed energy with which Min returns from the Prophet's. "There was such energy and firmness about the way she walked that Mrs. Hedges's eyebrows lifted as she craned her neck for a further look" (p. 138). And as the novel progresses, Min serves as Lutie's foil for Petry. Lutie becomes more hopelessly lost, in her pursuit of the American Dream; but Min follows the Prophet's instructions and manages to protect herself long enough from Jones to make up her own mind about what she wants to do. The contrast between the two women has never been examined by critics—but Petry clearly offers Min's alternatives, if not Min herself, as models for Lutie. How might the novel, and Lutie's life, have been different, for example, had she gone to the Prophet David for help when Bub is arrested instead of the white lawyer who wants to charge her two hundred dollars? Might the Prophet have been able to tell her she didn't need a lawyer?

Min, then, despite her limitations, lives by the same instincts Lutie Johnson rejects when she refuses to listen to her Granny's voice. Min knows, when she goes to see the Prophet David, that she is "committing an open act of defiance for the first time in her life" (p. 127). We never see Lutie Johnson defying anything or anybody in her world—until her rage becomes so uncontrollable that she commits murder. It is true that Min's situation is different from Lutie's; where Lutie wants a better life for herself and her son, Min, not a mother, wants only to survive. She excuses and explains why she moves from man to man "because a woman by herself didn't stand much chance; and because it was too lonely living by herself in a rented room" (p. 133). Petry doesn't give us any alternatives to Min's situation—yet Min displays a certain heroic dignity in deciding to leave Jones. Unlike Lutie, who despairs of ever leaving the street, Min makes her decision and carries it out. Unlike Lutie, who cannot interpret the "pattern against the sky" which ought to help her follow her instincts instead of burying them, Min can read signs. As she packs to leave, "she took a final look at the sky"(p. 355). She wants to get herself moved "before the snow started"—and in a novel where natural forces of wind and snow alternately reveal and obscure the reality of the street (and in which descriptions of wind and snow frame the novel, in its opening and closing paragraphs), Min recognizes the timeliness of her decision. She glances at the street which she is about to leave and thinks, "It wasn't somehow a very good place to live, for the women had too much trouble, almost as though the street itself bred the trouble" (p. 355).

In a closing scene with Jones, in which the super enters the apartment surprised to see Min at home instead of at work, Min explains her presence by saying that " 'My heart was botherin' me.' " As she speaks, she realizes that it is, indeed, her heart that is threatened, as she feels her heart "making a sound like thunder inside her chest" (p. 360). The scene recalls Bub's own feelings of vulnerability just a few pages earlier in the novel as he runs home from school, having bought his mother a present with money he has earned "working" for Jones, and finds himself pursued by Gray Cap and other boys: "his heart was thudding so hard, he thought it was just as though it had been running, too . . . . He could almost see it—red like a Valentine heart with short legs kicking up in back of it as it ran" (p. 337). Jones's impotence and rage, when Mrs. Hedges tells him that Min has left, leads him to set up Bub once and for all—Min may have escaped him, he thinks, but Bub, and Lutie, will not.

Before Min leaves, she discovers the opened letters addressed to strangers and realizes that "Jones was doing something crooked. He was up to something that was bad"(p. 365). Unfortunately, she leaves without even trying to find out what—and without being able to warn or save Bub. Still, the scene depicts Min as finally smarter than Lutie, more savvy. And Min will survive, away from this particular street. When she meets the pushcart man who arrives to move her belongings, she says softly to herself, " 'A body's got the right to live' " (p. 368). And Min leaves the novel as well as the street with a "soft insinuation in her voice" for the pushcart man. She is clearly on her way to another small apartment with another man, this one whose strength is apparent in his back muscles which bulge as he pushes the cart.

Min is not the perfect foil for Lutie—who rightly aspires to a better life than Min will have with yet another live-in "husband"—but Lutie, with all of her own strengths, combined with some of Min's, might have made more of her situation. Instead of idealistically looking to the American past, Lutie needed to see the founding as it really was: a deistic setting in motion, in which, for white people, there is no place for black people except on the street. Only Min escapes—because Lutie is even more alone than Min, cut off from the possibilities of both black and women's community by her aspirations to be Benjamin Franklin—or to be a mother deity in her own right, for Bub.

Deism and motherhood combine their forces, as the novel moves to its close, as remnants of American myth. In the depiction of Lutie's fall into despair as Boots's murderer, the novel reflects on the tragedy by which motherhood becomes Lutie's only alternative to the street, within the parameters of her attempts to make a decent life and to rise in society. The perversion of the mother in the portrait of the madam/madonna Mrs. Hedges finds its ultimate grotesqueness in Lutie—who believes that against all other odds she can protect her son. Therefore she refuses to allow him to shine shoes, to become the typical black boy in white society, yet contributes to her own fall by insisting on money as the ultimate value. After all, Bub does not initially agree to steal letters out of mailboxes—he only suppresses his own misgivings about working for Jones when Lutie, in her disappointment that Boots will not pay her for singing in his band, finds herself unable to control her own rage. " 'Damn being poor!' " she shouts as she prepares Bub's dinner. " 'God damn it!' " (p. 325). And so Bub turns to Jones.

But for all of her efforts to protect him from the street, Lutie abandons her son at the novel's end. *The Street* depicts the world Bub will grow up in as worse than indifferent, worse than deistic: he is now motherless as well. Lutie's departure reinforces the indifference of the landscape in the street world white people have made; yet her departure, though cruel, seems fated. She was "marked down" to fail as a mother when she was "marked down" for Junto. The particular indifference of white society comes to seem much more planned and much less an accident of nature than the deist's conception of the eighteenth-century universe. The reader is left, above all, with Bub's isolation hovering in the background. His *own* "god"— his mother—departs, leaving him to his fate. And Petry doesn't need to dramatize Bub's reaction to his abandonment—she has already done so in the earlier scene in which, when Lutie leaves Bub alone to go out to sing, he finds himself "swallowed up in darkness," afraid to look and afraid not to look around him in the empty apartment, "here alone, lost in the dark, lost in a strange place filled with terrifying things" (pp. 217–18). On second and subsequent readings of the novel, this scene, in which Bub lies terrified, yet in which he bravely tells his mother good-bye, becomes one of the most painful for the reader. For we know, when we read it, that when she leaves him for good, at the end, he won't have a chance to tell her good-bye.

Mrs. Hedges, whose apparent omniscience and indifferent curiosity lead the reader to perceive the connection between Lutie's references to Franklin and the novel's larger deism, also leads Lutie to the novel's denouement. As Lutie leaves the apartment building to go to Boots's for the last time, Mrs. Hedges reminds her of the " 'very nice white gentleman, dearie' " who wants to sleep with her. At first Lutie merely fumes; then she starts thinking more clearly, and at last she gives form to the forces of the street: "It was Junto" (p. 418). In her final appearance in the novel, Mrs. Hedges reminds us of her role as madam. The deity/goddess who seems so much a part of the landscape of the street has failed to mother. And when Lutie, following her murder of Boots, abandons Bub and buys a one-way train ticket to Chicago, Petry's vision is complete. The feeling of the failure of the idea of America, its possibilities, its "dream," is conveyed in the feeling of the failure of the mothers/madams to help their children. The image of "homelessness" or "absence of mother" which Petry gives her reader when Lutie leaves Bub is more terrifying than the absence of God.

Yet in the failure of the mothers to listen to their grannies, or to turn to the black community and the women's community for wisdom, solace, and help, the novel portrays social desolation in fundamental human terms. If we focus not just on the novel's deism, on the withdrawal of human agency by which the street operates, but see it instead as systematically alienating children from their "mothers"—that is, from their roots (and root doctors)—and orphaning them culturally, then the betrayal of democracy for black people in Petry's novel becomes the destruction of human feeling in the world. Mrs. Hedges's eyes become every bit as powerful and empty as the eyes of Doctor T. J. Eckleburg, which emerge from the landscape of the "valley of ashes" in F. Scott Fitzgerald's *The Great Gatsby*.[10] Despite her ultimate failure as a model for the women on the street, Min therefore points (minimally?) to the novel's meaning. In not wanting to be "put out" from Jones's apartment, she fights for human survival, and for the survival of women. She does not want to be "put out" from the human circle.

Ironically, then, the only "pattern against the sky" which the novel creates is, after all, motherhood—but a motherhood not of biology but of human connection, in which the Prophet David becomes the symbol of nurturing power in the black community, the force capable of countering the perverted indifference of feeling represented by Petry's portrait of Mrs. Hedges. Like the snow at the end of the novel, which "gently" obscures "the grime and the garbage and the ugliness," *The Street* does offer its readers an alternative in the vision of a black community which might embrace its grandmothers, its folklore, and the survival of human feeling, a street which might become, and thereby transform, "any street in the city"—even the street in Lyme, Connecticut, on which Petry shows us white people, like Mr. Chandler's brother, blowing their brains out.

In so doing, *The Street* stands as a connecting link in a fictional tradition that looks back to Zora Neale Hurston's portraits of black community and folklore and looks ahead to those contemporary novels by Marshall, Alice Walker, Morrison, and Bambara (and Ralph Ellison and James Baldwin and Al Young) which have taught readers to rediscover, reassess, and reclaim the human values signified by folk community in black fiction. Such fiction really proclaims our declaration of independence—our refusal to be any longer enslaved by human indifference in any form, in any culture.

Notes

1. In A. Robert Lee, ed., *Black Fiction: New Studies in the Afro-American Novel Since 1945* (New York: Barnes & Noble, 1980), p. 43. Gross is quoting Ann

Petry, *The Street* (New York: Houghton Mifflin, 1946), pp. 63–64. In making references to this edition, I will cite further page numbers in parentheses in the text.

2. "Ann Petry's Demythologizing of American Culture and Afro-American Character," included in this volume, Chapter 6.

3. Since its publication in 1946, *The Street* has been applauded by some critics and reviewers, damned by others. James W. Ivy, who first interviewed Petry for *The Crisis* (in February 1946; the interview is reprinted in Roseann P. Bell, Bettye J. Parker, and Beverly Guy-Sheftall, eds., *Sturdy Black Bridges: Visions of Black Women in Literature* [Garden City, N.Y.: Anchor Press/Doubleday, 1979], pp. 197–200), in a subsequent issue delivered a vicious attack on Petry in his review of *The Street* (*Crisis* 54 [May 1946], pp. 154–55). In a contrasting review from *Phylon* in the same year (7:98–99), Lucy Lee Clemmons called the novel "good reading . . . . Despite the sordidness, the squalor, the bitterness, there is a fundamental understanding of basic human qualities and realism concerning Negro life." And Alain Locke, in a review of Petry and other black writers who had published fiction during 1946, assesses both the novel and its controversy and concludes that *The Street* is "the artistic success" of 1946. Calling the novel "the cleverest kind of social indictment," he describes Petry's characters as symbolic of "the environment which made them," concluding that "in realism, that is the height of art" (*Phylon* 8 [1947]:21).

More recently, Petry's Lutie Johnson has frequently been termed "the female counterpart of Bigger Thomas" (see, for example, Alfred Maund, "The Negro Novelist and the Contemporary Scene" [*Chicago Jewish Forum* 12 (1954): 28–34]; or Robert Bone, *The Negro Novel in America* [New Haven: Yale University Press, 1958], who calls the novel a *roman à thèse* and an "eloquent successor to *Native Son*"). Other critics have moved beyond either attacking Petry's portrait of Harlem life or undercutting the value of her achievement by comparing her to Richard Wright. David Littlejohn, for example, advises the reader to skip the novel's "sordid plot" but praises its "female wisdom, the chewy style" with which Petry creates "people made out of love, with whole histories evoked in a page" (*Black on White* [New York: Grossman Bros., 1966], p. 155). Arthur P. Davis (*From the Dark Tower* [Washington, D.C.: Howard University Press, 1974]) calls the novel Petry's "most impressive," although he too characterizes it as "a depressing work" which implies "that the black poor in the ghetto do not have much of a chance to live decent and meaningful lives, to say nothing of happy lives" (p 194).

The most incisive analysis emerges from Addison Gayle, Jr., who explores the novel's naturalism and suggests that Petry "has paved the way for future black writers" by portraying America as "an oppressive place for black people," thereby beginning "the exploration for realistic ways of combating the deterministic universe" (*The Way of the New World* [Garden City, N.Y.: Anchor/Doubleday, 1975], p. 196).

4. In his biography, *Benjamin Franklin: Philosopher and Man* (Philadelphia: J. B. Lippincott Co., 1965), Alfred Owen Aldridge notes that Franklin organized his Junto in the fall of 1727 (p. 39), although he did not become a member of the Masons until February 1731 (p. 44).

5. Aldridge, p. 40.

6. Herbert M. Morais, *Deism in Eighteenth Century America* (New York: Russell & Russell, 1960), uses the representation of the universe as a machine

set in motion by an Efficient Cause (p. 54) and cites the deists' "central concept of God as a Passive Policeman" (p. 56).

7. See Edwin Gittleman, "Jefferson's 'Slave Narrative': The Declaration of Independence as a Literary Text," *Early American Literature* 8 (1974), pp. 239–56, for a fuller discussion of the original draft of the Declaration, as well as for the text of the anti-slavery grievance, pp. 252–53.

8. Gayle, p.196.

9. I'm thinking especially of Marshall's *The Chosen Place, The Timeless People* (1969), Morrison's *Sula* (1973) and *Song of Solomon* (1977), Bambara's *The Salt Eaters* (1980), and Walker's *The Color Purple* (1982), all of which portray strong women who understand the power of black, female traditions.

10. (New York: Scribner's, 1925), p. 23.

8

Jubilee: *The Black Woman's Celebration of Human Community*

MINROSE C. GWIN

> " . . . I closed her eyes in death, and God is my witness,
> I bears her no ill will."
> Vyry Ware in *Jubilee*

Margaret Walker's *Jubilee* is a novel of celebration and culmination. It is also "a canvas," she writes, "on which I paint my vision of my world."[1] Throughout her life as literary artist and teacher, Walker has evoked her world as a place of possibility in which the principle of humanism generates in persons of all races vast potentials for love and fellow feeling. Through the years she has repeatedly used the term *humanism* to delineate her own philosophy of life and art, and on occasion has associated *humanistic values* with religion, with Afro-American writing, and with women. In 1975, almost a decade after *Jubilee* was published, she herself said that her concept of humanism had expanded greatly in the past twenty to twenty-five years.[2] Although Walker at times has become disillusioned with organized religion as "the tool of a very racist society," *Jubilee* often reflects her

---

This essay has been expanded and appears as a chapter in *Black and White Women of the Old South: The Peculiar Sisterhood in American Literature* (Knoxville: University of Tennessee Press, 1985).

early commitment to basic Christian concepts. More significantly, the novel suggests her own insistence upon an organic connection between humanism and religion in which "even the highest peaks of religious understanding must come in a humanistic understanding— the appreciation of every human being of his own spiritual way."[3] In a profound sense, black literature emerges, she believes, from "the unbroken tradition of humanistic values that did not spring from renaissance Europe, but developed in Asia and Africa before the religious wars of the Middle Ages." Walker's definition of humanism synthesizes natural, religious, historical, and moral elements. Hers is an organic philosophy of human life which embodies

> a recognition that we are part of nature and the historical process, that we are implicit in the dynamic evolving of mankind to ever higher planes of being, that all life must be richly developed in spirit rather than mere matter, and that one must regard the sacred nature of a brother as one values his own privacy and his own inner sanctity.[4]

What she calls her "new humanism" carries with it "a new respect for the quality of all human life" and therein must be squarely opposed to racism. Afro-American literature, she believes, "is a reservoir of black humanism." It is the standard-bearer of the values of "freedom, peace, and human dignity." It is what America, black and white, needs.[5]

Walker's humanism is a faithfulness to what she sees as "the living truth of the human spirit."[6] Her world, as she believes it is and as she creates it to be, is thus inhabited by a flawed human race with enormous capacity for moral insight and spiritual change which affirm rather than deny humanist values. In *Jubilee* those characters with the greatest of these capacities are black people who endure slavery, war, and Reconstruction to emerge in profound and steadfast solidity as wounded but victorious soldiers in the cause of individual freedom. Above all, *Jubilee* celebrates the ability of the southern Afro-American to move through the baptismal fire of the mid-nineteenth century and actually to become regenerated and whole through suffering. The novel is about more than black suffering and endurance. It is about freedom of self through the acknowledgment of a self-imposed bondage to the human duty of nurturance of others. And it celebrates that freedom in women and men of all races who bind themselves to one another in such a way.

Walker speaks of her novel as a culmination. It is a life's work. Its origin was in the stories of her maternal grandmother, Elvira Ware Dozier, who kept young Margaret up past bedtime with tales of slavery times and the survival of those times by her own mother, Walker's great-grandmother, the indomitable Vyry of *Jubilee*. Grandma, as young Margaret called her, would grow indignant when accused of telling the child "tall tales" and would retort,"I'm not telling her tales; I'm telling her the naked truth."[7] That "naked truth," born of the black oral tradition, germinated in Walker's mind long before she actually began work on the book in 1934 when she was a senior at Northwestern. Walker put her project aside then, but throughout the years she worked on the novel piecemeal, poring over Civil War histories and researching oral slave narratives whenever possible. She became a poet and university professor, wife and mother. In 1964 she began writing in earnest on the novel which she would use as a dissertation for the Ph.D. at the University of Iowa. "On the morning of April 9, 1965, at ten o'clock," she writes that she typed the last words: "So, when I say that I have been writing *Jubilee* all my life, it is literally true. It has been a consuming ambition, driving me relentlessly."[8]

Yet *Jubilee* is a work of culmination in a more significant sense. It is a synthesis of folk tradition, imagination, and moral vision. It is, at once, realistic and visionary. Much like Harriet Beecher Stowe's *Uncle Tom's Cabin*, *Jubilee* is a paradoxical, difficult novel.[9] As Arthur Davis suggests, Walker's characters—black and white—are stereotypes based on southern myth.[10] Yet, like so many of Stowe's stereotypical creations, Walker's characters paradoxically spring into life and liveliness surpassing their obvious symbolic designations. The heroine Vyry, who survives and endures white cruelty and oppression to return love for hatred, becomes not just Every Black Woman, but every human being who still believes, like Walker, in a "common humanity [which] supersedes race."[11] Walker's novel is about race and class in the South during the period before, during, and after the Civil War; yet her writings and speeches throughout her life articulate *Jubilee*'s ultimate messages—that, as Walker puts it, "history is not just one solid page of black and white," [12] that forgiveness is possible, that love is redemptive and regenerative.

In its insistence upon resolution and forgiveness, *Jubilee*, published in the turmoil of the mid-sixties, may also be seen as a natural culmination of American fictional and autobiographical treatments of the mid-nineteenth century—particularly the Civil War—and of the profoundly ambivalent relationships between black and white southern women during that chaotic period of history. As Phyllis Klotman points out, the novel presents history from the black woman's perspective. Vyry is the focus—moral, physical, and spiritual—of *Jubilee*. From the death of her mother, Sis Hetta, in 1839, to news of the imminent birth of her fourth child at the end of the saga, we see the events of thirty years through the eyes of this larger-than-life black woman of the nineteenth-century Deep South.[13] As in women's slave narratives of the nineteenth and early twentieth centuries, Vyry's life *is* the book. Her movement from slavery through the vicissitudes of war to freedom parallels her burgeoning sense of who she is and what she stands for. All the while she gathers strength and self-knowledge and, as her white folks crumble under the barrage of war, she takes charge of their welfare as well as of her own and that of her children. Through this process of growth on southern soil, a process that in the slave narratives was usually the result of an escape north, Vyry— like real black women such as Harriet Jacobs—comes to know herself and her own capacities for endurance and love. *Jubilee* is a novel of Vyry's becoming. In its last pages, when she proclaims the message of Walker's humanism, one has the sense of immense possibility for this black woman who rejects racial bitterness at her southern heritage by revealing that she herself forgives the one white who most shamefully mistreated her, "Big Missy" Salina Dutton.

Vyry's profession of forgiveness toward her dead mistress releases wells of bitterness and hatred in the relationships between black and white southern women of the mid-nineteenth century, in life and in literature. This is a fictional nineteenth-century black woman's gesture of conciliation rendered by a real black woman writer of the volatile sixties. As such, it is a significant black acknowledgment of cross-racial female bonds of suffering which are so much a part of such white American fiction as Stowe's *Uncle Tom's Cabin* (1851), William Faulkner's *Absalom, Absalom!* (1936), and Willa Cather's *Sapphira and the Slave Girl* (1940). *Jubilee* does not so much oppose violence and love as it presents them as catalysts which create Walker's humanistic vision of life. Love is born out of violence in this fiction; it is a peculiarly female regenerative process that saturates and thereby dilutes racial bitterness with sisterhood and maternal nurture. This process of conciliation is a harbinger of what Walker called in 1970 the "new consciousness" of a nonracist society.[14] *Jubilee* is, in fact, a supreme example of Walker's own assertion that "Afro-American literature is a reservoir of black humanism" and perhaps also her exhibition of the "hope for a better world . . . founded on a new humanism instead of the old racism."[15]

At the same time *Jubilee* may be read as a moral resolution of fictional and autobiographical treatments of interracial relationships among nineteenth-century southern women. Walker's fictional construct of racial reconciliation is embodied in Vyry's charitable feelings for white women. Whether such a reconciliation opens this novel to James Baldwin's earlier criticisms of oversimplification and distortion of reality in other literature about blacks is a pertinent issue.[16]

Vyry's limited articulation of Walker's humanistic values does perhaps make life simpler than it is. In some ways, though, Walker's philosophy of humanism complicates life and renders fiction about race a more complex genre. History for Walker comes in shades of gray, as does its fictional mimesis. Issues of race lose clarity when considered in the light of Walker's humanism. Yet such issues become even more urgent in such a light. Walker believes that specific white people have been unjust to specific blacks. She does not believe that all whites are evil, just as she does not believe that all blacks are good. Like that of Christ, Vyry's path is the hardest to follow because it is, at once, the most simple and the most complex. Baldwin would perhaps chastise Walker for writing still another "everybody's protest novel" which imposes theological simplification upon the complexity of life. Yet Walker's vision of life has its own power. Speaking through Vyry's voice, she summons up the multi-layered quality of that life in which individuals of all races live in a mixed state of grace and disgrace, good and evil. Vyry's voice is the voice of good will, of duty, of a willingness to love and serve. It is the articulation of some of the best human impulses. Yet it is Walker's voice rather than Vyry's which moves us. Vyry herself is a simple woman. She does not come to her decision to forgive past cruelties out of a fullness of consciousness that would make such a gesture fictionally dynamic. It is Walker's vision of human reconciliation that is complex and significant; its fictional counterpart seems thin by comparison and less developed in *Jubilee* than imposed upon it.

This is a black woman's voice in a black woman's novel. Yet it is a counterpoint to other voices in black and white literature about southern women during the mid-nineteenth century. In *Uncle Tom's Cabin* several of Stowe's fictional women develop close cross-racial bonds in their mutual battle against a rapacious patriarchy in the slave South. Yet those bonds such as that between Mrs. Shelby and Aunt Chloe are always based on the racist presumption of white superiority. Women's slave narratives and journals by plantation mistresses show that in the reality of the southern experience sexual jealousy and mutual distrust often precluded meaningful female bonds. Such bonds as were developed were often predicated upon the assumption by the slave woman of a demeanor of inferiority and servility. Affection based on such bonds seems to have been more real to the white woman than to black, and remained only as long as the black woman stayed in her place. White women such as Mary Chesnut or Susan Smedes seem blind, or at best myopic, in regard to the real plight of the slave women, whose hardships at the hands of their southern white "sisters" are related by Harriet Jacobs and Elizabeth Keckley, both of whom faced the two-headed monster of the slavocracy, a lustful master and a jealous mistress.[17]

In the twentieth century, Faulkner's *Absalom, Absalom!* probes most profoundly the volatile, often violent connection between black and white women in the nineteenth-century South. Perhaps more than any other writer in the nineteenth and twentieth centuries, Faulkner, ironically a southern white male, plumbs the depths of ambiguity in these women's relationships, and in so doing seems to see in those complex connections a paradigm of southern racial experience. His explorations of these relationships take various forms: the enduring bond forged between Judith Sutpen and Clytie by common suffering, the sexual competition between Judith and the octoroon which eventually merges into human sympathy. Yet Rosa Coldfield's shocked recognition of Clytie's white Sutpen heritage and her anguished, questioning cry of ". . . *sister, sister?*" becomes Faulkner's true metaphor for the mysterious power of racism which supplants human kinship with terror and antipathy. In a more limited way Cather, a southerner turned Midwesterner, sees in Sapphira Colbert and her perverse cruelty to her slave Nancy a shocking case history of a woman's jealous madness—a study in evil. Slavery nurtures Sapphira's egocentricity and gives her the power to try to destroy the young black woman whose youth and health mock her own age and infirmity. Yet, at the same time, Cather depicts a complex woman who is admired by others of her women slaves and whose memory is evoked lovingly in the epilogue of the book—by a black woman. Just as the slave girl Nancy frees herself, so does the Sapphira of Till's imagination, who faces death with dignity and grace, and shows consideration for others in her final hours. These cross-racial female relationships reflect above all else the complex mixture of good and evil in human nature and human conduct. Cather creates a world where no one, particularly not Sapphira in her wheelchair, is ever free. In *Sapphira and the Slave Girl* slavery becomes a metaphor for all human bondage, past and present.

Except for the slave narratives, these literary treatments of cross-racial female relationships during this time and in this place are all from a white point of view; and black women characters are either, like Stowe's Aunt Chloe or Cather's Till, presented stereotypically or, like Faulkner's Clytie, become inscrutable. What Robert Lively has pointed out concerning Civil War novels in particular may apply to these three American novels about the nineteenth-century South—such white literary treatments, he writes, "have failed to enter slave minds or revivify slave ambitions; Negro characters have remained, for the most part, lacking necessary elements of unique individuality."[18]

Jubilee responds to these novels in the sense that it presents the slavery experience and cross-racial female relationships from the viewpoint of the black woman. Eight years after the publication of *Jubilee*, Walker said in conversations with Nikki Giovanni that she was still interested in "the black woman in fiction perhaps because I'm a black woman and feel that the black woman's story has not been told, has not been dealt with adequately."[19] The peculiarly female connection in *Jubilee* between natural creative principles of life and spiritual creativeness synthesizes much of what is positive in women's relationships in the earlier novels and autobiographies. Walker associates womanhood as it is personified in Vyry with burgeoning growth and fertility. Vyry's nurturance of white women is part of Walker's concepts of creative physicality and humanism. Such creativity, Walker wrote in 1980,

> cannot exist without the feminine principle, and I am sure God is not merely male or female but He-She—our Father-Mother God. All nature reflects this rhythmic and creative principle of feminism and femininity: the sea, the earth, the air, and all life whether plant or animal.[20]

In the same essay Walker suggests that the key to humanism lies in the traditional female sphere and in the woman writer who values that sphere. She sounds much like Stowe when she writes a century later:

> The traditional and historic role of womankind is ever the role of the healing and annealing hand, whether the outworn modes of nurse, and mother, cook, and sweetheart. As a writer these are still her concerns. These are still the stuff about which she writes the human condition, the human potential, the human destiny.[21]

Vyry is such a woman and such a symbol. And it is her connections with white women—whether those women be cruel, helpless, or kind—that reflect Walker's humanism and her own. It is also these fictional bonds that symbolically reconcile under what Walker believes to be the humanistic mantle of black fiction the profoundly ambivalent feelings among these women of this time and this region. The issue is whether this is a meaningful reconciliation or whether it is a facile distortion of far deeper and more painful conflicts.

Certainly Vyry's early struggles seem painful enough. The novel opens when Vyry is two years old with the death in childbirth of her mother, Sis Hetta, who had been since her early adolescence the concubine of the master of the Georgia plantation, John Dutton. Vyry is his daughter. After her mother's death, the child is taken to the Big House where she spends most of her time trying to stay out of the way of Dutton's wife Salina, the "Big Missy" of the plantation who, instead of taking a motherly role with her half-white step-daughter, takes perverse pleasure in tormenting the child whose pale face is a flesh-and-blood emblem of her husband's infidelity. "Big Missy" Salina is a woman of steel, a real ogre reminiscent of Jacob's Mrs. Flint; yet she also is a fictional exaggeration of glorified white southern womanhood. The overseer Grimes describes her as

a lady, . . . a fine, good lady. She nurses the sick far and wide, white and black. She knows how to handle niggers and keep a big establishment; how to set a fine table, and act morally decent like a first-class lady. She's a real Christian woman, a Bible-reading, honest-dealing, high-quality lady who knows and acts the difference between niggers and white people. She ain't no nigger-loving namby-pamby like that s.o.b. pretty boy she's married to.[22]

Salina's "Christianity" is in ironic contrast to her tortures of Vyry. When the child forgets to empty the chamber pot from the room of her half-sister Lillian, Big Missy throws the contents in her face. Soon after the death of Vyry's first surrogate mother, Mammy Sukey, the girl has the misfortune to break one of Salina's china dishes. Big Missy responds by hanging the child by her hands in a closet, where she loses consciousness until her father finds her. Yet, it is Lillian, Salina's daughter and Vyry's half-sister, who meets her father as he returns to the plantation with the words, "Oh, Poppa, come quick, Vyry's hanging by her thumbs in the closet and I do believe she's dead" (p. 37). Dutton rescues Vyry, and forbids his wife to mistreat her, not so much on humane grounds, but because "someday she'll be grown-up and worth much as a slave" (p. 37). Salina obviously associates Vyry with her husband's sexual appetites, and vows to "kill her and all other yellow bastards like her" (p. 37).

Just as the female principle is linked to creative humanism in *Jubilee*, so is the ideal of motherhood. The book begins and ends with the bearing of children. Sis Hetta fails in her attempt to bear a child, but Vyry at the end of *Jubilee* is expecting her fourth and has reconciled white and black interests through her willingness to aid in the delivery of other women's children. It is this maternal framework and emphasis which, by contrast, mark Salina as an evil force. By all natural laws, the white woman, as the wife of Vyry's father, has certain maternal obligations to the mulatto orphan. In the southern context, it is understandable that she refuses to fulfill any natural obligations. But, instead of casting Vyry to the care of others and forgetting her, Salina tortures and torments her as if she, by being her mother's child, were innately guilty of some unforgivable sin. Like Cather's Sapphira, Big Missy becomes Jung's Dark Mother—a perversion of the generative principle, the primal threat to life and growth. Young Vyry has two surrogate mothers: Mammy Sukey, whose death leaves her devastated, and (most important) Aunt Sally, the Dutton cook, who shares food, warm times in her cabin, cooking lessons, and maternal affection with her adopted daughter. Without warning, the Duttons decide to sell Aunt Sally. As her black mother is dragged away sobbing pitifully, young Vyry cannot soak in the horrible reality of the experience. It is Big Missy, the Dark Mother, who shatters the child's dazed state:

> Then Vyry found herself shaking like a leaf in a whirlwind. Salt tears were running in her mouth and her short, sharp finger nails were digging in the palms of her hands. Suddenly she decided she would go with Aunt Sally, and just then Big Missy slapped her so hard she saw stars and when she saw straight again Aunt Sally was gone. (p. 85)

Just as Rosa Coldfield's slap seems to seal the violent connection between white and black women, Big Missy's blow physically evokes separation—both between herself and the black-white child fathered by her husband, and between the child and her foster mother, Aunt Sally. Rosa's slap is a recognition. Big Missy's is a rejection. Both blows embody in the space of a single instant the misuse of power by southern white women; both are indictments of that misuse and of its ultimate victimization of black women. Such epiphanic moments in *Jubilee* provide the novel with emotive translations of history, and thereby with a vividness and intensity which Walker does not achieve in her descriptive historical passages. Big Missy's separation of Vyry from her surrogate mother and the slap which irrevocably seals that separation confront us with the dark side of southern history and make us feel its terror.

Big Missy's cruelties occur in the first section of the book, which presents the antebellum period. The mid-section, about the Civil War, focuses on the general decline of the Dutton family. Salina loses husband, son, and son-in-law to the war. The only real grief she seems to feel is at the death of her son Johnny; yet she supports the Confederacy until its fall and then dies suddenly of a stroke, making good her wish never to see the slaves freed. The focus in this mid-section is upon Vyry's resiliency and her care of the white women as their family disintegrates, a smoldering symbol of the waste and ruin of the Lost Cause. Vyry is also burdened with the care of two children by her marriage to Randall Ware, a free black who had gone north before the war.

As Salina loses control of the plantation and of herself, Vyry takes care of her half-sister Lillian and her children. When Lillian loses her husband to the war and Salina dies of a stroke, Lillian begs Vyry not to leave her alone on the plantation. Throughout this period directly after the war, Lillian gradually sinks into a mindless state and Vyry has to take more and more control of the plantation. She single-handedly plows some land to plant vegetables, and persuades other black women on the deserted farm to help her plant corn, collards, peas, okra, tomatoes, onions, and other food crops for themselves and the children, black and white, under their care. Lillian, who has lost brother, father, mother, and husband in close sequence, begins to lose touch with reality: she "seemed to pay less attention to what was going on around her as the days passed, but she smiled and gave her approval to their plans" (p. 277). When Lillian is attacked by Yankee soldiers and becomes permanently addled as a result, Vyry moves with her children to the Big House to take care of her white sister. As Lillian, a symbolic wreck of the Old South, sinks deeper and deeper into madness, Vyry—an emblem of the budding New South—shelters and nurtures her. She becomes more of a concerned mother to Lillian than the selfish Salina ever was. She saves fresh eggs and fresh buttermilk for her. Yet, regardless of her sister's efforts, Lillian slips further into permanent lethargy, as she rocks for hours, "apart from all around her" (p. 297).

This mid-section of the saga is Vyry's ascendancy. She moves from the frightened slave child who ducks behind corners to avoid Big Missy to the mainstay of what is left of the white family. Her endurance is the thread which knits this section—and the whole novel—together into a rendering of the indomitability of the Afro-American heritage. Her loyalty to Lillian also shows the practical application of humanistic values which Walker felt the black woman was particularly attuned to. When it appears that Randall Ware is not returning for her and the children, Innis Brown, who has helped her on the plantation, persuades her to marry him and to leave to find their own home. Yet Vyry will not desert Lillian without making sure she is taken care of. She sends for John Dutton's sister Lucy to come take Lillian and waits until she arrives before leaving. Meanwhile she becomes Lillian's mother, nurses and sustains her as her mind dissolves with the old Confederacy. She has deep family feeling for her white sister, and she truly grieves for "Miss Lillian," as her mind wanders farther and farther from reality:

> All this saddened Vyry. She felt terribly unhappy over Miss Lillian and it seemed so strange that things had turned out this way for the little golden girl she had always adored since she was a slave child herself growing up in the Big House. (p. 304)

Vyry's affection for Lillian remains throughout her years with Innis Brown. When she goes to visit Lucy Porter and her husband several years later, she weeps at Lillian's deterioration. To Lillian's repeated assertions, "I'm not crazy. I know who I am. I know my name. My name is Lillian," Vyry responds, "I know you ain't crazy, and I know you knows who you are. Honey don't you fret none. I knows you knows your name" (p. 412). In her soothing words, Vyry shows her recognition of Lillian's former identity and her kinship to her. She instinctively forgives her white sister for her thoughtlessness of the past years of slavery, and she mourns Lillian's loss of identity and sanity. Throughout her travels with Brown in their search for a permanent home, Vyry carries over that same openness and willingness to comfort and support white women of the merchant and share-cropper classes. Walker pictures many of the "poor Whites" of rural Georgia and Alabama after the war as being in worse condition than Vyry and her family. Often, too, white sharecroppers are depicted as having intense resentment against the newly freed blacks because of the economic competition they present. Vyry and Innis become the victims of Klan violence and are forced to move when their house, which they built themselves, is burned down. Throughout these experiences and hardships, though, Vyry responds to the needs of white women while at the same time retaining her own sense of self. Nor does she let prejudice against blacks deter her from doing what she sees as her duty to fellow human beings, who happen to be white.

When she and Innis find a white family still living in a sharecropper's shack that they have made arrangements to inhabit, Vyry recognizes poverty and actual hunger in the white wife and her six thin ragged children. She immediately asks to be allowed to cook supper outside and, to her husband's astonishment, begins to make supper in a huge wash pot. Her preparations for the meal seem ritualistic:

> First she heated water from the well and scalded two big fat chickens. Then after she had dressed them she had Innis half-fill the big iron wash pot with water. Into this she put the cut-up chickens, a rabbit cut

up, fat salt pork in hunks, a pan full of potatoes and onions, a jar of
okra, tomatoes and corn mixture, salt and pepper, and let the pot boil
a long time until the aroma of the food began to rise on the wind. (p.
348)

Drawn by the smell of food, the white woman confides in Vyry that
she and her family have eaten nothing but "fried meat grease and
hominy since day before yestiddy" (p. 348). Always calling the white
woman "ma'am," Vyry charitably feeds her and her family. She helps
the woman circumvent her husband's pride by pretending that the
whites are doing her a favor by helping her eat an unplanned surplus
of food. In the morning, she serves the white family hot food before
they set out. In order to meet the family's needs, she maintains a
subservient pose, one which she was trained for as a slave. Yet, at
the base, her brief encounter with this poor white woman shows Vyry
to be in control, just as she was in control with Lillian. Strangely,
after years of bondage, she does not seem concerned with power in
her relationships with whites. She adapts a mode of behavior concerned only with ministering to the needs of others, regardless of race
and regardless of the poses she must adopt in order to do good. Her
duty is to others—wherever that responsibility leads, she will follow.

In her relationship with another white woman later in the novel,
Vyry becomes more assertive and less self-effacing. Her assertiveness
comes perhaps from the knowledge that Mrs. Jacobson, her employer,
is a self-sufficient woman who does not really need her in the same
way that Lillian and the poor white woman did. In her characterization of Mrs. Jacobson, Walker seems to criticize the white woman
for failing to see Vyry, who becomes her cook, as a wife and mother
with her own responsibilities and as a person in her own right. Mrs.
Jacobson is willing to help Vyry as long as it suits her purposes. She
allows her to bring her three children to work with her and she is
sympathetic to the idea of elementary education for blacks. She even
promises to find a book for Vyry's daughter Minna. But when Vyry
wants to quit her employment to help Innis with their house and
farm, so as to allow her two older children the chance to go to school,
Mrs. Jacobson becomes bitter and accusatory. She complains,

"I understand how you colored people don't want to work the way you
useta. What's more you won't work the way you useta. You expect
everything to come dropping in your laps, houses and land and schools
and churches and money, and you want to leave the white people
holding the bag." (p. 373)

The message of Mrs. Jacobson's disgruntlement is that any white female's relationships with a black woman must be predicated on her staying in her place as a servant and caretaker of white interests. Vyry breaks that code, and thereby reaps the wrath of her employer who hitherto has been supportive. The old codes of slavery times are still operable as Vyry seeks a new life and new relationships with white women. Yet, again, Walker sees human behavior and morality in complex terms. When the Browns are burned out of their newly built house by Klansmen, it is Mrs. Jacobson who offers Vyry the old job back in town and who sends bedding and clothing to the distraught black family. Mr. Jacobson gives them money to travel on. Significantly, though, the white influential Jacobsons do not offer to protect the black family against further trouble from local hoodlums and agree that the Browns have little choice but to move on. The Jacobsons treat the Brown family as a charity case. They give the Browns things that are simple to give; they withhold real support and friendship.

Small wonder that Vyry sinks into a depression after being burned out of her home and, soon after, losing a child at birth. What pulls her from her despair and lethargy, though, is a pilgrimage to Georgiana and "Miss Lucy," her father's sister who has taken over the care of Lillian. Recognizing the limitations of illiteracy and race in 1870, she makes the trip to get the Porters' help in recording claim to new property. Conscious of their debt to her for Lillian's care after the war, they agree to help her. Yet it is just as much Lucy Porter's support and encouragement that cheers and sustains Vyry, who has realized with the loss of her house that the Reconstruction world is far from safe. Lucy counsels Vyry not to worry and insists that the Porters will make sure the Browns' land remains in their hands. Unlike "Big Missy" Salina, Lucy Porter—actually Vyry's aunt—seems to have a maternal feeling for the daughter of her brother and responds to her warmly and genuinely. Even their relationship, though, is based on the premise that the black woman needs the white woman to take care of her, that Vyry cannot function in the postwar society without a white sponsor. Though this may be a realistic assumption, it does preclude true sisterhood between the two women.

Yet Walker's ultimate vision of life is optimistic. She chooses not to explore the dark web of racism and ambivalence in cross-racial female relationships as Faulkner has done, or find in these relationships the mysterious mixture of human nature as Cather pursues it in *Sapphira and the Slave Girl*. But in Walker's last spiritual vision of what is possible in these women's relationships, *Jubilee* powerfully suggests the infinite potential of human love through the regenerative principle and the overcoming of those dichotomous boundaries of race which so immured black and white women of antebellum, Civil

War, and Reconstruction periods. The events leading to this reconciliation begin ironically with Vyry's passing for white. Although Vyry
as a former slave has always thought of herself as black, she is light
enough to pass. When she and her family camp out near Greenville,
Alabama, she begins to sell eggs and butter in town. Though she does
not attempt to pass, she is treated like a white woman. Still leery
about building a house in the area, she listens quietly to racist talk in
order to gauge white feelings about blacks. Walker captures poor
white sentiment in the monologue of an old woman who doesn't even
have a dime to buy Vyry's eggs but offers her a cup of water and her
warped resentments of blacks' moving into the area:

> "Them peoples ain't got no business in here, at all. They was much
> better off in slavery, and I says that's where they needs to be right now.
> Why, it's tore up our country just something awful! Instead of us pros-
> pering like we thought we was gonna after the war and everything,
> them grand rascals what the Yankees has brung down here ain't done
> nothing but set us back a hundred years. No telling when we'll git a
> living wage, and they even got the nerve of trying to open up mixed
> schools." (p. 420)

With her pale features Vyry becomes privy to chilling talk of Klan
tortures and murders, and peevish complaints that "niggers" have
taken white folks' rights. Her hopes fall for making a home in the
area.

It is her relationship with a young white woman and their common
experience with the struggles of giving birth that reverse the force of
racism which has swept the Browns from "pillar to post." On one of
her trips into the white settlement, she becomes an emergency
"granny" to this young woman and probably saves the baby by calm-
ing the mother and showing her how to give birth. She cares for the
young mother and child, and misses church on the following day to
return to check on Betty-Alice Fletcher and her baby, hushing Innis's
complaints with an articulation of her philosophy, "I feels like it's my
duty to help anybody I can wheresomever I can" (p. 429). In a dramatic
scene Vyry, whom the Fletchers assume is white, listens to racist
myths from the mouth of the white woman whose baby she has
delivered. Betty-Alice parrots her husband's assertions that "all black
nigger mens wants white women" and "nigger mens is got tails" (p.
430). Vyry can stand no more and discloses her racial identity and
the falseness of these myths. To the Fletchers and to Betty-Alice's
parents, Vyry discloses in a flood of frustration and despair her feelings about the racism and violence she and her family have had to

endure. Linked to the whole family, particularly to Betty-Alice, through her participation in their regeneration in the birth of a child, she calls upon each of them to acknowledge her humanity and that of her family:

> " . . . I does feel real bad and hurt deep down inside when I goes around and hears all the things the white folks is saying bout the colored peoples. What's so bad and what hurts so much is half the time they don't know what they talking about, they doesn't even much know us and what they saying is all lies they has heard and stuff they has made up. Me and my husband and my chilluns is been from pillar to post since the war. We ain't been ables to stay nowheres in peace. We's been in a flood and we's been burned out when six white mens purposely set fire to our brand-new house right in front of our very eyes . . . . We ain't even much knowed who they was. We's got us a place now out on the Big Road and we's been planning to build in this here community, but after all the terrible stuff I has heard just going round selling vegetables and eggs and stuff I'm scared for us to build, and I'm gwine tell my husband we's gotta be moving on." (pp. 432–33)

Mrs. Shackleford, Betty-Alice's mother, is the one who responds:

> "Well, I'm sho sorry to hear that. I can tell you is a good woman and a Christian woman, too. I thank God for what you done for my child and I wants you to know I wishes you well." (p. 433)

This *connection* between Vyry and the two white women, mother and daughter, through the common female experience of giving birth results in meaningful interracial communication. Vyry thus extends the black circle of community, later embodied in the reconciliation of her two husbands at her own table, into a second larger circle of interracial community. Walker's vision of peace, sympathy, and common goals linking all people into one human race becomes a reality of shared food and shared labor when the white members of the community, motivated both by good will and by Vyry's willingness to serve as community midwife, come to help the Browns build their long-awaited house. This is a moving and sweeping scene, and one which embodies Walker's celebration of creative humanism. The men in the community work together to build the house, while the women have a quilting bee. As they sew busily, Vyry moves among them "with her generous spirit of hospitality" (p. 440), herself the seamstress sewing together black and white people and their lives and affections. This quilting scene is a picture of the human race, the female human race, making the one and many patterns of life through love, sympathy, and sisterhood.

It is to this ideal of sisterhood that Vyry speaks at the end of the book. And as she speaks, she takes on at the same time a mythic voice, Walker's voice, a profoundly caring voice. To Randall Ware's cynical view that whites only have use for blacks when blacks have something they want, Vyry responds that all people need one another, that Ware has "no God" in him and is eaten up with hatred. She bristles when Ware refers to her sister Lillian as stupid, and harshly criticizes his willingness "to try to beat the white man at his own game with his killing and his hating" (p. 482). At this, the climax of the book, Vyry returns to her childhood and "Big Missy" Salina, the first white woman in her life and the most treacherous. In her account of what she endured under this ogre of a woman and her expression of forgiveness of such depths of human and female cruelty, Vyry shows herself to be truly a spiritual paragon. She tells Ware:

> "Big Missy was mighty mean to me from the first day I went in the Big House as a slave to work. She emptied Miss Lillian's pee-pot in my face. She hung me up by my thumbs. She slapped me and she kicked me; she cussed me and she worked me like I was a dog. They stripped me naked and put me on the auction block for sale. And worsetest of all they kept me ignorant so's I can't read and write my name, but I closed her eyes in death, and God is my witness, I bears her no ill will." (pp. 483–84)

These are marks of the suffering servant. Vyry's words are reminiscent of Christ's "Father, forgive them for they know not what they do."

Vyry's spirit of forgiveness is a fictional expression of the redemptive power of love. It is more what Walker hoped her great-grandmother was than what she knew her to be. Walker admits this point:

> Insofar as Vyry's lack of bitterness is concerned, maybe I have not been as honest as I should be, taking the license of the imaginative worker, but I have tried to be honest. My great-grandmother was a definite product of plantation life and culture. She was shaped by the forces that dominated her life. In the Big House and in the Quarters, she could not react any other way. Her philosophy of life was a practical one, and she succeeded in getting the things she wanted and prayed for. She realized that hatred wasn't necessary and would have corroded her own spiritual well-being.[23]

In reconstructing her grandmother in the simple and forgiving Vyry, Walker—writing most of her manuscript during the Civil Rights movement of the sixties—appears to suggest black humanism as an answer to America's racial conflicts. It is not so much Vyry's gesture itself which is significant, but Walker's association of this loving black woman and her simple act of forgiveness with the black writer's complex commitment to humanistic values of "freedom, peace, and human dignity." Like Vyry, but in a fullness of consciousness which she lacks, the black literary artist celebrates life and "the highest essence of human spirit."[24] This is what Walker means by humanism. By its very nature, such a vision embodies, at once, the necessity to rebel and the willingness to reconcile. Vyry's act of forgiveness is not a passive acceptance of white cruelty, but an assertion of ontological black self in the face of it.

Like Faulkner and Cather, Walker presents the volatile relationships of these black and white women as inextricable from the complex whole of the southern racial experience. Like that of the women's slave narratives, her point of view is that of the black woman. Though her white characters are often as stereotypical as Stowe's black ones and though her Vyry does not come to her moment of forgiveness and reconciliation in a fullness of consciousness, Walker's *Jubilee* transubstantiates Vyry's simple gesture into real vision. That vision is realized, significantly, in the southern black woman's forgiveness of the perverse and vicious cruelty of the southern white woman. *Jubilee* culminates more than one hundred years of American literary struggle with the paradoxical South and its women, fictional and real, white and black. At the same time, it celebrates the power of black humanism in a book which is part history and part fiction—a synthesis of life and literature.

As our great writers have shown, guilt at failure in human relationships is the inexorable white burden of southern history. In *Jubilee* the black woman's forgiving gesture suggests not so much an abatement of black pain or a lifting of white guilt as a greatly simplified paradigm of Walker's belief that we can redeem ourselves by extending our sense of human community—whether white, black, male, female, South, North—in ever-widening circles. Baldwin would say perhaps that Vyry, like Uncle Tom and Bigger Thomas, "has accepted a theology that denies . . . life" rather than affirming its complexity.[25] Vyry's gesture of forgiveness does come too easily. Yet it is undeniably significant that the black woman writer, descendant of a slave woman who suffered greatly at the hand of her mistress, renders that gesture and the vision of human community which it implies. It is she—as Southerner, as Afro-American, as woman—who has a particular right, and perhaps also a particular need, to evoke such a vision. For Walker's present, and for our own, *Jubilee* illuminates, in a black woman's forgiveness of her white sister, a regenerative response to the southern past.

Notes

1. Margaret Walker, *How I Wrote Jubilee* (Chicago: Third World Press, 1972), p. 28.
2. Charles Rowell, "Poetry, History and Humanism: An Interview with Margaret Walker," *Black World* 25 (December 1975), pp. 11–12.
3. Ibid., p. 12.
4. Margaret Walker, "The Humanistic Tradition of Afro-American Literature," *American Libraries* 1 (October 1970), p. 853.
5. Ibid., pp. 853–54.
6. Ibid., p. 851.
7. Walker, *How I Wrote Jubilee*, p. 12.
8. Ibid., pp. 16, 23.
9. This may account for the dearth of critical treatment of *Jubilee*. Of the few critical articles, the most comprehensive is Phyllis Klotman, " 'Oh Freedom'—Women and History in Margaret Walker's *Jubilee*," *Black American Literature Forum* 11 (Winter 1977), pp. 139–45. See also Joyce Pettis, "The Black Historical Novel as Best Seller," *Kentucky Folklore Record* 25: 3 (1979), pp. 51–59; and Bertie Powell, "The Black Experience in Margaret Walker's *Jubilee* and Lorraine Hansberry's *The Drinking Gourd*," *CLA Journal* 21 (December 1977), pp. 304–11. Considerations of *Jubilee* and Walker as a novelist are notably absent in such studies or collections as Robert Hemenway, ed., *The Black Novelist* (Columbus, O.: Charles E. Merrill, 1970); Edward Margolies, *Native Sons: A Critical Study of Twentieth Century Black American Authors* (Philadelphia and New York: J. B. Lippincott, 1968); and Roger Rosenblatt, *Black Fiction* (Cambridge: Harvard University Press, 1974). Arthur P. Davis allocates some attention to the novel in *From the Dark Tower* (Washington: Howard University Press, 1974), pp. 181–84; as does Barbara Christian, *Black Women Novelists* (Westport, Conn.: Greenwood, 1980), pp. 71–73. One of the most illuminating analyses of Walker's novel may be found in Blyden Jackson's entry on Walker in *Lives of Mississippi Authors 1817–1967*, ed. James B. Lloyd (Jackson: University Press of Mississippi, 1981), pp. 444–46.
10. Davis, *From the Dark Tower*, p. 184.
11. Walker, "The Humanistic Tradition," p. 854.
12. Nikki Giovanni and Margaret Walker, *A Poetic Equation: Conversations Between Nikki Giovanni and Margaret Walker* (Washington: Howard University Press, 1974), p. 16.
13. Klotman, " 'Oh Freedom!' " p. 140.
14. Walker, "The Humanistic Tradition," p. 854.
15. Ibid., p. 854.

16. James Baldwin, "Everybody's Protest Novel," *Partisan Review* 16 (June 1949), pp. 578–85; rpt. Elizabeth Ammons, ed., *Critical Essays on Harriet Beecher Stowe* (Boston: G. K. Hall, 1980), pp. 92–101.

17. See Mary Chesnut, *Mary Chesnut's Civil War*, ed. C. Vann Woodward (New Haven and London: Yale University Press, 1981); Susan Dabney Smedes, *Memorials of a Southern Planter*, ed. Fletcher Green (Jackson: University Press of Mississippi, 1981); Harriet Jacobs, *Incidents in the Life of a Slave Girl*, ed. L. Maria Child (1861; rpt. New York: Harcourt Brace Jovanovich, 1973); Elizabeth Keckley, *Behind the Scenes or, Thirty Years a Slave, and Four Years in the White House* (1868; rpt. New York: G. W. Carleton, 1968). Bibliographies of other journals by white women are available in Catherine Clinton, *The Plantation Mistress: Woman's World in the Old South* (New York: Pantheon, 1982); and Anne Firor Scott, *The Southern Lady: From Pedestal to Politics 1830–1930* (Chicago: University of Chicago Press, 1970). For bibliographies which list women's slave narratives separately, see Erlene Stetson, "Studying Slavery," in *But Some of Us Are Brave*, ed. Gloria Hull, Patricia Bell Scott, and Barbara Smith (Old Westbury, N.Y.: The Feminist Press, 1982), pp. 82–84; and Stetson, "Black Women In and Out of Print," *Women in Print—I*, ed. Joan Hartman and Ellen Messer-Davidow (New York: MLA, 1982), p. 97.

18. Robert Lively, *Fiction Fights the Civil War* (Chapel Hill: University of North Carolina Press, 1957), p. 55.

19. Giovanni and Walker, *A Poetic Equation*, p. 91.

20. Margaret Walker, "On Being Female, Black, and Free," in *The Woman Writer on Her Work*, ed. Janet Sternburg (New York: Norton, 1980), p. 96.

21. Ibid., p. 106.

22. Margaret Walker, *Jubilee* (Boston: Houghton Mifflin, 1966), p. 26. Subsequent references will be designated parenthetically.

23. Walker, *How I Wrote Jubilee*, p. 25.

24. Walker, "The Humanistic Tradition," p. 851.

25. Baldwin, "Everybody's Protest Novel," p. 585.

9

Chosen Place, Timeless People: *Some Figurations on the New World*

HORTENSE J. SPILLERS

> "Once a great wrong has been done, it never dies.
> People speak the words of peace, but their hearts
> do not forgive. Generations perform ceremonies of
> reconciliation but there is no end."
> [From the Tiv of West Africa; Epigraph to the Novel]

In the approach from Fort-de-France to Trois Ilet, the Martiniquan land lifts off the Caribbean in soft folds of tiered country. One imagines that the fictitious Bournehills of Paule Marshall's *Chosen Place, Timeless People* presents to the mind's eye a similar prospect from the vantage of the sea. But the perception of a specific geographical place in the Caribbean might matter less to Marshall's overall intentions for this novel than the sheer magnitude of mimetic life that it captures. A study of politics and society in an English-speaking Caribbean community and the turbulence that is stirred when representatives of corporate America are introduced to it, *Chosen Place* was published in 1969.[1] The novel is now available again in Vintage paperback after having been out of print for several years. The plausible reasons why the novel was, for all intents and purposes, "lost" until the fall of 1984 will not occupy my attention beyond this note, but I observe the absence as more than odd, given the nimble orchestrations of this work. In fact, when I recall my own limited acquaintance with the fabled Caribbean "Horseshoe," most northerly point projecting ninety miles off the southeastern tip of the United States, I imagine *Chosen Place* as its most definitive mimesis.

This essay, then, though it guards against the superlative degree of praise and assertion, is my attempt (1) to inquire into Marshall's achievement by suggesting that the novel requires of its readership the suspension of simplistic expectations (the "quick read") and (2) to pinpoint the ways and means by which I think such suspension is encouraged. Although the work does not confront the reader with an opacity or impenetrability of surface, it demands, I think, as much care of the detail from the reader as the detail has received from the writer. We can expect here no straightforward vindication of various public tastes regarding race, ethos, and gender; no facile condemnation of victors or celebration of victims, but, rather, a staged dialectics of human involvement that will reinvoke, I believe, our best hopes for a New World humanity.

In 1981, Feminist Press reissued Marshall's *Brown Girl, Brownstones.*[2] *Chosen Place*, in perspective with *Brown Girl, Praisesong for the Widow* (1983), and the writer's short stories, not only corrects the limited view of her career that we have at the moment, but also comprehends Marshall's project as a writer within an enlarged scope of fictional operations.[3] With *Chosen Place*, it is as if Marshall brings to a head her own writing past and future in rich continuity with the present. To that extent, I would consider this novel not only the "impression point" against which we might gauge and contemplate Marshall's efforts up to the moment, but also one of the most engaging works of fiction created by an African-American writer within the last half century of American creative effort.[4] With that in mind, we can well regard Paule Marshall's career as a significant point of intersection between feminist and creative discourse.

Any attempt to summarize *Chosen Place* is ultimately frustrating since single threads of it disappear into the whole, integrated fabric. But I would offer a simple pattern of four concentric circles as a useful paradigm for grasping the novel's dynamically related parts. I am proposing that these four circles of involvement—myth, history, ritual, and ontology—identify the primary structural and dramatic features of the work and that our understanding of character and motivation takes shape against this architectonics. Although the various contents of the text may be seen to alternate their emphasis from one

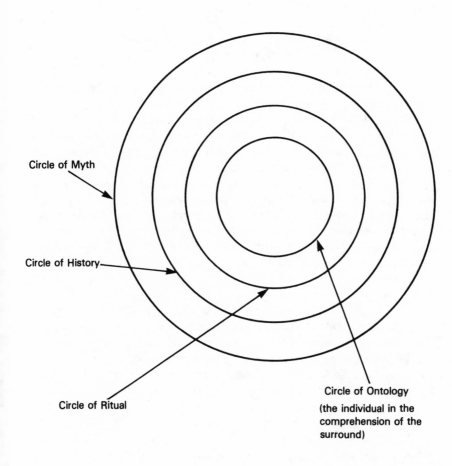

Circle of Myth

Circle of History

Circle of Ritual

Circle of Ontology

(the individual in the
comprehension of the
surround)

circle to another, we are compelled to keep the novel's wider scheme of mutual engagements in mind.

I think it is correct to say that the work is agent-centered, as the diagram suggests that the "circle of ontology," or the point at which we locate character, becomes the comprehensive ring on an interlocking sequence of changes. This locus designates the nuclear, or fundamental, unit of more encompassing relationships that open out, in turn, into the realm of the timeless, here represented by the "circle of myth." Between outermost and innermost is poised the world of human history, and the realm of history is figuratively repeated in the daily activities of the community through its ritualistic and symbolic play. The agent, at the relatively still point of a multiple impingement, embodies the resolution of the metaphors of experience that surround her or him. Ontogeny here repeats phylogeny: the individual both makes and is made by the collective history, as we also imagine that this subtle shimmering and shading of meanings continuously obverts. In other words, the individual agent is both the origin *and* end of a complex figurative progression. The characters embody, therefore, a noble synecdochic purpose because they are the part that speaks for the whole, just as the whole is configured in their partialness.

We can go back and forth between part and whole without loss of radiance or structural value. Merle Kinbona, worldly black female, indigenous to Bournehills, and Saul Amron, sophisticated Jewish anthropologist from academic America, Stanford University specifically, are the principal agents. The web of conflict between hostile cultures eradiates from their erotic encounter, and we experience both characters against the background of entangling social and political events.

To say that *Chosen Place* is agent-centered is to argue that other elements in the Burkeian pentad—agency, act, scene, and purpose—are deployed through an equality, or economy of means.[5] The agent is not overwhelmed by forces of necessity, either demonic or divine, nor is the scene of his or her activity so suppressed in the reader's awareness that the characters become disengaged from a concrete ground of meaning. The agents stand solidly within a specific temporal/spatial sequence at the same time that they lose none of its partial and particular illuminations. For instance, we are not allowed to forget that Merle and Saul stand for their representative cultures, converging at a given moment, and simultaneously manifest their own individuality of character in all its contingency of possibilities.

Set against a background of vegetal lushness, *Chosen Place* might well have been inspired by the author's ancestral home Barbados that also provides the scenery for some of her short stories as well as the source of memory and myth in *Brown Girl, Brownstones*. Whatever Caribbean scene the novel brings to mind, we perceive Bournehills, the fictitious country of the novel, as a continuum of geopolitical and cultural moments surrounded by Marshall's order of the timeless. The Caribbean itself converges with the Atlantic, and their interaction describes a point of dramatic emphasis. This shifting tempo of breaking waters and altering colors in a confluence closes the links of the notorious "Middle Passage." The currency of exchange between waterways engenders a wealth of metaphorical referents. In that way, Old World, sub-Saharan Africa connects geographically and figuratively with Bournehills of the New World. The geographical nexus of motives is completed by Stanford and mainline Philadelphia, points of origin for two of the main characters; both the United States and the Caribbean are read, consequently, by way of the economics of captivity and their implications for the contemporary world. With Bournehills at the center of Marshall's scenic apparatus and Bourne Island and Spiretown related to it in triangular proximity, we move freely between seaport, hillside, and suburban aspects of a continuous cultural and geographical progression.

The sociology that Bournehills generates is as complicated as its terrain. There are the common people, who have names and faces in the novel, and there are more of them than most contemporary fiction attempts. The various ritualistic activities of Marshall's fictional world so refine our sense of the people that a reader's intimations of anonymity complement the affecting presences of the work rather than hinder their impact. Above the folk in the social hierarchy is the local ruling class, which dominates in the name of the absentee landlords. Treacherous both to their own people and the overlords, the local rulers are occasionally attractive, well-educated abroad, own expensive things, some of them droll and amusing. Beyond the surrogate rulers, or lateral to them, are the social critics of local society, Merle Kinbona among them, and they are the "conscience" of their people, even as their own is troubled. These free-floating agents, suspended between cultures, provide the basic stress points on which the action turns.

The cast of "aliens" in the novel is mostly European in origin, with an Australian thrown in for variety. The most powerful foreign presence, however, is that of the United States, newcomer conjoined with impunity to the neo-imperialist axis of nations represented in the life and economy of Bournehills. The American interest is embodied in the Philadelphia Research Institute that has created, in turn, an entity called the Center for Applied Social Research. The latter organization ostensibly carries out programs of social and technological "betterment" in Third World communities. Its director, Saul Amron, and his assistant, Allen Fuso, are both moved in the most profoundly personal way to confront aspects of their own system of values. Essentially, no one in Bournehills is "bettered" by their presence, but for them, this tenure of research in the Caribbean—not their first— will be their last and most devastating because they are brought to consider that the humanity they must heal is their own.

One of the major plot lines of the novel involves Saul, his wife Harriet, and Merle in what could be considered the climax of the novel, but Marshall provides the reader with points of culmination and climax, as the structure of the whole is as spectacular and intricate as a bridgework. The Saul-Harriet-Merle triangle identifies the primary complicating device of the novel, and we see the tale of Vere Walkes, parallel to it, as an interesting simplification of the motives of revenge, sexual jealousy, and death that haunt the triangle.

Harriet Shippen Amron stands at the apex of a venerable mercantile/ corporate interest, linking issues of family and inheritance. The powerful Shippen family of mainline Philadelphia owns the major shares in the United Corporation of America, which in turn, makes the largest contribution to the Center for Applied Social Research. This elegant calculus of economic motives yokes the Philadelphia Research Institute, the Center for Applied Social Research, and the United Corporation of America in an unholy trinity of affluence and complicity.

As the "son" and heiress-apparent to the Shippen empire, Harriet has the means and the authority to do whatever she pleases with the massive benefits that accrue to her patronymic. She decides for love and marries the seductive Amron with the intention of promoting him through her organization as far as his considerable abilities will take him. Merle intervenes out of no premeditated sexual desire or scheming, and Harriet, wishing to save her marriage, will see to it that the Bournehills project in the Caribbean is destroyed. Confronting Saul concerning his liaison with Merle, Harriet does not get the answers she has expected. Saul does not denounce the black woman as he might have and as she anticipated, and Harriet takes the next step. Attempting to blackmail the woman out of Bournehills (or "whitemail" from another point of view), Harriet is frustrated in her wishes. Remembering painfully what it has meant for her to function as the custodial mascot of a powerful white woman, Merle refuses Harriet's offer of money. She will not take a dime of it, and Harriet, fearing that Merle's refusal will ultimately destroy her marriage, walks into the sea and drowns.[6]

Most of Marshall's people are the poor, employed in the Cane Vale Sugar Refining Factory, whose closing is a subtle study in the ways and means by which powerful moneyed interests in the island work from a distance. These characters and the caretakers appear in the novel episodically, but their role is altogether essential to the intricate social and narrative engineering of the whole. George Clough, the editor of the local newspaper; his wife Dorothy, carrying on quite openly with prominent local barrister Lyle Hutson; Mr. Deanes, Bournehills Member of Parliament—are not simply parasitic on the island's energies, but in the dynamics of local leadership, they are indispensable to the tissue of lies and betrayal that keeps the people groaning under the onus of oppression.

Among the people are Vere Walkes, returned to Bournehills from a period of migrant labor in Florida; his great aunt Leesy Walkes; "Ten Ton" and "Stinger," the caneworkers; the pregnant woman Gwen, and a host of other figures who provide the splendid noises, colors, and mobilities in the background. During the week of Carnival, when all the novel's elements of suspense are resolved, Vere corners his target in her "Valley of the Dolls" and whips her, but will lose his life in the Whitmonday motor race and in the ancient laughing stock of a vehicle, his fire-red Opel, brought lovingly back to life. The events of closure happen quickly, but we have been prepared for them all along. The feelings of loss, of tragic outcome, built on a solid structure of entangling relationships, are palpably rendered, but we gain satisfaction in beholding each movement choreographed to a fine point.

The context, or ground of human operations here—the Atlantic and the Caribbean—constitutes a first order of figurative procedure. I would assign preeminent place to the great waterways not only because their intersection provides the steady plangencies of background, but also because they name mysterious origins and provide the primary point of connection between past, present, and future; black and white; African and European; and two radically different aspects and degrees of the capitalist synthesis. The individual agents of both cultural integrities are captivated by the social and political currents engendered by the great oceans. This surrounding figuration lends the novel its chief imagistic strategies since it embodies Marshall's expression of the mythic as well. Assuming a constitutive status that does not interfere with the humanity poised against it, the sea worlds, in standing for the Ineffable, allow us to experience humanity under its auspices.

Intruded at decisive narrative moments, changes denoted in the outward appearance of the seas delineate the seasons of the year in Bournehills. By way of these conjoined natural phenomena, Bournehills tells its own local time. But just as importantly, cosmic rhythms are transmuted from an impersonal neutrality of meaning into a specific historical entitlement because they "speak" to a specific people. I would suggest that this interplay between microcosmic and macro-cosmic detail, or the universal and the particular evocation, and its consequent dispersal throughout the Collective Unconscious life of Bournehills humanity locates a model for mythic formations. In other words, myth depends upon the efficacy of the particular in order to bolster and safeguard its profoundest secrets. If, as Roland Barthes argued, myth is a discourse ordained by history, then *Chosen Place* offers a fruitful source of investigation in relationship to this collusive program. The dynamic give-and-take between human and Other yokes a particular humanity and signs of the Ineffable in harmonious order. In this way, all things are full of human value, and the fictional universe throws back an anthropomorphic reflection everywhere, even from its most distant point. The following passage provides an example:

> It was the Atlantic this side of the island, a wild-eyed, marauding sea the color of slate . . . lined with row upon row of barrier reefs, and with a sound like that of the combined voices of the drowned raised in a loud unceasing lament—all those, the nine million and more it is said, who in their enforced exile, their Diaspora, had gone down between this point and the homeland lying out of sight to the east.[7]

The relationship that the author establishes in this dialectical display[8] is analogous to the perspective between the synchronic and diachronic axes of time. In its transitory character, the diachronic dimension repeats, in linear fashion, the depths of experience (the synchronic), or that content not immediately available to the seeing eye. "Dailiness" does not exhaust the potentialities of the synchronic, but, rather, participates in the rules of behavior that determine its identity.[9] If, then, we can posit a basic structure of meanings, we can anticipate the outline of particular cases in light of it. Marshall does not mean that Bournehills is stuck, consequently, in its history of betrayal and oppression, but that the scene against which it enacts and reenacts its history has been decided by origins that must be appeased, at least recognized and named out loud.[10] The transatlantic slave trade, the historic provenance of Bournehills, is thoroughly me-diated through a number of peak points. But the trade and its human and social currencies become the basic archetypal and memorial sym-bol-pattern that asserts itself in the cultural and daily activities of the community.

By way of this eternal order, Bournehills society is shown in a paradox of motion—a movement on the verge of a successive movement, whose failure to complete itself renders a theme for art and the impasse of would-be revolutionary change. The following passage demonstrates the artistic usability of paradox, but its intrusion into the arena of politics lays claim to a stroke of fatalism, as Merle will painfully discover. As she and her cohorts of the Center for Applied Social Research, recently met at the local airport by Merle and Leesy Walkes, churn toward Westminster Hill, they see this scene: Overlooking Bournehills at its summit, Westminster curves around an isolated village in "a wide arc to slope gradually to the sea." The moment that the sea appears behind them, "two royal palms, looking like pylons," suddenly rise up "ahead in the fields on each side of the steep road. Tall, incredibly straight, their fronds tossing in the wind like the headdress of a Tutsi warrior, the trees crowned the high ridge called Cleaver's which marked the ascension of the land. As Merle spurred [the Bentley] up the sheer lift to the top, the palms stepped swiftly toward them, growing taller as they advanced" (p. 99).

The royal palms that dominate attention here organize the visual field in such a way that the angle from which we see them contains land, sea, and hillside in a brilliant perspective of textural differences. The emerging, retreating, advancing palms are not moving, despite the falsifying verbs of mobility, but the eye moves for them, pinpointing their stark and majestic isolation. In this discrete moment of perception, the narrator's palms assume a degree of artifice, roughly comparable to the poet's jar on a hill in Tennessee. The power of art, in the novelist's and poet's case, the verbal art, to declare its status in the midst of natural things not only represents whimsicality turned aggressive, but also lends an analogy on levels of symbolic meaning that come to occupy nature itself, focusing and instructing human consciousness by way of gestures of symbolic dominance. Marshall's narrator suggests a way of seeing that is so forceful of insistence that of all the other prospective modes of visual organization, *this* one seems the most likely, the most "natural."

It does not matter that the Center for Applied Social Research will not live beyond this novel, or that other characters could occupy this space/time continuum and see something else, or a different arrangement of the same thing. It does not matter that Merle's Bentley is moving off a scene that it will not retrace. Swinging against a seascape of parallel and divergent identities, the royal palms fixate in consciousness as a gift of eternity.

In this scene, a "protocol of unveiling"[11] orchestrates the narrative into an iconographic emphasis so that we vividly see movement and stability, natural and human, trapped by the same text. The constant interplay that Marshall achieves in the novel between the diurnal and the unchanging, or the transitory and the eternal (as the kaleidoscope of our vision shifts with the turning car) is captured on a number of levels—iconic, rhetorical, dramatic, and imagistic. The novel, then, is the *situation* of two *conflicting* principles that Marshall would confront. Merle and Saul, with their particular fever and dis-ease, are the wellspring of a dialectics in the making, one that will discover in the agents' promised resolution of trouble, a new way to flourish in Bournehills society, and in the USA for that matter. They become the woman and the man of the New World, only if . . . .

The distinction between the momentary and the momentous lapses across categories of naming and experience and discloses a shared context of value between them. Merle and Saul must reacquaint themselves with human requirements that take them beyond the call of ego. In short, it is the movement back and forth and among the things of the daily world and the things that we might assign to brooding eternity that Merle and Saul must discover. The conflation of transitory and permanent nominative features here engenders what I would call Marshall's "circle of history," whose rich schemes of human continuance point us in two directions at once—West Africa and Europe, the United States and the Caribbean. The individual agent, concentered in the "circle of history," is obligated to discover his or her own particular relationship to historical content and rename, metaphorically speaking, herself or himself in light of the discovery. The clash of cultures and histories renders a specific text, captured in the varying sentimental education of the major characters. Saul speaks the language of intellectual culture and the gestures of alienation. He eventually perceives himself not only estranged from those around him, but also cut off from the crucial emotional resources of his own past. Albeit for quite different reasons, Merle, whose culture retains intimate contact with elements of its originary African source, shares with Saul some of the same symptoms of self-alienation. Both characters, who can no more participate now in the indigenous worlds of their respective mother-tongues, which they have, in effect, abandoned, as Western technological communities can return to the age of the wheel, verge on a profound personal synthesis as the novel closes.

Aspects of Saul's and Merle's individual and converging dramas unfold on a historical background that articulates the urgencies of *difference* primarily by way of the dynamics and psychodynamics of ritual. To that extent the circles of history and ritual are overlapping. We assign to them, however, a contrastive meaning and function for the sake of analysis and to suggest their relationship to the world of overwhelming natural phenomena that does not depend on human or human mimetic agents to decide its sufficiency. Though one relies here on the spatial arrangement of the concentric circles to hint the distance and discreteness of contents, the novel itself reads ritual into history and history into the eternal without break. Concentricity is as close as we can come to the unimpeded and massive ripplings of meaning that the novel engages.

It is accurate to say that the realm of history evades an explicit text here, except by a structure of inference that rests solidly on the historical information that the reader already commands. It is drawn into the diagram, nonetheless, not only because the ritualistic configurations of Bournehills make no sense without the historical echo, but also because the community raids its exquisite silence and sublime ageless witness for the very authority that gives the everyday and seasonal life its special richness. Insofar as a "natural" historical progression transcends the individual agent in the allotment of time and space to items in an array, insofar as history is collective doing that subsumes and exceeds the individual's, it is proximate to the eternal in this scheme, if not a secondary and inferior version of it. At least one might read Marshall's intentions that way: Hundreds of years past, those "nine millions and more, it is said," were captured in their African homelands and transported like cattle across the vast Atlantic and held under coercive conditions by their captors. *This* narrative is not directly repeated since we already know it well, but it is insinuated into the interstices of structure with unfailing, refractive accuracy. In the ritual ceremonies of the Bournehills community, this transatlantic origin displaces scripture, or becomes a class of scripture that offers a compendium of *potential* interpretations. The "other" historical narrative—that of the owners and captors—does not bear explicit repeating either and for the same reason as the narrative of captivity. We have not had the one without the other.

As we recognize the purposes that the homologously opposed encodations of history and culture serve in the novel, we are nevertheless called upon to experience character and the situations of character in dynamic interplay. The Burkeian definition of irony,[12] the getting in motion of all the competing subperspectives of a particular picture, finds an exact translation here. The novel has, then, no "good guys" or bad ones, though it does confront and contrast two radically disparate mimetic conditions. If there is an "enemy" here, it is the American capitalist machinery, indicted for what it has also done to its own children. The troubled humanity of Marshall's agents draws the sympathies immediately toward the human particular, as the war of ideologies roars in the background.

The intricate mediations that Marshall achieves come to focus most impressively in the Bournehills annual Carnival held during the season of Lent. This structure of central episodes is culminant, if not climactic: (1) We discover, for instance, who the woman is that Vere has loved for an age, has had a child with, and has followed and harassed for the whole of the story; (2) On the final night of Carnival, Merle tells her terrible secret to Saul (cf. n. 6) concerning the London interlude and her Kenyan husband's betrayal ten years earlier. In turn, Merle hears Saul's tale of the loss of his first wife Sosha and his subsequent guilt, and Harriet searches the streets of Bournehills for him. Merle's and Saul's mutual sorrow, rehearsed in a graceful comedy of wit and high charm, leads to mutual need and the bedroom of Merle's childhood near Cassia Boardinghouse, owned by Leesy Walkes. On orders from London, Cane Vale Sugar Refining Factory is closed down, leaving scores of men jobless, and Vere Walkes is killed in his Whitmonday race Opel. In its microcosmic economy of structure, Carnival leads to revelations and resolutions.

Bournehills Carnival comes but once a year, and that's almost too often. The society is literally open to anything and everyone, and everyone comes, including strangers, who are absorbed by Carnival activity. Since everybody feels right at home in an atmosphere of exaggeration and spectacle, the temporary loss of identity does not matter, and the indigenous and the exotic populations are divested of degrees of difference. Carnival throws us in the midst of a massive societal mobility that appears to generate, proceed, and conclude in a unanimity of conduct and underlying value.

One of the intriguing aspects of the celebration depends on time itself. Bordered on either side by the historian's "normalcy," Carnival decisively punctuates the order and flow of experience and expectation. That this interruption of accepted order involves the masses gives it spatial depth in the same way that an environment—in its sequential recurrences—appears unbroken. The very idea that the members of a society may be captivated at the same time by a single overwhelming notion, whose central intent is movement, startles the senses. But what is more, the society at the time has no destination, except itself. Movement, then, seems splendidly literal and erratic. That the agents dance a range of motor behavior in the disguise of costume and in the witness of countless others hands Carnival over to the territory of the hyperbolic. In an atmosphere of licensed exaggeration, amplified mood and desire, Carnival verges on chaos. The participant/observer/reader experiences it as a moment of awful bliss.

The Carnival scenes are structured progressively and episodically as though its activities were a mode of fiction. We would suggest that

Carnival is a fiction in a fiction since the agents duly acknowledge its special character. As if by their own will, they actively choose to suspend that system of actions and reflexes by which we have come to know them, imbuing their character with a contrastive signature of behavior. The reader experiences the content of Carnival as an accretion of various narrative and rhetorical energies. Marshall's invocatory lyricism here precisely marks a *beginning*, and we are suddenly in the presence, by implication, of suggestive antiquities. Day stalled for an hour, breaks slowly,

> so that the entire coast, including the sandhills and Westminster's dark steepled spur and the guesthouse on its rocky ledge, including too, the great boulders rearing up out of the surf and resembling ancient ruins in the uncertain light: Zimbabwe, Stonehenge, the huge heads on Easter Island, testimony to man's presence, monuments to his ingenuity and grace, witness of his inevitable passing—all this stood poised between the . . . blanched fire of the moon and the first subtle suggestion of day. (p. 251)

The slaughter of Leesy Walkes's white sow—the sacrificial animal of this Sunday's pigsticking—is no ordinary event, for which the foregoing excerpt has already prepared us. The language requires that the listening intensify because it is clear that a "Call" is being given. "Entire coast," for instance, is not assigned a predicate, nor "all this" a specific antecedent. This grammatical symptom, the mode of anacoluthon, with its impacted modifiers, pointing in this case in multiple imagistic directions beyond the local scene, denotes a strategy of preaching, or the lecture platform. The conventional relationship between subject and verb lapses in the sheer euphonious overflow of nominatives. Strategically preliminary to Carnival, the slaughter of the sow introduces to these scenes the dynamics of sacrifice, as the victim, in apparent knowledge of its imminent death, takes on gestures vaguely human.

This elaborate practice, beginning in blood and slaughter, renders a sort of eucharistic analogy, robbed of piety and embodied holiness. Marshall, however, intends neither satire nor humor in the rites of communion that end the scene. The men pass the rum bottle, and everybody will have a bite of roasted pig tail. The overlap here between violence and communion outlines an economy of symbolic meanings: The spilling of blood has brought together individual characters in a replay of the rites of brotherhood. Saul, understanding that something at least complicated is taking place, has been troubled before now at the beginning of his stay by certain elements of the ritual—the blood, the flies, the smells, the ravenous dogs. But he eventually overcomes his initial sqeamishness; his feelings this morning, however, assume far greater complexity and agitation: "For some reason he had been unduly affected by the death of this particular animal, perhaps because its eyes had taken on what appeared to be a kind of intelligence at the end, making him wonder for a fleeting moment whether something human wasn't being offered up on the battered table." Puzzled by the apparent change that comes over the men performing the slaughter, Saul is moved by the "sudden harshness with which they had set upon the pig, the coldly methodical, ruthless way they had laid bare its hide, revealed an aspect of them which he had never seen acted out so graphically before" (pp. 258–59).

If Saul is disturbed by this moving display, then the narrator provides good reason for it. The instrumentalities of communion, laid bare at the approach of dawn and proceeding, virtually instinctively, in a repetition of certain ancestral patterns of belief might suggest that both the ritual and the collective response to it represent a cultural mode of operation that exactly contradicts Saul's own. One's *group membership*, defined along a hierarchy of social, cultural, and genetic functions, takes precedent over the unique wish that is supreme, from Saul's agonized point of view. The bone of contention that drives the argument of the novel is that this scenic mode of Caribbean society is invaded by another cultural emphasis. Quite removed from his own ancestral imperatives, Saul confronts his destiny alone. As if unaccompanied by any source of power and instruction that does not come from himself, Saul precisely demonstrates the "existential predicament" of "technological man," to express what we mean in shorthand. Embodied in Saul's terror of the unfamiliar, the unresolved, and in Merle's burden of her own troubled past, the dilemma of the isolated person becomes the element of irony that lends *Chosen Place* its complexities of dramatic procedure.

That Saul, the cultural agent of institutions of technological and bureaucratic means, is repelled by the spectacle of Bournehills society is a proper response for him. From where he comes, the techniques of "sacrifice" and celebration are far more deadly precisely because the society pursues its ends by antiseptic displacement—the "victim" is removed from sight—and the agents are not allowed an open and acceptable way to exercise their violent tendencies. In the mode of crime and punishment, we recognize little ground for figurative play, few strategies for rationalization that the agents are fully allowed to see. I am not suggesting that Bournehills society is any more or less violent, criminal, and permissive than another, but that its modes of ritual expression provide a metaphor for violence beyond that of the juridical initiatives that characterize certain power aspects of Saul's natal community.[13]

As an extension of the weekly Sunday ritual, Carnival imposes hierarchical order. Who the performers are is never open to debate as the act of slaughter points to an undisputed male function. Unusual male prerogative in this instance is neither appropriate nor probable as a question. A hierarchy of decisions is implied in the act since it involves various social elements and functions in a well-defined place. That the ceremony itself releases an elaboration of learned masculine skills would suggest a transfer of traditions from one generation of males to another. This structure of authority, display, and sanction—whatever we might come to make of its aesthetic choices and its styles of gender segregation—confronts the reader both as cultural content and as an analogy on a discursive order. We can try to investigate this convergence as it sheds light not only on the structure of the Carnival scenes, but also as it lends wider interpretive possibilities to the whole structure.

If we look at Carnival as though it were a coherent grammar, we might examine its related parts in this way: The syntax of Carnival and Carnival events determines the principles of meaning, or the rules by which a certain set of givens is "marshalled into orderly array." Agents are bound by a covenant whose procedures evince a display of exactly demarcated roles. The act itself does not vary much across time, we imagine, as its original meaning is buried along with the original actors. To that extent, *Chosen Place* traces the grammar of a mythology. Looking at mythology from the point of view of Roland Barthes's definition, we witness the healed rupture between linear and memorial functions of time.[14]

Myth as a "discourse ordained by history" does not contradict the point we made earlier, that Marshall's myth-making yokes a specific humanity and signs of the Ineffable in an imposed order of harmony. Freeing up "Ineffable" to include certain human, as well as extraordinary, events or the impressive acts of natural phenomena, we could say that Marshall's implied presences of the past—the "nine millions and more" in the African Diaspora; the evoked icons of Zimbabwe, and the founding members of the indigenous African-American culture of Bournehills, whose names and deeds are legion—become aspects of a mythical *lexis*. These presences are as irretrievable to the present as the originating act of murder and sacrifice. Carnival, then, is rendered Marshall's master sign and controlling figure that allows her, through a plurality of dramatic and narrative means, a concise articulation of overlapping texts. Contemporary Bournehills is made one with its past, with its deepest memories, so that ongoing and linear time dips down into the reservoir of collective experience and repairs the apparent fissure between then and now through the systematic repetition of certain inherited cultural gestures.

It seems, then, that we have disclosed the following plausible relationships: The Diaspora, the numbers of ancestors involved in it, and the terrible causes that provoked it in the first place are among the items to be arranged or interpreted; Carnival provides not only the patterns and the rules of an interpretation, as in the syntax of a grammar, but also a context in which an interpretive display might occur. This system of elaborately replicated recurrences, convoking the entire community, locates the replay of a common wealth, binding once again members of tribal order in a common purpose, in a sense of well-being. If we think of a grammar as a language or a discourse, then we might suggest that the totality of Carnival in Bournehills allows us to understand more precisely why this work is entitled *Chosen Place, Timeless People*. The agents in that regard do not belong simply to themselves, in their discrete time and place. Their renewal is altogether essential to a redemptive historical scheme that must play itself out.

In the parade of bands episode that follows the slaughter of the sow, the narrator's vivid portrayal of movement takes us to the heart of Bournehills' social giftedness and ingenuities. On the road at dawn the Monday morning after the Sunday pigsticking, the Bournehills band will reenact the legend of Cuffee Ned, the chief cultural hero of the island and leading figure of slave revolt. The story goes that once upon a time the island was owned by one Percy Bryam, wealthy British planter, and the islanders were his subjects. On the night of the revolt, Bryam himself was taken captive by Cuffee Ned and the estate-house and Pyre Hill set ablaze. Whether or not Cuffee Ned, eventually repulsed, resisted singlehandedly a British regiment at Cleaver's High Wall for *three* or *six* months is contended with passion in Delbert's Rumshop in Spiretown on the first night that Saul visits the place. But the finer points of military strategy and the correct gauge of human probabilities hold far less importance for the interlocutors than the powerful symbolisms of the case. Cuffee Ned perfectly embodies Bournehills' idea of subversion that is rehearsed in various New World historical narratives—Haiti's Touissant L'Ouverture and Nat Turner and Denmark Vesey of the southern United States share the same heroic constellation.

Starring Ferguson and "Stinger," both serving in a dual role of agency, the Pageant of Revolt, in sheer pyrotechnical display, is unrivaled by any other project or scene in the parade. The characters relive the fall of Percy Bryam and the transcendance of Cuffee Ned annually, complete with howls, screams, man-in-night-cap, knife thrusts, a hillside, and a fake fire—all atop the float of the Bournehills band: "The pitched battle raged, the hill seethed, Stinger [as Cuffee Ned] paraded his captive [Ferguson as Percy Bryam] before the crowd, and far up front . . . the steelband boys sent their mallets winging over the drums in a new song—a fast-paced, stirring hymn of jubilation and victory" (p. 285).

The representation of a natural historical sequence, richly layered by the accretions of real and textual time, provides an analogy on the processes of interpretation. The event that originates the new readings has its own unassigned temporal status, whose value is transformed and altered from one version of Bournehills society to the next. In other words, Cuffee Ned's triumph over the owners assumes such overdetermination of value that it might as well have happened *out of* time; just as the events of the Diaspora, Cuffee Ned's Revolt threatens to lose its historical status, or specificity in time, verging, instead, on pure priority, a category of "in the beginning." The "truth" of one generation's reading of this historical sequence over another generation's might vary according to the rules of fiction, but the inaugurating scene is always implied in the present version. All the pointed historical references, held here in simultaneity, are made manifest by a kind of shorthand. These strategies of displacement and selection that acquire believability in visual and aural dimension stand also for those particular aspects of dramatic meaning that might have fallen out along the way. These typologies of repetition that take full advantage of the inherited narratives, both oral and written, move toward the ironic figure, the subperspectives in motion all at once. Because Carnival is avidly reiterative, its ritual modes figure forth the powerful imagery of all time and the actually imagined communal well-being that the Carnival seeker would repossess and "refigure."

The Circle of Ritual in the surround of history and culture in the surround of myth comes to focus on individual agents. If irony is the juxtaposing of competing subperspectives, then the dialectical motion that it implies culminates in the meeting of Saul and Merle, whose ambivalence and complexity of feeling make them both strangers, for quite different reasons, to Bournehills society. Merle assumes a repertoire of correct and loving gestures toward the motherland, the sole powerful figure who confronts the managers of Cane Vale Factory when it is closed for work. But the truth is that her relationship to it is occasionally hysterical and self-serving. She suspects that it is so, but is led to acknowledgment by a foreigner and through the emotional hardware of a foreign culture. Because Saul's talkativeness and meddling into the private business of others whom he likes make her comfortable, Merle is "read" by the man in ways that Leesy Walkes, for instance, would neither presume nor attempt. Merle's culture gives her sanctuary from offense and deliverance. With the text of his feelings etched deeply on his conscience, Saul finds use for *his* version of the foreign and through a foreigner's (Merle's) insistence. Both he and Merle leave each other speaking, having penetrated the core of a mutual silence, even though they both have *talked* incessantly and love has brought it about.

I mean little that is erotic and romantic by "love" in this instance. Even though the attempt is difficult, I have tried to imagine the concept of love in its full dimensional play as a *ground* or background of acts. Kenneth Burke describes it as "the realm of the appetites generally . . . the realm of the nursing child, the nursing mother, the cat purring affectionately at the promise of food; sexual coupling, parental affection, feasts, harvests, trodden grapes, spilled cornucopias, the realm of *ubertas* . . . of the seasons and climates."[15]

If love is the "fullness everywhere": of generation, the generosity, then it is also the burden of human and material things and the source of their generation. The woman in Brueghel's engraving of summer has her imagistic counterpart in Marshall's women and men under the heft and curse, borne gracefully atop the skull, of portions of sugar-cane harvest. As if the power to bear this fecund load sought a kind of figurative displacement, Marshall's women are fertile childbearers. Piety makes us search for love under the entitlements of ease, facility, peace, and kindness, but it seems that the ceaseless labor of having, bearing, begetting, sharing, providing, under whose signs we imagine the spectacle of female and male born and borne endlessly beneath the tyranny of necessity and desire, renders love the most mandatory, yet agonizing, of human activities. In this region of complications and oppositions love is an entanglement, earthbound, just as we are mortally, fatefully bound to both. "Love" as I mean it here is that site of inexorable enactments and reenactments that determines the unfolding of character.

As the principal embodiment of a technological order, Saul must learn the lessons of love in the sense I have described. The society from which he comes "would seem to represent all that attains its culmination in the faculty of intellection. In its noblest aspects, it is wisdom, reason: *veritas*."[16] If the realms of *ubertas* and *veritas* show quite different orders of human and human mimetic experience so that a technological sufficiency marks a point of qualitative change, then Marshall's narrative dialectic appears vividly exposed as it counterpoises agents of cultural disparity. Interestingly enough, Merle and Saul belong to the same order of expectation and desire, need the same kind of healing that a Bournehills might provide. This opposition of motives between the principal agents and the principal agency and scene of the work brings Merle and Saul to the foreground in the final and most inward reverberation of the four concentric circles.

We have already seen in one instance Saul's unease during a selected ritual occasion. But there are other moments that compel similar responses in him. Observing laborers in the cane fields on a usual day of work, Saul carefully traces the agonistic progression of Stinger and Gwen from early morning through the afternoon. Burdened by the unrelieved demands of physical assertion, the scene is claimed by *ubertas*, as we are aware of the human body converted into an instrument of production. The women bear the load away, as the men cut the cane and gather it into great sheaves. Saul is dazed by the scene unfolding before him, "his eyes inflamed by the sun." It seems to him that the cane, while giving an impression of retreating, "had all the time been swiftly regrouping, replenishing their ranks, so that there was now as many of them as when the cutting began" (p. 162).

Stinger presses on, but as noon approaches and passes, he is shaken, in a state of collapse. What Saul experiences, watching on the cane slopes, is tantamount to illness. His head pounds, his eyes burn, he is unable to breathe, and he gropes his way down. The sun, shortly, spins before him "like Ezekiel's great flaming wheel in his stricken gaze." That Saul is the old name of the converted Paul on the road to Damascus is a figurative link pressed into service. In this astonishing context, sunlight is driving and insistent. It impels the workers, it hounds the watchers. Palpable enough as sheer physical energy, the light acquires a visionary dimension, "struck" occurring in too close proximity to words that suggest a dancing brain and an unsteady gaze not to have an other-determined reference. Saul is overcome by double vision, and the twin subjects of this ecstatic upsurge his mother and a senile figure from his childhood. He literally comes back to himself on the road to Spiretown, as Merle watches him from the driver's window of the Bentley: " 'Are you finding out all about us?'," eyes narrowing, scrutinizing.

There is no acceptable answer, nor one intended, to Merle's smirking question, and she herself has no idea that, in this moment of assumed moral superiority, she is as vulnerable to observation as Saul. If we claim that love has brought them to this state of emotional exchange, then we mean to say that love is no longer vague or intense desire and yearning, repulsion and attraction, alone, and in that order of contradictory responses, but a background against which the agent is thrown at the same time that he or she is moved to assume its properties. In this instance, love is not only the given—the scene of the encounter—but also the objective, insofar as it describes an aim, a destination for Saul and Merle. Love also becomes, then, a function of agency, wreaking quite obvious changes of mind and heart in the agent.

The leap from illness to a new seeing, or Saul's immersion in content, translated into a catalyst of re-vision, sums up the narrator's apparent intentions for this scene. Saul's reward for presenting a rich receptivity to the surface of Bournehills society is an absolute drowning in its phenomena. To that extent, his seeing and feeling expose him to a crucifixion of the senses. The repetitions of agony as they occur in the evocative material burden of the scene and in thematic replay along lines of related and divergent stress capture the agents in a world of now-shared values, the laborers, because they must confront economic necessity, and Saul, because he witnesses their lack of freedom and is engaged by it. If we say that empathy makes him see, then we get things only halfway correct because Saul does not stay for resolutions. They take place within him as he slowly comprehends. Standing in another's place has brought him to his own standing, induced by directly physical means.

Saul's customary method of understanding and engagement is "abstract," and "reception" and "extension" are assigned by him to an inferior status of recognition. In that regard, his representability as an agent of "intellectual" culture is solid. But here, in the midst of a mindless fertility, taking place in an infinite progression and regression of exact appearances and in the presence of a natural force of unusual persistence and uniform intensity, the intellect verges on the rediscovery of the muted connection between "love" and "work." The pregnant woman Gwen and the pregnant harvest figuratively announce the link, but the scene crosses its wires and takes hold of a broader imagery. The unborn will repeat the moment and figures now not only in a collective nervous system, but also a geopolitical synthesis, an entire structure of culture through the mother. Sexual coupling and its aspects of nurture are seen in their relationship to the symptoms and objects of wealth—family, private property, and the state. Bournehills does not have a program of "birth control," or a manipulated fertility rate, and as long as necessity constrains it, the women of Bournehills will experience their biological status as the preeminent mode of an economic will not their own. Marshall's narrator says none of this, sustaining her chosen figurative alliances within the delegated narrative means. But since the novel places contrastive degrees of mimetic experience side by side, it allows interpretation to range freely within the borders of related grammars. We might also assume that Bournehills, in order to free itself, to free its people, from the onus of necessity awaits a new Cuffee Ned for its time.

Saul comes to realize that the Center for Applied Social Research, with himself leading this tour of duty, has nothing to teach Bournehills, but that Bournehills is precisely instructive to him in terms of a profoundly personal invasion. Because he cannot escape the scene or its implications; because he can no longer evade the powerful magnetisms and repulsions of love, here robbed of romantic feature, he must succumb to an immediate intuition of the basic human circumstance—in its dance with matter, and a dance without words: "He stumbled past Gwen, her head weaving in its subtle dance as she meticulously picked her way down amid the debris. The dead eyes didn't notice him" (p. 163).

Having acquired the codes of a technological efficiency beyond Bournehills' wildest imaginings, Saul embodies, at once, a cross section of human history and an image robbed of such knowledge. While an ideology of race, unpronounced in the interest of thematic subtlety, is neither asserted by Saul nor explicit in any of his acts, it is nonetheless there, embedded and subversive in the very idea of the anthropological project that he mounts.

In the meantime, Saul has forgotten decisive aspects of his own Jewish past, as the striking vision of his mother and certain poignant memories of his first wife reawaken in him. Whether he likes it or not, or chooses it or not, on the cane slopes with another timeless people and as he is instantly seized by a recognition no longer enthralled to the mysticisms of race, Saul's brotherhood declares itself as the inevitable copulative. Before he completes his stay in Bournehills, he knows, inchoately, that to live in the realms of *ubertas* and *veritas* at the same time designates the terrible contradiction, the virtually unimaginable human destiny not yet achieved that the heart must somehow imagine and make good. Technological agent must recover feeling, memory, extension, generosity, and receptivity—those elements that cluster under the name of compassion, here replayed in the communal remembrance of the ancestors—just as the body once enslaved is now set free to readdress the world.

Saul has a future, Bournehills has a future. Their mutual meeting and exchange demarcate the new dialectics of a New World culture that *Chosen Place, Timeless People* would contemplate.

Notes

1. *The Chosen Place, The Timeless People* (New York: Harcourt, Brace and World, 1969). All direct quotations from the novel come from this edition.

2. *Brown Girl, Brownstones,* with an Afterword by Mary Helen Washington (Old Westbury, N.Y.: The Feminist Press, 1981).

3. Given the definitive character of the novel, it seems perfectly earmarked for a quite different placement in the writer's career. According to the imitative organic and evolutionary model by which an audience perceives the processes of art to go on, one conventionally expects that the big work comes later, rather than sooner, in a career because we assume that the artist is "growing" in the practice of the craft. *Chosen Place* tends to counter such anticipation, following *Brown Girl, Brownstones* by a decade and preceding *Praisesong* by approximately the same number of years. Both *Brown Girl* and *Praisesong* are structured around single central figures. But what is more, the context of their respective drama is foreshortened by an interiorization of scenic detail: The fictions of Selina Boyce (*Brown Girl*) and Avey Johnson (*Praisesong*) unfold along a monochromatic scale of impressions—they embody the central consciousness of the respective works, either by way of concealed narration or stream-of-thought narrative devices. *Chosen Place,* contrastively, is negotiated by a subtle blend of omniscience and concealed strategies that seek to widen the exterior space, as individual characters are "stretched" to the proportions of the surround. The novel, then, repeats not only a certain thematic configuration, but also subsumes its own immediate literary past by elaborating a persistent theme against a complicated background of broader historical and cultural point; the work, in its "lateness," achieves a kind of priority. I am borrowing here from Harold Bloom's *Map of Misreading* (New York: Oxford University Press, 1975). Although Bloom's scheme is made to work comparatively, among generations of male writers within the traditional English and American literary categories of alignment, the idea is flexible in its application to some women writers whose careers do not conform so exactly to the sequential prerogatives of Bloom's system of Freudian displacements: literature as an Oedipal elaboration of father/son antagonisms.

4. Barbara Christian provides a thorough analysis of Marshall's work, in perspective with that of Alice Walker and Toni Morrison, in *Black Women Novelists: The Development of a Tradition, 1892–1976* (Westport, Conn.: Greenwood Press, 1980).

5. The pentad of terms is adopted from Kenneth Burke's *Grammar of Motives* (New York: Prentice-Hall, 1945), "Introduction: The Five Key Terms of Dramatism," pp. x–xvi.

6. Professor Judith Fetterley has discussed parts of the novel with me, and in her opinion, the work is homophobic. Although the relationship between Merle and her London patroness, remembered by the reader during Merle's conversation with Harriet, is not, to my mind, a major thematic issue in the novel, we should pause to consider it as an illustration of the sorts of conflicts that arise among discontinuous reading and interpretive communities.

Briefly, Merle returns to Bournehills after many years abroad in London. In the course of things, she has lost husband and child in a scandal that erupts when her husband believes, quite correctly or wrongly, that she has had a love affair with a woman. Her East African husband doesn't wait for explanations, but abandons Merle instead, taking back with him to Kenya their young daughter. For Merle resolution is imminent in her decision to have the will to confront that loss and to actually travel to East Africa in search of this crucial aspect of her past. As I read the narrator's intentions, Merle's recitation of this phase of her life to Saul throws several nuances into play: As a young woman from one of the commonwealth communities in the metropolitan city, Merle has become friends with a powerful Englishwoman. It is not absolutely certain that their encounter is sexual, but I assume that it is and that the ambiguity concerning it in Merle's mind is intended to show her ambivalence along a number of stress points. For instance, Merle is decidedly confused in her feelings for the mother culture; and this engenders, consequently, a structure of nervous traits that we might regard as a neurasthenic constellation. She suffers periods of exhaustion—some of this is melodramatic self-indulgence, I believe—when she must take to her bed, refusing to see anyone, with the probable exception of Leesy Walkes.

As Merle tells her story, she must end her relationship with the Englishwoman because she feels exploited by the dynamics of power. There are grounds here for an "inequality"—Merle is younger, poorer, and not only black-skinned and colonized, but also, primarily, *not* English *culturally*. I believe that this intrusion of subtlety into the matrix of political power is the feature of reading that an American audience—or aspects of it—might miss. It is also the provenience of the complicated relationship between the colonized, or formerly colonized, community and the metropolitan center *outside* the novel that inspires the Fanonian vision of the New World Negro. (Cf. *Black Skin, White Masks*, trans. Charles Lam Markmann [New York: Grove Press, 1967]; *The Wretched of the Earth*, trans. Constance Farrington [New York: Grove Press, 1968]. Fanon's particular contributions to articulating the problematics of culture and history in dominated communities is well known. For a recent discussion of the role of language in Fanon's view of "open" and "closed" cultures, see Chester Fontenot's *Frantz Fanon: Language as the God Gone Astray in the Flesh*, University of Nebraska Studies: new series no. 60 [Lincoln: University of Nebraska Press, 1979].)

Merle is the "cultural inferior" in the eyes of English society, and according to elaborately observed racial coding, the white "liberal" does not say as much directly any more than it is not entirely possible for the subject to believe that it is "true" of *her* in *their* eyes. My impression is that Merle has also been adoring of her friend in the spirit of "groupie." Whether "straight" or homoerotic, we know that inequality between lovers, for whatever reason, equals oppression. In my reading, Marshall's character and narrator are getting at the particular dynamics of colonial politics and its involvement on the intimate ground of feeling. When Harriet Amron, as the moneyed powerful other, confronts Merle Kinbona, it is that powerful other who can buy affection or buy it off that Merle remembers about the London liaison.

The conflicted readings that might cluster around the novel point steadily toward the requirements of a dialectics of reading that will not choose one mighty and irrevocable interpretation of women's texts, but an *epistemological ground* for locating centers of interpretation. Recent interest in the evaluative dynamics of critical reading and the formation of reader communities in response to texts has generated some important work, among them Professor Fetterley's own *Resisting Reader: A Feminist Approach to American Fiction* (Bloomington: Indiana University Press, 1978); Barbara Hernstein Smith, "Contingencies of Value," *Critical Inquiry* 10:1 (September 1983), pp. 1–37; Stanley Fish, *Is There a Text In This Class?* (Cambridge: Harvard University Press, 1980).

7. *The Chosen Place, The Timeless People*, p. 106. The page numbers of subsequent quotations will be noted in the text.

8. What is conventionally designated the "pathetic fallacy" becomes for Marshall a dialectical engagement. Proscription against it is fairly useless because the novel embodies an overwhelming figure of carefully choreographed and juxtaposed disparities. The entire effect of the work depends upon one's seeing the well-defined particular in light of an indivisible whole, and vice versa. Unlike Margaret Walker's big novel of the same decade, *Jubilee*, Marshall's work, though not explicitly arguing the point, gives the agent the potential resources to remake her/his world more nearly in accord with the right. Under whatever disguise, "God" does not wait offstage to spring his own. In this world of human particularity, women and men must rely on each other, admittedly not as much as any of them would like, and their motives are richly mixed and complicated.

9. I am drawing here on Ferdinand de Saussure's distinction between the diachronic and synchronic dimensions of language. *The General Course in Linguistics*, eds. Charles Bally and Albert Sechehaye, trans. Wade Baskin (New York: McGraw-Hill, 1966).

10. Ralph Ellison's *Invisible Man* demarcates a similar intersection between the elements of autobiography and history as the main character cannot be emancipated until he has experienced in his own career certain figurative peak points of the historical order in which he is rooted. (New York: The Modern Library, 1952.)

Marshall's own *Brown Girl* poses the obsession of history as the puzzle that young Selina Boyce, like "invisible man," must discover and somehow absorb before the "plunge outside history" can assume its critical meaning and function.

11. Roland Barthes, *The Fashion System*, trans. Matthew Ward and Richard Howard (New York: Hill and Wang, 1983), p. 16. The description of garments of fashion offers the viewer an order for seeing the garment "and this order inevitably implies certain goals." Similarly, Marshall's narrator negotiates a seeing of aspects of natural order that elaborates it as an extension of a discursive order.

12. "Irony arises when one tries, by the interaction of terms upon one another, to produce a *development* that uses all the terms. [emphasis Burke] Hence, from the standpoint of this total form (this 'perspective of perspectives'), none of the participating 'sub-perspectives' can be treated as either precisely right or precisely wrong." (Appendix D, "Four Master Tropes," p. 512, *A Grammar of Motives*.)

13. In attempting to understand the structure of sacrifice deployed in Marshall's work, I have had recourse to René Girard's *Violence and the Sacred*, trans. Patrick Gregory (Baltimore: The Johns Hopkins University Press, 1977). I also borrow the term "natal community," richer in its cultural implications than "race," from Barbara Christian, cf. n. 4.

14. I am drawing here on Roland Barthes's startling adaptation of De Saussure's linguistic program. In his contemplation of myth as a mode of discourse, Barthes reads the healed split between "past" and "present" in mythic patterns as the convergence between a linear and memorial extension of time. Even though Barthes regards the process of myth-making as fundamentally conservative, even reactionary, cultural praxis, his scheme suggests an image for grasping modes of time and their impact on human consciousness. "Myth Today," *Mythologies*, trans. Annette Lavers (New York: Hill and Wang, 1972), pp. 109–159.

15. Burke, *A Grammar of Motives*, p. 122.

16. Ibid.

10

Lady No Longer
Sings the Blues:
Rape, Madness, and Silence
in The Bluest Eye

MADONNE M. MINER

Robert Stepto begins a recent interview with Toni Morrison by commenting on the "extraordinary sense of place" in her novels. He notes that she creates specific geographical landscapes with street addresses, dates, and other such details.[1] His observations certainly hold true for Morrison's first novel, *The Bluest Eye*, set in a black neighborhood in Lorain, Ohio, in 1941. Reading *The Bluest Eye*, I feel as if I have been in the abandoned store on the southeast corner of Broadway and Thirty-fifth Street in Lorain where Pecola Breedlove lives, as if I have been over the territory traversed by the eleven-year-old black girl as she skips among tin cans, tires, and weeds.

Morrison's skill in creating this very specific place accounts, in part, for my sense of the strangely familiar, the uncanny, when I read her novel—but only in part. While reading, I am familiar not only with Pecola's neighborhood but also, in a more generalized way, with Pecola's story. The sequence of events in this story—a sequence of rape, madness, and silence—repeats a sequence I have read before. Originally manifest in mythic accounts of Philomela and Persephone, this sequence provides Morrison with an ancient archetype from which to structure her very contemporary account of a young black woman.

In the pages which follow I want to explore intersections between these age-old myths and Morrison's ageless novel.

For an account of Philomela, we must turn to Ovid, who includes her story in his *Metamorphoses* (8 A.D.). According to the chronicler, this story begins with an act of separation: Procne leaves her much-loved sister, Philomela, to join her husband, Tereus, in Thrace. After several years, Procne convinces Tereus to make a trip to Athens and escort Philomela to Thrace for a visit. In Athens, Tereus barely manages to curb the lust he feels for Philomela. He caresses her with his eyes, watches possessively as she kisses her father good-bye, and uses each embrace, each kiss,

> . . . to spur his rage, and feed his fire;
> He wished himself her father—and yet no less
> Would lust look hideous in a father's dress.[2]

Arriving in Thrace, Tereus drags Philomela into a dark wood and rapes her. The virgin calls out the names of father, sister, gods, but to no avail. Having indulged his lust, Tereus prepares to leave this "ringdove . . . with bloodstained plumes still fluttering" when she dares cry out against his sin:

> "I'll speak your deed, and cast all shame away.
>   . . .
> My voice shall reach the highest tract of air,
> And gods shall hear, if gods indeed are there."[3]

Tereus cannot tolerate such sacrilege against his name, so he perpetrates yet another rape: with pincers he

> . . . gripped the tongue that cried his shame,
> That stammered to the end her father's name,
> That struggled still, and strangled utterance made,
> And cut it from the root with barbarous blade.[4]

Deprived of speech and lodged in "walls of stone," Philomela weaves the tale of her plight into a piece of fabric, which she then sends to Procne. When Procne learns of her sister's grief and her husband's treachery, she determines upon a most hideous revenge; she slays the son she has had with Tereus and feeds his remains to the unsuspecting father. While Ovid's story ends with this feast, popular mythology adds yet another chapter, transforming Philomela into a nightingale, damned forever to chirp the name of her rapist: tereu, tereu.

Obviously, male-violating-female functions as the core action within Philomela's story. Under different guises, this violation occurs several times: first, when Tereus ruptures the hymen of Philomela; second, when Tereus ruptures the connecting tissue of Philomela's tongue; and, finally, when he enters her body yet again ("Thereafter, if the frightening tale be true,/ On her maimed form he wreaked his lust anew"[5]). With each act Tereus asserts his presence, his sensual realm, and denies the very existence of such a realm (encompassing not only sensuality, but the senses themselves) to Philomela. As if to reinforce the initial violation, Tereus, following his act of rape, encloses Philomela in silence, in stone walls. He thereby forces her to assume externally imposed configurations instead of maintaining those natural to her.

If man-raping-woman functions as the most basic "mythemic act"[6] in Philomela's story, the most basic mythemic *inter*-act involves not only this pair, but another: father and sister of the rape victim. When, for example, Ovid notes that Tereus, lusting for Philomela, "wished himself her father," and when the chronicler describes Philomela, in the midst of the rape, calling out her father's name (for help, of course, but for what else?) he sets the act of violence within a familial matrix. Thus, we cannot limit consideration of this act's motivations and ramifications to two individuals. Interestingly enough, however, just as the basic mythemic act (man raping woman) robs the woman of identity, so too the mythemic interact; dependent upon familial roles for personal verification ("mother of," "sister of," "wife of"[7]) the female must fear a loss of identity as the family loses its boundaries—or, more accurately, as the male transgresses these boundaries.

Having noted the most important structural elements in Philomela's story, we cross an ocean, several centuries and countless historical, racial, and class lines before coming to the story of Pecola. Despite obvious contextual differences between the two stories, structural similarities abound. Individual mythemes from Philomela's story appear, without distortion, in that of Pecola. First, in various ways and at various costs, the female figure suffers violation: by Mr. Yacobowski, Junior, Bay Boy and friends, Cholly, Soaphead. Second, with this violation a man asserts his presence as "master," "man-in-control," or "god" at the expense of a young woman who exists only as someone to "impress upon." Third, following the violation/assertion, this woman suffers an enclosure or undesirable transformation; she cowers, shrinks, or resides behind walls of madness. Finally, the most characteristic example of violation/assertion/destruction occurs within the family matrix; Cholly Breedlove rapes his own daughter, violating a standard code of familial relations. We now might look more closely at individual instances of mythemes structuring the Pecola story.

An early, and paradigmatic, example of male transgression and subsequent female silence occurs in the "See the Cat" section. Junior, a tyrannical, unloving black boy, invites a rather credulous Pecola into his house, ostensibly to show her some kittens; like Philomela, Pecola has no idea of the dangers involved in trusting herself to a male guide. Once inside, engrossed in admiration of the furnishings, she forgets about Junior until he insists that she acknowledge him:

> She was deep in admiration of the flowers when Junior said, "Here!" Pecola turned. "Here is your kitten!" he screeched. And he threw a big black cat right in her face.[8]

Pecola immediately responds to this unexpected penetration by sucking in her breath; metaphorically she draws herself inward. She then attempts to flee, but just as Tereus confines Philomela behind stone walls, Junior confines Pecola behind the wall of his will:

> Junior leaped in front of her. "You can't get out. You're my prisoner," he said. His eyes were merry but hard . . . . He pushed her down, ran out the door that separated the rooms, and held it shut with his hands. (pp. 73–74)

Male realms expand as those of the female suffer an almost fatal contraction.

Junior does not actually rape Pecola. Morrison, however, duplicates the dynamics of the scene between Junior and Pecola in a scene between Cholly and Pecola, where rape *does* occur. Eleven-year-old Pecola stands at the sink, scraping away at dirty dishes, when her father, drunk, staggers into the kitchen. Unlike Tereus and Junior, Cholly does not carry his victim into foreign territories; rather, Pecola's rape occurs within her own house, and this fact increases its raw horror (Morrison denies us the cover of metaphor and confronts us directly with a father's violation of his daughter). As Morrison explains, several factors motivate Cholly, but the two thoughts floating through his besotted brain immediately prior to his penetration of Pecola point, once more, to his desire for confirmation of his presence. First, a gesture of Pecola's, a scratching of the leg, reminds him of a similar gesture of Pauline's—or, more accurately, reminds him of *his own* response to this gesture. He repeats his response, catching Pecola's foot in his hand, nibbling on the flesh of her leg, just as he had done with Pauline, so many years before. Of consequence here is not Pecola's gesture, but Cholly's belief that he can regain an earlier perception of himself as young, carefree and whimsical by using this girl/woman as medium. When Pecola, however, unlike the laughing Pauline, remains stiff and silent, Cholly shifts to a second train of thought, a second stimulus to self-assertion: "The rigidness of her shocked body, the silence of her stunned throat, was better than Pauline's easy laughter had been. The confused mixture of his memories of Pauline and the doing of a wild and forbidden thing excited him, and a bolt of desire ran down his genitals, giving it length" (p. 128). Thus, on a literal level, Cholly expands as Pecola contracts:

> The tightness of her vagina was more than he could bear. His soul seemed to slip down to his guts and fly out into her, and the gigantic thrust he made into her then provoked the only sound she made—a hollow suck of air in the back of her throat. Like the rapid loss of air from a circus balloon. (p. 128)

As in the episode with Junior, Pecola sucks inward, but without positive effect; like a deflating circus balloon, she *loses* the benefits of lifegiving oxygen and the power of speech.

To enforce this silence, Cholly need not cut off Pecola's tongue or imprison her behind stone walls. The depresencing of Pecola Breedlove takes a different form from that of Philomela. Upon regaining consciousness following the rape, Pecola *is* able to speak; she tells Mrs. Breedlove what has happened. But as Mrs. Breedlove does not want to hear and does not want to believe, Pecola must recognize the futility of attempted communication. Thus when Cholly, like Tereus, rapes a second time, Pecola keeps the story to herself; in silence this eleven-year-old girl steps across commonly accepted borders of reason and speech to enter her own personal world of silence and madness. Pecola's "self" becomes so crazed, so fragmented, that it conducts conversations with itself—and with no one else:

> "How come you don't talk to anybody?"
> "I talk to you."
> "Besides me."
> "I don't like anybody besides you . . . ."
> "You don't talk to anybody. You don't go to school. And nobody talks to you." (p. 153)

Of course, when Pecola comments that her mirror image does not engage other people in conversation, she engages in self-commentary;

"I" and "you" are one and the same. Tragically, even when combined, this "I" and "you" do not compose one whole being. Claudia's description of the mutilated Pecola leaves no doubt that she no longer exists as a reasonable human being; like Philomela-turned-nightingale, the "little-girl-gone-to-woman" undergoes a transformation:

> The damage done was total . . . . Elbows bent, hands on shoulders, she flailed her arms like a bird in an eternal, grotesquely futile effort to fly. Beating the air, a winged but grounded bird, intent on the blue void it could not reach—could not even see—but which filled the valleys of the mind. (p. 158)

Silent, isolated, insane: Pecola cannot escape.

In depicting the effects of rape on one young woman, Morrison sets into motion a series of associations that take their cue from gender. Men, potential rapists, assume presence, language, and reason as their particular province. Women, potential victims, fall prey to absence, silence, and madness.[9] An understanding of the powerful dynamics behind this allotment of presence/absence, language/silence, reason/madness along sexual lines contributes to an understanding of the painful truths contained in Philomela's story, in Pecola's story, and in the story of yet another rape victim: Persephone. While clearly related to the Philomela myth, that of Persephone differs in certain details which, when brought to *The Bluest Eye*, prompt an even richer reading of the novel. Before engaging in an application of Persephone's story to that of Pecola, however, we might look at three different renditions of the Persephone myth, each of which may advance our understanding of the way Persephone's and Pecola's stories intersect mythopoetically.

Homer sets a springtime mood of warmth, gaiety, youthfulness, and beauty as he begins his rendition of Persephone's story:

> Now I will sing/of golden-haired Demeter,
> the awe-inspiring goddess,
> and of her trim-ankled daughter,
> Persephone,
> who was frolicking in a grassy meadow.[10]

When Pluto, god of the underworld, abducts the "trim-ankled" young woman (and surely it is not mere coincidence that Morrison specifies Pecola's ankles as a stimulant to Cholly's desire) this mood changes abruptly; in terror, the virgin shrieks for her father, Zeus. While noting that Persephone directs her shrieks to her father, Homer also comments on the virgin's hopes relative to her mother:

Still *glimpsing* the earth,
the brilliant sky,
the billowing, fish-filled sea
and the rays of the sun,
Persephone vainly hoped *to see* her mother again.[11]

Homer establishes a causal connection between rape and the loss of a particular *vision*. He further substantiates this connection in Demeter's response to her daughter's rape, a punitive response which involves Demeter's changing the world so that its occupants will no longer see fruits and flowers:

She made that year
most shocking and frightening
for mortals who lived on the nourishing earth.
The soil did not yield a single seed.
Demeter kept them all underground.[12]

The goddess imposes a sensual deprivation on mortals parallel to the sensual deprivation suffered by her daughter (note that *The Bluest Eye* opens with a statement of similar deprivation: "Quiet as it's kept, there were no marigolds in the fall of 1941"). By the end of the hymn, Demeter and Pluto reach a compromise; half of the year Persephone resides with her mother and the flowers grow; during the other half, Persephone remains with Pluto and the earth produces no fruits.

James Frazer, in *The Golden Bough*, relates another version of the Persephone story. In substance, Frazer comes very close to Homer; in detail, however, the two diverge, and Frazer's details reverberate in *The Bluest Eye*. First, Frazer provides more specifics about Persephone's "frolic"; the young woman gathers "roses and lilies, crocuses and violets, hyacinths and narcissuses in a lush meadow."[13] Individual flowers in Frazer's catalog call forth associations of importance to *The Bluest Eye*: the virginal lily, bloody hyacinth (taking its color from the slain youth, Hyacinthus, beloved of Apollo) and narcotic Narcissus (taking its name from the self-enclosed youth, Narcissus, capable of seeing only himself).[14] The mythic situation itself, flower picking, finds an analog in the novel as Pecola, on her way to the candy store, peers into the heads of yellow dandelions. Second, Frazer's more detailed description of Persephone's abduction and underworld residence might serve as metaphoric description of Pecola's state of mind following her rape: "the earth gaped and Pluto, Lord of the Dead, issuing from the *abyss*, carried her off . . . to be his bride and queen in the *gloomy subterranean world*."[15] Finally, when Frazer concludes the story, he notes that although the "grim Lord of the Dead" obeys Zeus's command to restore Persephone to Demeter, this Lord first gives his mistress the seed of a pomegranate to eat, which ensures that she will return to him. Tereus and Cholly also "give seeds" to women, thereby ensuring that the women never will be able to reassume their previously experienced wholeness.

In a very recent reworking of the Persephone story, Phyllis Chesler focuses most intently on the fate of this myth's female characters. Because she places women's experiences at the center of her version, Chesler begins with a chapter of the story which does not appear in Homer and Frazer: Persephone menstruates. Further, Chesler specifies the nature of certain acts and relationships that her male counterparts choose to obscure; she identifies rape as rape, fathers as fathers:

> One morning Persephone menstruated. That afternoon, Demeter's daughters gathered flowers to celebrate the loveliness of the event. A chariot thundered, then clattered into their midst. It was Hades, the middle aged god of death, come to *rape* Persephone, come to carry her off to be his queen, to sit beside him in the realm of *non-being* below the earth, come to commit the first act of violence earth's children had ever known. Afterwards, the three sisters agreed that he was old enough to be Persephone's *father*. Perhaps he was; who else could he be? There were no known male parents . . . and thus they discovered that in shame and sorrow childhood ends, and that nothing remains the same.[16]

Morrison, like Chesler, pays attention to female rites of passage; she includes a description of Pecola's first menstruation, an experience which bonds Pecola to her adopted sisters, Claudia and Frieda. Also like Chesler, Morrison insists on the paternal identity of the rapist (Pecola need not shriek the name of father as Philomela and Persephone do; father is right there) and emphasizes that the rape act brings one entire way of life to a close ("nothing remains the same"). This rapport between Chesler's Persephone and Morrison's Pecola surfaces in conclusions to the stories as well. Chesler writes:

> Persephone still had to visit her husband once each year (in winter, when no crops could grow), but her union with him remained a barren one. Persephone was childless. Neither husband nor child—no stranger would ever claim her as his own.[17]

Pecola's fate runs along strikingly parallel lines. Despite the offerings and incantations of Claudia and Frieda, Pecola miscarries and remains childless. Grown people turn away, children laugh, and no stranger attempts to share Pecola's world.

Structurally, the stories of Philomela, Persephone, and Pecola share the same blueprint: violated by a male relative, a young virgin suffers sensual loss of such an extreme that her very identity is called into question. In one brutally explicit scene Ovid conveys the terror of Philomela's sensual loss—Tereus severs his sister-in-law's tongue and deprives her of speech. As chroniclers of this same basic female experience, Homer, Frazer, and Chesler also must convey the terror of sensual loss. In their versions, however, *sight* rather than speech assumes priority, and they convey the terror of deprivation not in one explicit scene, but by depicting the ramifications of an altered vision. Of course, this particular emphasis encourages yet further consideration of the Persephone myth and Morrison's novel, the very title of which suggests an interest in the way vision structures our world. This interest, reflected in the novel's title (what does it mean to see through "the bluest eye"?) and in sectional titles (how does one "see mother," "see father"?) springs naturally from Morrison's more fundamental interests: how does the world see a young black girl? how does a young black girl see a world? and finally, what are the correspondences between presence/absence, vision/nonvision, male/female?

As described by various psychologists and psychoanalysts,[18] the processes of identity construction and personal integration involve an extremely sensitive and constantly shifting balance between seeing and being seen—so that, for example, only after an infant sees itself reflected in the mother's eyes (that is, given a presence) can the infant, through its own eyes, bestow a presence on others. Throughout *The Bluest Eye*, Morrison provides several examples of the ways sex and race may prompt a dangerous distortion of this visual balance. An early instance of this distortion, and subsequent personal disintegration, occurs during an exchange between Pecola and Mr. Yacobowski, white male proprietor of a candy store on Garden Avenue.[19] Pecola enjoys her walk to Mr. Yacobowski's store. Many times she has seen that crack in the walk, this clump of dandelions. Having seen them, she grants them a reality, a reality which redounds to include Pecola herself:

> These and other inanimate things she saw and experienced. They were real to her. She knew them . . . . She owned the crack . . . she owned the clump of dandelions . . . . And owning them made her part of the world, and the world part of her. (p. 41)

Such a happy rapport between viewer and vision is short-lived, however. When Pecola enters the candy store and comes under Mr. Yacobowski's eyes, her existence, as well as the existence of her world, become matters of doubt. Mr. Yacobowski *does not see* her:

> Somewhere between retina and object, between vision and view, his eyes draw back, hesitate, and hover. At some fixed point in time and space he senses that he need not waste the effort of a glance. He does not see her, because for him there is *nothing to see* (pp. 41–42, my italics)

In effect, this scene parallels previously described rape scenes in the novel: male denies presence to female. Pecola cannot defend herself against this denial: "she looks up at him and sees the vacuum where curiosity ought to lodge. And something more. The total absence of human recognition—the glazed separateness" (p. 42). Nor can she defend her world; walking home, she rejects dandelions she formerly has favored. They, like Pecola herself, certainly will not satisfy standards that the blue eyes of a Mr. Yacobowski may impose:

> Dandelions. A dart of affection leaps out from her to them. But they do not look at her and do not send love back. She thinks "They are ugly. They are weeds." (p. 43)

Before contact with this white male, Pecola creates belief in both a world and a self; following contact with Yacobowski, her conjuring powers impaired, she abandons the effort.

A second example of visual distortion finds Pecola face to face with Geraldine, one of those "brown girls from Mobile and Aiken" able to construct inviolable worlds by imposing strict boundaries between the acceptable and the unacceptable, the seen and the unseen. Unlike Mr. Yacobowski, Geraldine does *look* at Pecola, but, like Yacobowski, Geraldine does not *see* Pecola; she sees only a series of signs, a symbolic configuration. Thus, when Geraldine returns home and discovers a shrieking son, a frying feline on the radiator, and an unfamiliar black girl in her living room, she responds by distancing herself from Pecola. With no qualms whatsoever she relegates the young girl to the general category of "black female who is an embarrassment to us all", or, "black female whom we would prefer to keep out of sight":

> She looked at Pecola. Saw the dirty torn dress, the plaits sticking out of her head, hair matted where the plaits had come undone, the muddy shoes with the wad of gum peeking out from between the cheap soles,

the soiled socks, one of which had been walked down into the heel of
the shoe. She saw the safety pin holding the hem of the dress up . . . .
She had seen this little girl all of her life. (p. 75)

Pecola, for Geraldine, serves as symbol of everything ugly, dirty, and
degrading. Physically as well as symbolically, Geraldine must negate
Pecola, must deny the ragged eleven-year-old access to her world.
The woman who does not sweat in her armpits or thighs, who smells
of wood and vanilla (pp. 70–71) says to Pecola, *quietly* says to Pecola:
" 'Get out . . . . You nasty little black bitch. Get out of my house!' "
(p. 75). In other words, get out of my world, out of the vision I
construct before and about me. Pecola leaves. As she leaves, she
hangs her head, lowers her eyes; incapable of defending herself
against visual distortion, Pecola attempts to deny vision altogether.
But, even here, she fails: "she could not hold it [her head] low enough
to avoid seeing the snowflakes falling and dying on the pavement"
(p. 76). These snowflakes, falling and dying, suggest the visual perimeters of Pecola's world. In an earlier comment, Morrison gener-
alizes as to the nature of these perimeters: "She would see only what
there was to see: the eyes of other people" (p. 40). As these eyes do
not see her, or see her only as a sign of something other, Pecola loses
sight of herself.

Although Pecola's encounters with Mr. Yacobowski and Geraldine
serve as the most complete and sensitively drawn examples of visual
imbalance, they merely reenforce a pattern of imbalance begun much
earlier in Pecola's life—for that matter, begun even before Pecola sees
the light of day, while she is in Pauline's womb. During the nine
months of pregnancy, Pauline spends most afternoons at the movies,
picking up an education in white values of beauty and ugliness. Morrison describes this education as yet another violation of male on
female, white on black. There, in a darkened theater, images come
together, "all projected through the ray of light from above and behind" (p. 97). This ray of light resembles a gigantic eyeball (apologies
to Emerson) which defines the boundaries of existence and which, of
necessity, projects a white male vision. Having absorbed these silver-
screen values, Pauline conjures up "a mind's eye view" of her soon-
to-be-born child more in keeping with white fantasy than black reality.
Upon birth, Pecola gives the lie to this view, and Pauline expresses
her disappointment:

So when I seed it, it was like looking at a picture of your mama when
she was a girl. You know who she is, but she don't look the same . . . .
Head full of pretty hair, but Lord she was ugly. (p. 99)

As various psychologists attest, the mother's gaze is of primary importance in generating a child's sense of self. Tragically, Pauline looks at her infant daughter and then looks away.

Morrison's novel contains repeated instances of Pecola's negation as other characters refuse to see her. *The Bluest Eye* also provides numerous instances of Pecola's desire to hide her own eyes, thereby refusing to acknowledge certain aspects of her world. Morrison articulates this desire for self-abnegation most explicitly in a postscript to her description of a typical fight between family members in the Breedlove home. Mrs. Breedlove hits Cholly with a dishpan, Cholly returns the blow with his fists, Sammy strikes at Cholly while shouting "you naked fuck," and Pecola covers her head with a quilt. The quilt of course cannot completely block out this scene, so Pecola prays that God will make her disappear. Receiving no response from the man in the sky, she does her best on her own:

> She squeezed her eyes shut. Little parts of her body faded away. Now slowly, now with a rush. Slowly again. Her fingers went, one by one; then her arms disappeared all the way to the elbow. Her feet now. Yes, that was good. The legs all at once. It was hardest above the thighs. She had to be real still and pull. Her stomach would not go. But finally it, too, went away. Then her chest, her neck. The face was hard too. Almost done, almost. Only her tight, tight eyes were left. They were always left.
>
> Try as she might, she could never get her eyes to disappear. So what was the point? They were everything. Everything was there, in them. (p. 39)

These paragraphs forcefully convey Pecola's desire and her notion of how she might realize it. If Pecola were to *see* things differently, she might *be seen* differently; if her eyes were different, her world might be different too.[20] As Morrison deals out one ugly jigsaw piece after another, as she fits the pieces together to construct Pecola's world, we come to understand the impulse behind Pecola's desire, as well as its ultimate futility. When boys shout at her, " 'Black e mo Black e mo Ya daddy sleeps nekked' " (p. 55), Pecola drops her head and covers her eyes; when Maureen accuses her of having seen her father naked, Pecola maintains her innocence by disclaiming, " 'I wouldn't even look at him, even if I did see him' " (p. 59); when Maureen attacks her yet again Pecola tucks her head in "a funny, sad, helpless movement. A kind of hunching of the shoulders, pulling in of the neck, as though she wanted to cover her ears" (p. 60). By covering ears, eyes, and nose Pecola attempts to shut out the testimony of her senses. Reminded of her own ugliness or that of her world, she repeatedly resorts to an elemental self-denial.

Pecola quavers when Mr. Yacobowski and Geraldine refuse to acknowledge her. She shrinks in fear when Maureen and Bay Boy insist on acknowledging her ugliness. Quavering and shaking, Pecola *does* maintain a hold on her world and herself—until Cholly smashes her illusions about the possibility of unambivalent love in this world. Throughout the novel, Pecola ponders the nature of love, pursues it as a potentially miraculous phenomenon. On the evening of her first menstruation, for example, she asks, " 'How do you do that? I mean, how do you get somebody to love you' " (p. 29). And, after a visit to Marie, Poland, and China, Pecola ponders, "What did love feel like? . . . How do grownups act when they love each other? Eat fish together?" (p. 48). When Cholly rapes his daughter, he commits a sacrilege—not only against Pecola, but against her vision of love and its potential. Following the rape, Pecola, an unattractive eleven-year-old black girl, knows that for her, even love is bound to be dirty, ugly, of a piece with the fabric of her world. Desperate, determined to unwind the threads that compose this fabric, Pecola falls back on an early notion: the world changes as the eyes which see it change. To effect this recreation, Pecola seeks out the only magician she knows, Soaphead Church, and presents him with the only plan she can conceive. She asks that he make her eyes different, make them blue—blue because in Pecola's experience only those with blue eyes receive love: Shirley Temple, Geraldine's cat, the Fisher girl.

In its emotional complications, Soaphead's response to Pecola's request resembles Cholly's response to Pecola's defeated stance; both men move through misdirected feelings of love, tenderness, and anger.[21] Soaphead perceives Pecola's need and knows that he must direct the anger he feels not at her, but rather at the God who has encased her within black skin and behind brown eyes. But finally, when Soaphead decides to "look at that ugly black girl" and love her (p. 143), he violates her integrity in much the same way Cholly violates her body when he forces open her thighs. Prompted by the desire to play God and to make this performance a convincing one, Soaphead casts Pecola in the role of believer. Thus, although he *sees* Pecola more accurately than other characters do, he subordinates his vision of her to his vision of self-as-God. He later boasts in his letter "To He Who Greatly Ennobled Human Nature by Creating It":

> I did what you did not, could not, would not do. I looked at that ugly little black girl, and I loved her. I played You. And it was a very good show! (p. 143)

Of course, the script for this show sends Pecola into realms of madness. Even Soaphead acknowledges that "No one else will see her blue eyes" (p. 143), but Soaphead justifies himself first on the grounds that "she will love happily ever after" and then, more honestly, on the grounds that "I, I have found it meet and right to do so" (p. 143). In other words, Soaphead's creation of false belief is not necessarily right for Pecola, but for himself. Morrison substantiates this assessment of Soaphead's creation a few pages later, when she portrays its effect on Pecola. Imprisoned now behind blue eyes, the schizophrenic little girl can talk only to herself. Obviously, this instance of male-female interaction parallels earlier scenes from the novel: "rape" occurs as Soaphead elevates himself at the expense of Pecola.

In *The Raw and the Cooked* Lévi-Strauss observes: "There exists no veritable end or term to mythical analysis, no secret unity which could be grasped at the end of the work of decomposition. The themes duplicate themselves to infinity."[22] Although the stories of Philomela, Persephone, and Pecola do not form a composite whole, each of them, with its varied and individual emphases, contributes to a much larger woman's myth, which tells of denial and disintegration, which unveils the oft-concealed connections between male reason, speech, presence and female madness, silence, absence. As a young black woman, Pecola assumes an especially poignant position in this growing complex of mythic representations; she is absent (and absenced) in relation to the norms of male culture and in relation to the norms of white culture. Ultimately, I read Pecola's story as a tragic version of the myth; this twentieth-century black woman remains behind blue eyes, an inarticulate, arm-fluttering bird. But I cannot read *The Bluest Eye* as tragedy; Claudia, our sometimes-narrator, *speaks*, as does Morrison, our full-time novelist. Thus, although the novel documents the sacrifice of one black woman, it attests to the survival of two others—a survival akin to that of Philomela or Persephone—filled with hardship, but also with hope.

Notes

1. Robert Stepto, " 'Intimate Things in Place': A Conversation with Toni Morrison," in *The Third Woman*, ed. Dexter Fisher (Boston: Houghton Mifflin, 1979), p. 167.

2. A. E. Watts, trans., *The Metamorphoses of Ovid* (Berkeley: University of California Press, 1954), p. 131.

3. Watts, p. 133.

4. Ibid., p. 133.

5. Ibid., p. 133.

6. I take this term from Claude Lévi-Strauss. For an explanation of Lévi-Strauss's *modus operandi* see Robert Scholes, *Structuralism in Literature* (New Haven: Yale University Press, 1974), pp. 68–74.

7. "From her initial family upbringing throughout her subsequent development, the social role assigned to the women is that of serving an image, authoritative and central, of man: a woman is first and foremost a daughter/ a mother/a wife." Shoshana Felman, "Women and Madness: The Critical Phallacy," *Diacritics* 5 (1975), p. 2.

8. Toni Morrison, *The Bluest Eye* (New York: Pocket Books, 1979), p. 73. I will include all further page citations from Morrison's novel within the body of my text.

9. An observation from Shoshana Felman about Balzac's short story "Adieu" condenses many of the associations described. Felman notes: "the dichotomy Reason/Madness, as well as Speech/Silence, exactly coincides in this text with the dichotomy Men/Women. Women as such are associated both with madness and with silence, whereas men appear not only as the possessors, but also as the dispensers, of reason, which they can at will mete out to—or take away from—others . . . . Masculine reason thus constitutes a scheme to capture and master, indeed, metaphorically RAPE the woman" (p. 7).

10. Penelope Proddow, trans., *Demeter and Persephone, Homeric Hymn Number Two* (Garden City, N. Y.: Doubleday, 1972), n.p.

11. Ibid., my italics.

12. Ibid., n.p.

13. Sir James George Frazer, *The Golden Bough* (New York: Macmillan and Company, 1950), p. 456.

14. According to Frazer, in the original Homeric myth Persephone, drawn by the sight of narcissuses, moves beyond the reach of help. The choice of this particular plant as lure is of interest not only because of the Narcissus myth, but also because of recent psychoanalytic readings of this myth. These readings stress the importance of a child's progression through a stage of narcissistic self-love and suggest that this progression can occur only with the help of a mother-figure who assures the child of external love.

15. Frazer, p. 456.

16. Phyllis Chesler, *Women and Madness* (New York: Avon Books, 1973), p. xiv.

17. Ibid., p. xv.

18. See, for example, D. W. Winnicott, "Mirror-role of Mother and Family in Child Development," in *The Predicament of the Family*, ed. Peter Lomas (New York: International University Press, 1967), pp. 26–33; Heinz Lichtenstein, "The Role of Narcissism in the Emergence and Maintenance of a Primary Identity," *International Journal of Psychoanlysis* 45 (1964), pp. 49–56.

19. Why specify "Garden Avenue"? Perhaps Morrison wants to suggest that Pecola's experience is the twentieth-century urban counterpart to Persephone's experience in an actual garden?

20. "If she looked different, beautiful, maybe Cholly would be different,

and Mrs. Breedlove too. Maybe they'd say, 'Why look at pretty-eyed Pecola. We mustn't do bad things in front of these pretty eyes' '' (p. 40).

21. Compare, for example, Cholly's response (pp. 127–28) to that of Soap-head (p. 137).

22. Lévi-Strauss, *The Raw and the Cooked* (New York: Harpers, 1969), p.5.

11

Recitation to the Griot: Storytelling and Learning in Toni Morrison's Song of Solomon

JOSEPH T. SKERRETT, JR.

Pilate

> Being you, you cut your poetry from wood.
> The boiling of an egg is heavy art.
> You come upon it as an artist should,
> With rich-eyed passion, and with straining heart.
> (From "The Egg Boiler"
> by Gwendolyn Brooks)

Literary success brings popular admiration and critical attention, and Toni Morrison's work has been singled out for a variety of creative characteristics—narrative experimentation in the great Faulknerian modernist tradition, the successful absorption of the lessons of Latin American "magical realism," the masterful presentation of black women of all ages and conditions as figures of capable imagination. The critical cohort has dealt with those elements in some detail.[1]

But Morrison is a complex writer and part of her complexity is that

---

An earlier version of this paper was presented in the Folklore Section of the South Atlantic Modern Language Association's annual convention on November 6, 1981, in Louisville, Kentucky.

while she is contemporary, literary, and experimental, she is at the same time solidly grounded in the culture of the black American community. If Morrison's protagonists are always the "single, separate persons" of American individualism, then the community from which they have become isolated and alienated is always the community of shared beliefs, practices, stories, and histories that is the folk heritage of Afro–Americans. Toni Morrison is an inheritor as well as an innovator. Her predecessors—especially Zora Neale Hurston and Ralph Ellison—actively sought to bring the rich resources of the folk heritage under the transforming hands of the novelist. The lessons of these masters have not been lost on Morrison.

This is not to suggest that she merely "picks up where they left off." Rather, I think, inspired by their example, Morrison has looked very carefully at the way folk processes inform Afro-American life, and she produces highly concentrated images of that relationship that advance her complex vision of its meaning. Like Hurston and Ellison, she lives in this culture comfortably and finds in it all the resources needed for a full and satisfying moral universe. Nonetheless, what she sees when she looks at the behavior of black folk is different from what Hurston and Ellison see, and so her images—her inclusions and exclusions, her emphases and contrasts—are significantly different.

Like Hurston's and Ellison's, Morrison's fiction relies heavily on images of folk processes of communication.[2] In *Song of Solomon* in particular, fictional replications of these folk processes dominate the narrative. Milkman's search for the meaning of his life is carried out through a set of interactions that increase in intensity—a verbal battle, a physical challenge, a hunt, a love affair—among others. But what hurls Milkman into this series of experiences is a story, his father's story of lost treasure. Seeking material value, Milkman discovers history—his place in the story of his ancestors—and that discovery gives him self-understanding.[3]

Storytelling is the primary folk process in Toni Morrison's fictional world, and *Song of Solomon* contains many stories. Surrounding the central narrative of Milkman's growth to effective manhood are the stories that fill out the context that defines that manhood: the story of the black community and its place in the city; the story of his parents' marriage; the story of his friend Guitar's family; the story of the Seven Days; and, of course, the story of his ancestor Solomon. The novel also contains a variety of storytellers—or perhaps I should call them informants, for in the folkloric sense, they aren't all storytellers.

Like all of us, Milkman is born into a world brimming with mystery and hidden significance. On the day before his birth Robert Smith, the local insurance agent, tried to launch into flight from the roof of Mercy Hospital. Milkman will not come to understand the meaning of this act for over thirty years. But not because he hasn't heard the story. Robert Smith's story never means anything to Milkman until Guitar tells him the story of the Seven Days, and it does not become significant to him until he can relate Mr. Smith's effort to fly to that of his ancestor Solomon—and ultimately to his own.

Milkman's ignorance is in part a result of his resistance to the significance of the stories he is told. He lacks a connecting imagination. He believes, as he tells Guitar, "Unless it happens to you, you can't understand it" (p. 85). But it is in part a result of how he is taught.

Milkman's parents, Macon and Ruth, are not effective informants for Milkman. Their narration of their own parts of the mystery of his heritage is partial, egocentric, defensive. Macon, for example, tells twenty-two-year-old Milkman his version of the marriage only after Milkman has struck him down for slapping Ruth. He claims that nothing he is about to tell his son is "by way of apology or excuse. It's just information" (p. 70). But this is misleading—Macon wants Milkman to feel that his attitude toward Ruth is justified by her "incestuous" relationship with her father. Milkman's response to these contradictory messages is, of course, confusion. Wondering why his father has told him this story, Milkman's confusion turns to anger:

> If he wanted me to lay off, he thought, Why didn't he just say that? Just come to me like a man and say, Cool it. You cool it and I'll cool it. We'll both cool it. And I'd say, Okay, you got it. But no. He comes to me with some way-out tale about how come and why. (p. 76)

Similarly, when Milkman confronts his mother at the cemetery, she also tells her story as an act of self-justification. Her version is pathetic, not vengeful, but equally melodramatic: "she began in the middle of a sentence as though she had been thinking it all through since she and her son left the entrance to Fairfield Cemetery" (p. 123). The effect of hearing Ruth's story is to leave Milkman incredulous.

Milkman's parents cannot provide him with the key to understanding and identity. To each of them, he is an extension of self, not really an independent person at all. His father, Macon, a coldly rational and conventional bourgeois, thinks that Milkman's access to his "information," his rational, cause-and-effect "tale of how come and why" will clarify reality for Milkman. But Milkman wonders what use this story can be for him. He sees no place for himself in this history. Similarly, Ruth, an emotionally distorted and indirect person, tells her side of the family story, ending with a rhetorical question that only serves to chill Milkman's imagination, for answering the question "What harm did I do you on my knees?" is either to exonerate Ruth and believe his father a murderer or to condemn Ruth and believe his father's vision of her incestuous love for her father.

It is only Pilate for whom storytelling is *not* self-dramatization, self-justification, or ego-action. Pilate is Morrison's most complex and concentrated image of an Afro-American in touch with the spiritual resources of Afro-American folk traditions. She is a conjuror, having supplied Ruth with "some greenish-gray greasy-looking stuff" (p. 125) to put into Macon's food to revive his sexual interest in her. She is a voodoo priestess who puts an end to Macon's efforts to abort the resulting pregnancy by placing "a small doll on Macon's chair in his office. A male doll with a small painted chicken bone between its legs and a round red circle painted on its belly" (p. 132). A celibate and a teetotaler, she supplies the community with homemade intoxicants. And Pilate embodies the image of the black blueswoman, for her song is not the spiritual of an old woman, but the sad, ever-relevant blues of the lost man, flown away, departed, leaving the beloved behind in suffering and pain. Most importantly, I think, Pilate is a teller of tales. If the communicative act of storytelling is central to the action of *Song of Solomon,* then the form, content, and context of Pilate's storytelling is a key element.

Pilate's interactions with Milkman—and with others—are informed by processes of narration that have little to do with the patterns of self-protection and self-justification we have seen in Macon and Ruth. When Milkman and Guitar visit her in the winehouse, she immediately strikes toward them the pose that is central to her self-concept—that of teacher, preceptor, exemplar. Macon tells his son, " 'Pilate can't teach you a thing you can use in this world' " (p. 55), but he is absolutely wrong. Pilate begins by teaching the boys how to *talk* properly:

> Milkman took a breath, held it, and said, "Hi." Pilate laughed. "You all must be the dumbest unhung Negroes on earth. What they telling you in them schools? You say 'Hi' to pigs and sheep when you want 'em to move. When you tell a human being 'Hi,' he ought to get up and knock you down." (p. 37)

She then proceeds to teach Milkman and Guitar her formula for the perfect soft-boiled egg. When she has their attention—"they sat in a pleasant semi-stupor, listening to her go on and on" (p. 40)—Pilate begins her story. Unlike Macon's story, it is not a defense of how she has lived. Rather, it begins as a defense of Macon, without whose brotherly love and protection she would have died in the Pennsylvania woods after their father was murdered. Her story is a complex structure, punctuated by questions from Guitar, moving from personal familial history, including the appearance of the ghost of Pilate's and Macon's father, to later experience back to the ghost until Milkman and Guitar are entranced:

> The boys watched, afraid to say anything lest they ruin the next part of her story, and afraid to remain silent lest she not go on with its telling. (p. 43)

But the storytelling session is ended. Pilate's formulaic closure is refrain/repetition and a dying fall:

> We just stood there looking at the stump [where the ghost of their father had been sitting]. "Shaking like leaves . . . .Shaking like leaves," she murmured, "just like leaves." (p.43)

Pilate's performance of her life story is not intended to amuse Milkman and Guitar, but to educate them. She gives them "a perfect egg"—the symbol of the beginnings of things. More than merely giving the boys an egg, she teaches them how to make eggs. Her lesson is both practical and spiritual; her method of timing the perfect softboiled egg is to go off and "do one small obligation" either to self or others, "like answering the door or emptying the bucket and bringing it in off the front porch" or even going to the toilet. Her story continues these lessons, showing Macon's daunting father as a frightened child, as incapable of doing something they now know how to do—"he couldn't cook worth poot" (p. 39)—and demonstrating the continuing relationship between the living and the dead. Though it will be nearly twenty years before Milkman comes to understand Pilate and her values, in her storytelling she is teaching him how to be a single, separate Afro-American person—independent and idiosyncratic—while also connected to a family, a community, and a culture.

Pilate takes a similar teaching attitude in her dealings with others. When Ruth hears that Hagar, Pilate's granddaughter, is trying to kill Milkman for breaking off their affair, she goes to Pilate's house to confront her. She tells Hagar that she will kill her if she hurts her son. Hagar tries to explain her love by saying

> "He is my home in this world."
> "And I am his," said Ruth.

"And he wouldn't give a pile of swan shit for either one of you."
They turned and saw Pilate leaning on the window sill.

Pilate attempts to give both Ruth and Hagar a lesson:

"Two-growned-up women talkin 'bout a man like he was a house or
needed one. He ain't a house, he's a man, and whatever he need, don't
none of you got it."(p. 138)

Hagar's near-madness means that the lesson is almost useless for her.
It only exacerbates her confusion and frustration. Pilate turns to Ruth
with a lesson that Ruth recognizes as, in part, ritualized and formulaic:

After the tension, the anger, followed by the violence of Pilate's words
to her granddaughter, this quiet social-tea tone disarmed her, threw
her too soon and too suddenly back into the mannered dignity that was
habitual for her. (p. 139)

As Pilate prepares her lesson by offering Ruth a ripe peach, Ruth
remembers her last visit to the winehouse, to ask Pilate's help in
preventing Macon from aborting her pregnancy.

"The last time I was here you offered me a peach. My visit was about
my son then, too." Pilate nodded her head and with her right thumbnail
slit the peach open. (p. 139)

Pilate's lesson for Ruth is that Milkman can't be killed by Hagar, not
because she won't continue to try, but because Milkman doesn't want
to die:

"He come into the world trying to keep from getting killed. Layin'
in your stomach, his own papa was tryin to do it. . . . . When he was
at his most helpless, he made it. Ain't nothing going to kill him but his
own ignorance, and won't no woman ever kill him. What's likelier is
that it'll be a woman save his life." (p. 140)

Pilate's argument for Milkman's safety in the world is a spiritual
notion, for, as Ruth now discovers, Pilate believes that people themselves decide upon death.

"Some folks want to live forever. Some don't. I believe they decide
on it anyway. People die when they want to and if they want to. Don't
nobody have to die if they don't want to." (p. 141)

Pilate then tells Ruth the story of her life, making it "deliberately long to keep Ruth's mind off Hagar" (p. 152). Here, as in the scene with Milkman and Guitar, Pilate's storytelling is an art of love and nurture, closely associated with food—an egg, a peach—and structured to meet the needs of others, not self. She means her stories—and her life— to benefit those around her, the people she loves. Some—like Hagar— are beyond her help; Hagar is the captive, in her imagination, of an entirely different set of values from those supported by Pilate's independence and idiosyncrasy. She has never learned to accept herself as a single, separate person. She feels incomplete without Milkman, "her home in this world"; and her death is the result of her interpretation of his rejection as her fault or responsibility. Pilate fails to reach Hagar with the very message that she announces at her funeral—that she was loved.

As a figure of a woman who has gained social and moral experience in the world which her community finds it difficult to absorb, Pilate's prototype or predecessor is Janie in Hurston's *Their Eyes Were Watching God*. Janie's telling of her life story to her friend Pheoby changes Pheoby's life. But Pilate is a larger figure than Janie. She is more than a woman who has found her voice and a satisfactory experience in tragic love. She has been an individual lover, but that is not seen as the great experience of her life. Nor is her motherhood or grandmotherhood. Like Mary Rambo in Ellison's *Invisible Man*, Pilate is a figure of motherly nurture in the folk tradition. But the range of aspects of the culture of which she is master suggests that Morrison most certainly does not mean to limit her to supporting roles.

On the contrary.

More like Janie than any other predecessor, Pilate represents the rich, complex, and often problematic aspects of culture which every individual must struggle to make serve his or her human needs. People fear Pilate, as they fear Janie, because her personal power goes beyond the conventions of her gender. Her navel-less belly is the symbol of her alienation, an alienation which is the ultimate cause of her radical individuality:

> Men frowned, women whispered and shoved their children behind
> them . . . when she realized what her situation in the world was and
> would probably always be she threw away every assumption she had
> learned and began at zero. (p.149)

Pilate functions as a priestess or *shaman*; she is a figure of power and mystery "kept . . . just barely within the boundaries of the elaborately socialized world of black people" by her love for other troubled people (p. 150). More than Janie in her unconventional man's overalls, Pilate is the frightening source of uncomfortable questions and liberating truths. Pilate has answered for herself her namesake's question, what is truth?; and she knows how she wants to live, what is valuable and necessary to stay alive. Having acquired "a deep concern for and about human relationships," Pilate becomes a kind of oracular figure, a spiritual teacher whose lessons are deeply important but not always accessible.

Indeed, Pilate's most necessary predecessor is Peter Wheatstraw, the junkman with the cart full of blueprints who greets the narrator of Ralph Ellison's *Invisible Man* early one morning in the street with a blues and a riddle. When Ellison's nameless narrator doesn't respond to his formulaic greeting "Is you got the dog?" with a proper formulaic response, the enigmatic bluesman accuses him of denying his heritage. Before their conversation is ended, he reminds the narrator of the cultural resources in his southern folkloric heritage that he will need to survive in the northern city:

> "You digging me, daddy?" he laughed. "Haw, but look me up sometimes, I'm a piano player and a rounder, a whiskey drinker and a pavement pounder. I'll teach you some good bad habits. You'll need 'em. Good luck," he said.[4]

Like Ellison's folk figure, Pilate is isolated but loving, reaching out to those in need of her knowledge. But she also requires her students to come up to the lesson, to enter into the act of communication. Pilate presents Milkman with a blues and a riddle. The song she is constantly singing—sang to Robert Smith as he prepared to fly off the roof of Mercy Hospital, sang with Reba and Hagar as her brother Macon watched through the window of the winehouse, sang to Milkman and Guitar during their secret visit—is her most important storytelling.

The song itself is a verse and chorus with a classic blues feeling,

> "O Sugarman don't leave me here
> Cotton balls to choke me
> O Sugarman don't leave me here
> Buckra's arms to yoke me
> Sugarman done fly away
> Sugarman done gone
> Sugarman cut across the sky
> Sugarman gone home." (p. 49)

Pilate sings this song in emotionally charged circumstances. When she sings it outside Mercy Hospital before Mr. Smith's attempt at flight, it serves to channel the anxiety of the waiting crowd, who "listened as though it were the helpful and defining music in a silent movie" (p. 6). But Pilate seems to be singing it to Mr. Smith, with irony, sadness, and support.

The context in which the song is sung during Milkman's and Guitar's visit is as Pilate's and Reba's response to their realization that Hagar needs something they can't give her. The act of singing is an act of reunification of the family: "Pilate began to hum as she returned to plucking the berries. After a moment Reba joined her and they hummed together in perfect harmony . . . . When the two women got to the chorus, Hagar raised her head and sang too" (p. 49). It thus functions as a blues, allowing Pilate, Reba, and Hagar to finger the jagged edge of their unhappiness as a way of mastering it.

But as Milkman discovers when he gets to Shalimar, Virginia, Pilate's song is also a kind of riddle. As he pieces together the clues from various informants, he realizes that Pilate's song is a variant of the chorus of a local children's game, and that the game tells the story of his great-grandfather who "flew off" and left an orphaned son Jake, who was Macon's and Pilate's father.

Milkman's involvement in solving the riddle requires him to abandon the supports of his bourgeois, urban life and reenter the folk world:

> Milkman took out his wallet and pulled from it his airplane ticket stub, but he had no pencil to write with, and his pen was in his suit. He would just have to listen and memorize it. He closed his eyes and concentrated while the children, inexhaustible in their willingness to repeat a rhythmic, rhyming act in game, performed the round over and over again. And Milkman memorized all of what they sang. (p. 306)

Most importantly, Milkman's learning who he is by assembling and connecting these bits of folk narrative makes him a whole and responsible man. Even before he decodes the children's game, Milkman, stripped of his city trappings and no longer in search of material treasure, is transformed into a better man. He offers to Sweet the loving human service which his sister Lena had accused him of being incapable of rendering. Their affair is a matter of mutual respect and shared service:

> She put witch hazel on his swollen neck. He made up the bed. She gave him gumbo to eat. He washed the dishes. She washed his clothes and hung them out to dry. He scoured her tub. (p. 289)

After he has decoded the game-song, his understanding embraces his own inadequacy. "From the beginning, his mother and Pilate had fought for his life, and he had never so much as made either of them a cup of tea" (p. 335).

He takes Pilate back to Virginia to bury her father's bones. She is shot by Guitar, now Milkman's deadly enemy. Dying, she asks for a song, and Milkman gives her back her own:

> "Sugargirl don't leave me here
> Cotton balls to choke me
> Sugargirl don't leave me here
> Buckra's arms to yoke me." (p. 340)

Mature at last, Milkman takes possession of his heritage, adding Pilate to its ever-changing history, and is possessed by it as well: "he could not stop the worn old words from coming, louder and louder as though sheer volume would wake her" (p. 340). Here, in what may prove to be his last moments of life, Milkman has become an improvising bluesman, denying the finality of death through the continuity of art. His song is a recitation to the *griot*, a demonstration of the efficacy of her lessons.

Pilate's teaching and example bring Milkman from confusion and alienation to community and creativity. His singing to her is the unselfish act of love he had never been able to extend before. And Milkman's improvisatory extension of the narrative behind Pilate's old blues chorus acknowledges his final understanding of what it means to be able to fly.

Notes

1. *Song of Solomon* has been examined closely twice by Marilyn Judith Atlas in "The Darker Side of *Song of Solomon*," *SSMLN* 10:2 (1980), pp. 1–13 and "A Woman Both Shiny and Brown: Feminine Strength in *Song of Solomon*," *SSMLN* 9:3 (1979), pp. 8–12. Susan L. Blake, in "Folklore and Community in *Song of Solomon*," *MELUS* 7:3 (Fall 1980), pp. 77–82, comments on the paradoxes that derive textually from Morrison's choice of a particular variant of the flying African's folktale. A. Leslie Harris, in "Myth as Structure in Toni Morrison's *Song of Solomon*," *MELUS* 7:3 (Fall 1980), pp. 69–76, relates the narrative pattern to European mythic structures. Wilfrid D. Samuels, in "Liminality and the Search for Self in Toni Morrison's *Song of Solomon*," *Minority*

Voices 5:1 and 2 (Spring and Fall 1981), pp. 59–68, explores Milkman's quest from an anthropological viewpoint.

2. I have tried to heed the warnings of the folklorists on the dangers inherent in attempting to relate a literary text to an existential performance. See Daniel Ben-Amos, "Toward a Definition of Folklore in Context," *Journal of American Folklore* 84 (1971), p. 9; Alan Dundes, "Texture, Text, and Context" in his *Interpreting Folklore* (Bloomington, Ind.: Indiana University Press, 1980), and Robert Hemenway, "Are You a Flying Lark or a Setting Dove?" in *Afro-American Literature: The Reconstruction of Instruction*, ed. Dexter Fisher and Robert B. Stepto (New York: MLA, 1979), pp. 122–52.

3. All page references to *Song of Solomon* are to the Signet edition (New York, 1978) and will be indicated in the text.

4. Ralph Ellison, *Invisible Man* (New York: Random House, 1952), p. 134.

12

The Wise Witches:
Black Women Mentors
in the Fiction of
Octavia E. Butler

THELMA J. SHINN

Being born black and female in contemporary urban America has taught Octavia Butler much about the uses—and abuses—of power. "To comprehend a nectar/Requires sorest need," Emily Dickinson has written, and Butler's understanding of social power certainly fits that definition. On the other hand, her recognition of personal power—survival power—comes from more direct experience. "The Black women I write about aren't struggling to make ends meet," Butler explains, "but they are the descendants of generations of those who did. Mothers are likely to teach their daughters about survival as they have been taught, and daughters are likely to learn, even subconsciously."[1] Not only have her black women learned "about survival," but also they transform that personal power into social power by teaching others.

Exploring what "mothers are likely to teach their daughters" brings Butler's fiction inevitably into comparison with the novels of other women. Annis Pratt has defined archetypal patterns, common to three centuries of women's fiction, which preserve female knowledge within the enclosure of patriarchal society as follows:

It gradually became clear that women's fiction could be read as a mu-
tually illuminative or interrelated field of texts reflecting a preliterary
repository of feminine archetypes, including three particularly important archetypal systems—the Demeter/Kore and Ishtar/Tammuz rebirth
myths, Arthurian grail narratives, and the Craft of the Wise, or
witchcraft.[2]

Each of these patterns can be found in Butler's fiction, providing a
framework for the transfer of knowledge, although one pattern governs each of the novels. Her first work, *Patternmaster* (1976), carefully
follows the grail quest, leading the quester Teray to Forsyth, California, where he must accept the role of Patternmaster from his dying
father, Rayal. "The Quest," Pratt quotes Jean Markale, "is an attempt
to re-establish a disciplined sovereignty, usurped by the masculine
violence of the despoiling knight, while the kingdom rots and the
king, the head of the family . . . is impotent." The quester must be
compassionate, even "androgynous," and must "restore a kingdom
punished for violating women." The grail itself, "as container of beneficence, feeder of the tribe, and locus of rebirth," symbolizes feminine power: "As 'mother pot,' 'magic cauldron' (with which Persephone can regenerate the dead heroes and heal the sick), golden bowl
of healing, etc., this archetype expresses women's generative and
regenerative powers."[3] In *Patternmaster*, Teray's older brother Coransee is the "despoiling Knight," violating Teray's prospective wife
Iray, demanding his Housemaster's right to sexual favors from the
independent healer Amber who accompanies Teray on his journey
and allowing the mistreatment of those under his care, as Teray discovers when the beaten and abused Suliana comes to him for help.
Rayal, suffering from Clayark's disease (a "gift" from the first returning starship which decimated the population of Earth and left
mutants in its wake), is impotent to stop the stronger Coransee, who
is also his son by his lead wife and sister Jansee. Teray is recognizable
as the appropriate successor by his "androgynous" qualities: his protection of Suliana and others like her; his willingness to recognize the
humanity in the feared and hated mutants the Clayarks; his unwill-
ingness to kill except for survival. Yet Teray is young, lacking the
necessary knowledge and skills to succeed in his quest. For these he
must turn to the first of Butler's black women mentors, Amber. Amber's knowledge has literally been transferred to her and her healing
skill has been brought through transition to a useful tool by her friend
and lesbian lover, the Housemaster Kai, suggesting an archetypal
Demeter/Kore pattern of "uniting the feminine generations."[4] She

seems to symbolize the grail in herself, literally regenerating Teray's body after his final fight with Coransee.

Butler's next two novels, *Mind of My Mind* (1977) and *Survivor* (1978), follow the pattern of rebirth and transformation myths. *Mind of My Mind* can be seen as what Pratt calls a "novel of development," and young Mary struggles against much of the poverty and violence common to "the multiple alienation of sex, class, and race" which "intensifies physical and psychological suffering for the young Black woman."[5] She grows up in a California ghetto with a prostitute mother and finds it necessary at times to protect herself from unwanted men by wielding a cast-iron skillet. But Mary is exceptional; her "transition" from adolescence to selfhood leaves her an active telepath, controlling minds of others like her through a Pattern. In giving birth to the Pattern, Mary gives birth to a new society in which she is the most powerful figure and gives rebirth to thousands of "latent" telepaths who have been suffering from their uncontrollable reception of human pain from everyone around them. However reluctantly, Mary has learned survival from her female heritage—from her mother Rina and her ancestress Emma (whose name means grandmother)—and she is ready to become another black woman mentor, leading "her people" to constructive utilizations of their individual skills.

Although Frances Smith Foster argues that Mary, despite her name, cannot fit the stereotype of the Black Madonna as defined in Daryl Dance's essay "Black Eve or Madonna: A Study of the Antithetical Views of the Mother in Black American Literature," she must admit later that Mary combines the traits "not only of Eve and Madonna, but also of God and Satan" into "a new kind of female character in both science fiction and Afro-American literature."[6] That new character has been defined by Phyllis J. Day as follows:

> The new women of science fiction, then, whether witch or Earthmother, are real people, strong people, and they are integral to and often protectresses of Earth and ecology. Moreover, they are part of an organic whole, a return to our premechanistic past, and they represent a force against man in his assumption of the right to dominate either women or Earth/Nature.[7]

Much of this applies to Mary, daughter of the godlike Doro and descendant of Emma (whose African name Anyanwu means "sun," as does Doro), combining the male and female principles represented by these two and ending the domination of Doro by absorbing his life into her Pattern, allowing herself to offer rebirth to those dependent on her: "Karl lived. The family lived . . . . Now we were free to grow again—we, his children."[8] In her new role, Mary is the archetypal female defined by Pratt: "the mothers and daughters in women's fiction seem also to be enacting the various aspects of the triple goddess, who was virgin, maternal figure, and old woman at one and the same time. The third figure of the triad, who has often been gynophobically perceived as 'devouring mother' or 'crone,' represents the wise older mother's knowledge of the best moment to fledge or let go of her children, a moment that, if precipitous or delayed, can lead the maternal element to become destructive."[9] So it is with Mary. Her third aspect becomes apparent when she draws strength from her people through the Pattern. If she lets go too late, she kills them. But unlike Doro, whose power depended upon killing his victims, Mary discovers that she doesn't have to destroy: "I'm not the vampire he is. I give in return for my taking" (p. 210). Doro finally recognizes that Mary is whole, "a complete version of him":

> She was a symbiont, a being living in partnership with her people. She gave them unity, they fed her, and both thrived. She was not a parasite, though he had encouraged her to think of herself as one. And though she had great power, she was not naturally, instinctively, a killer. He was. (p. 217)

As such, Mary fits Day's description of witch, as do the other "wise witches" of Butler's fiction:

> These capable women with power are most often called witches and considered deviant from their society. They are usually feared and hated by other tamed women, as well as by men. They are healers, wise women, religious leaders, or focal points for natural or preternatural powers. Their power is usually antimachine, though not always antitechnology—that is, they may use technologies but in a nondeterministic manner in which nature is enhanced rather than destroyed.[10]

In her role as Patternmaster, Mary will enhance what Doro has neglected by bringing the latent telepaths through transition, by providing unity for all Patternists, and by teaching individuals how to use their powers for the betterment of the community. Although Mary is hated at first, Butler reminds us that "people who must violate their long-held beliefs are rarely pleasant. I don't write about heroes; I write about people who survive and sometimes prevail."[11] Mary must kill Doro, but she does survive and she does prevail—teaching others to make the most of what they have and giving rebirth to the rejects of

the society into which she was born. Through her, Butler can trans-
mute her Afro-American heritage into archetypal human heritage and
achieve her aim by bringing "together multi-racial groups of men and
women who must cope with one another's differences as well as with
new, not necessarily controllable, abilities within themselves."[12]

Alanna's rebirth in *Survivor* (1978) is personal rather than communal, following the structure Pratt provides for woman's spiritual
quest into the self:

> Phase I: Splitting off from family, husbands, lovers
> Phase II: The green-world guide or token
> Phase III: The green-world lover
> Phase IV: Confrontation with parental figures
> Phase V: The plunge into the unconscious[13]

Butler's only novel set on another planet, *Survivor* offers alternatives
to today's prejudices for those who do not fit into the Pattern she has
created, to the nontelepathic "mutes." Unfortunately, the mutes have
carried their prejudices with them. As Missionaries of Humanity, they
have fought the Clayark threat by deifying the human image. Consequently, they are blind to humanity in any other guise—to the
humanity of the native Kohn, furlike creatures of various hues who
live in tune with their environment. Except for a few, their prejudice
extends as well to Alanna, an Afro-Asian who had survived as a "wild
human" after her parents had died protecting her from a Clayark
attack. Alanna had been adopted by the leader of the colony, Jules
Verrick, and his wife, Neila, despite the prejudices that would allow
these religious people to kill wild humans as if they were animals and
would further lead them to suggest that Alanna at least be put with
a black family. Clearly, hers is at best an uneasy relationship with her
society, making her a perfect candidate for a quest or rebirth journey
which, Pratt asserts, can "create transformed, androgynous, and
powerful human personalities out of socially devalued beings."[14]

Phase I is accomplished for Alanna when she is kidnapped with
some other Missionaries and some of the Garkohn natives with whom
they peacefully coexisted. The kidnappers are the Tehkohn, a native
group bluer in color than the predominately green-furred Garkohn.
Phase II is realized by something taken from rather than given to
Alanna, as is the usual pattern. This "ordinary phenomenon that
suddenly takes on extraordinary portent"[15] is the meklah fruit, which
has become the staple diet of the Missionaries as it is for the Garkohn.
Meklah, however, is addictive; withdrawal from it is so difficult that
only Alanna, owing probably to her wild human brushes with star-

vation and her incredible will to survive, is alive when the five-day "cleansing period" ends.

Alanna has learned that not all is good in the green world—Nature can offer poison as well as life. She needs to discover Phase III, "an ideal, nonpatriarchal lover who sometimes appears as an initiatory guide and often aids at difficult points in the quest."[16] Her lover turns out to be the leader of the Tehkohn, their Hao Diut. Diut rules because he is the darkest blue; before him, the Hao Tahneh, a female, had ruled. However, though Diut can offer her knowledge of and participation in a society which lives in tune with its environment—constructing dwellings which "mimicked the mountains around it in its interior as well as its exterior,"[17] fighting without weapons, even recognizing the animal jehruk "as their wild relative and they took pride in its ferocity" (p. 110)—he must also learn from her the limits he must put on his power before they can have a relationship "where differences existed, but were ignored" (p. 114). "We're not children squabbling in the inner corridors," she tells him. "You need not prove your strength or your coloring to me. We can talk to each other. Or we can go away from each other!" (p. 114)

Drawing on her memories of survival on Earth, Alanna is able to fit into this alien society much better than she could with the Missionaries. The shared knowledge of the green world, of working with rather than against nature, is lost on the Missionaries, whose walled settlement mars the natural landscape and who see all Kohn as animals. But Alanna is "rescued" from her new home, and in the process the life she has created there—a daughter Tien—is destroyed. She is forced into Phase IV, and her confrontation with her foster parents is bittersweet. While Neila could accept the changes in her daughter, Jules cannot condone the blasphemy of mating with "animals." Alanna must come to terms with her parents by doing all she can to enable them to survive, but then she must be rejected by them.

This rejection initiates the final phase, the plunge into the unconscious where Alanna must face her own actions and define her self. "I'm a wild human," she tells her foster parents. "That's what I've always been."

> She glanced at Jules. "I haven't lost my self. Not to anyone." And again to Neila. "In time, I'll also be a Tehkohn judge. I want to be. And I'm Diut's wife and your daughter. If . . . you can still accept me as your daughter." (p. 170)

Alanna has completed the quest for self and chosen that self above any social identity that would limit or enclose her, transforming even

Diut through her personal integrity. Unfortunately, she is not able to share her survival skills with the Missionaries. While she is willing to teach, risking her life for them, they are not willing to learn. Their prejudices limit their humanity and their possibilities for survival.

Butler's next novel, *Kindred* (1979), is a departure from the science fiction mode which has enabled her to fantasize societies accepting of her strong and independent black women. If the feminine archetypes provided a framework for her own mythos, that mythopoeic vision was allowed room to expand by the possibilities inherent in the contemporary mythological form. Patricia Warrick has identified three ways in which science fiction offers this expansion. First,

> The radical element in all the myths is their setting in the future. They describe a future time that will be different from the present in at least one significant way. In contrast, traditional myths typically are set outside time; they reflect all that is conceived to be eternal and unchanging in the universe.

Second,

> It seems safe to assume that in previous myths both the teller and the listener believed the story to be true. In contrast, the participants in a science fiction myth are very conscious that the story is not true; however, they do believe that in the future it just might be true.

And third,

> These earlier myths tend to be very clear in their meanings and their concepts of good and evil . . . . But science fiction myths have a quality of ambiguity about them. They are much less certain of what man's relationship to the natural world around him and to the cosmos is. Good and evil can no longer be easily labeled.[18]

Besides the acceptance of change and ambiguity in a probable future, science fiction also provides Butler with the one aspect her heritage neither as a black nor as a woman seemed to provide—freedom. This concept, central to everything she has written, drew her to the literary form where, as she explains,

> I was free to imagine new ways of thinking about people and power, free to maneuver my characters into situations that don't exist. For example, where is there a society in which men and women are honestly considered equal? What would it be like to live in such a society? Where

do people not despise each other because of race or religion, class or ethnic origin?[19]

Patternist society fits this description, but such a change is not without ambiguous results. The timelessness of the feminine archetypes and the experiences of the black woman have penetrated even Butler's fantasies to show that human beings will find new categories of prejudice—assigning subhuman status to mutes and Clayarks—and new abuses for power unless it is limited. Her communal solutions remain dependent on the humanity of its individual members: the compassion of the Patternmaster, the determination of others to preserve their freedom even if they must kill or die to accomplish this, and the willingness of all members of the society to overcome prejudice and accept differences. Only Tehkohn society seems potentially utopian, although the power hierarchy and stress on fighting separate it from most utopias.

Borrowing the vehicle of time travel from her science fiction, Butler turns in *Kindred* to apply her new understanding of power to the Afro-American experience today and yesterday. Dana, her contemporary black woman, finds herself mentor and healer to her own white slaveholder ancestor Rufus when he pulls her back through time over and over again to save him. Certainly feminine archetypes again underlie Butler's fiction, as Dana "controls death and rebirth," not only that of Rufus but her own as his descendant. This rebirth myth most closely relates to Pratt's Ishtar/Tammuz pattern, as "the hero can be released from death only through feminine power."[20] That feminine power can also be used to destroy, and is so used when Rufus has concluded the rape through which Dana's ancestress is conceived and furthermore has ignored the limits set on his power. "I'm not property, Kevin," Dana had assured her contemporary white husband. "I'm not a horse or a sack of wheat. If I have to seem to be property, if I have to accept limits on my freedom for Rufus's sake, then he also has to accept limits—on his behavior toward me. He has to leave me enough control of my own life to make living look better to me than killing and dying."[21] So too had Alanna set limits on Diut in *Survivor*:

> "And I have your bow and your arrows." She looked at me for a long time, her face already bruised and swollen, her eyes narrowed, the knife steady in her hand. "Then use them to kill me," she said. "I will not be beaten again." (p. 113)

Diut accepts and both survive; Rufus tests his limits once too often. The first time, he hits Dana when she objects to his selling a field hand out of jealousy: "And it was a mistake. It was the breaking of an unspoken agreement between us—a very basic agreement—and he knew it" (p. 239). In retaliation, Dana cuts her wrists, and the threat to her life returns her to the present. The next betrayal, attempted rape, forces her to overcome her compassion finally: "I could accept him as my ancestor, my younger brother, my friend, but not as my master, and not as my lover. He had understood that once" (p. 260). At the cost of her left arm, she kills him.

Dana is not a victim, as Beverly Friend concludes when she compares *Kindred* with novels by Eisenstein and Millhiser. Butler recognizes some truth in Friend's other conclusion "that contemporary woman is not educated to survive, that she is as helpless, perhaps even more helpless, than her predecessors,"[22] at least inasmuch as Dana accepts "that educated didn't mean smart. He had a point. Nothing in my education or knowledge of the future had helped me to escape" (p.215). But Dana has learned to heed women's knowledge; as Kai had fed Amber all she knew in *Patternmaster*, Dana seeks out the cookhouse because

> sometimes old people and children lounged there, or house servants or even field hands stealing a few moments of leisure. I liked to listen to them talk sometimes and fight my way through their accents to find out more about how they survived lives of slavery. Without knowing it, they prepared me to survive. (p. 94)

And, although Dana suffers a share of what her ancestors had endured in slavery and loses her arm in saving her life, she never becomes an object; she maintains control of her life and acts out of a sense of responsibility even while she recognizes the irony of her position as Rufus's mentor:

> I was the worst possible guardian for him—a black to watch over him in a society that considered blacks subhuman, a woman to watch over him in a society that considered women perennial children. I would have all I could do to look after myself. But I would help him as best I could. And I would try to keep friendship with him, maybe plant a few ideas in his mind that would help both me and the people who would be his slaves in the years to come. (p. 68)

Dana may, as Friend submits, be as much a slave as the heroines of the other two novels, but she does have heritage on her side—black women have survived slavery before.

Kindred shows that Butler's wise witches, her compassionate teachers armed with knives and cast-iron skillets, have survived and will survive, whether or not they are accepted by their society. Her consciousness of "the adaptations women with power must make in a patriarchal society,"[23] however, adds an African archetype to her mythology in her most recent novel, *Wild Seed* (1980). In *Mind of My Mind*, where we first met Emma/Anyanwu, Doro had told Mary that "Emma was an Ibo woman"(p. 95); so it seems particularly fitting that Sir James G. Frazer has specifically attributed the belief in shape shifting to her kinspeople: "They think that man's spirit can quit his body for a time during life and take up its abode in an animal. This is called *ishi anu*, 'to turn animal.' "[24] Anyanwu, a wild seed growing free in nature—not, until the beginning of this novel, under the control of Doro—has learned through an inner quest how to change her body, aging and becoming young again, hunting as a leopard or swimming as a dolphin. Symbolizing the adaptions she had made for survival in a patriarchy headed by Doro, four-thousand-year-old patriarch of what would become the Patternists, Anyanwu's shape shifting is the prototype for Alanna's chameleon ability, which she draws on in *Survivor* to save the Missionaries: "But deception is the only real weapon we have. We face physical chameleons. To survive, we must be mental chameleons" (p. 118). Alanna accurately labels this awareness "survival philosophy."

Shape shifting is also the source of the healing power that Anyanwu will hand down to the Patternists, ultimately to Amber and Teray of *Patternmaster*. Anyanwu heals herself by turning inward and changing the shape of the injured or diseased part until it is again healthy. The archetypal witch most reflective of its designation by Pratt as "Craft of the Wise," Anyanwu is clearly the female principle of life itself. This Great Mother has already been living three hundred years when Doro tracks her down and coerces her into his selective breeding program by threatening to use her children if she refuses. Typical of the black women who will follow her, however, she stays not out of fear of Doro or acceptance of slavery but out of compassion. In time she comes to recognize the truth in what her husband and Doro's son Isaac tells her: "I'm afraid the time will come when he [Doro] won't feel anything. If it does . . . there's no end to the harm he could do. . . . You, though, you could live to see it—or live to prevent it. You could stay with him, keep him at least as human as he is now."[25] When Anyanwu comes to feel that Doro is past learning from her, past feeling, she is ready to let herself die rather than be used by him. As Dana has challenged Rufus, as Alanna has challenged Diut, Anyanwu challenges Doro with the one thing beyond his control—her own life. Doro can destroy her, but he cannot make her live if she chooses not to. It is only when he sincerely recognizes and admits his need for her and his feeling for her that she decides to stay with him.

As much as Anyanwu offers her daughters as the Great Mother, she is not limited as this figure usually is. A living woman (*Wild Seed* begins in 1690, which puts her birth around 1390), she still fits Aldous Huxley's definition of "the principle of life, of fecundity, of fertility, of kindness and nourishing compassion; but at the same time she is the principle of death and destruction."[26] She, however, prefers not to kill and feels great remorse when she finds it necessary to do so. Nor is she an irrational force. Even science fiction, usually more open to ambiguity and change, has stereotyped men and women, as Scott Sanders observes:

> In much of the genre, women and nature bear the same features: both are mysterious, irrational, instinctive; both are fertile and mindless; both inspire wonder and dread in the hero; both are objects of male conquest. . . . Men belong to the realm of mind; women and nature, to no-mind. Women are the bearers of life; men are life's interpreters and masters.[27]

Yet Anyanwu, not the male principle Doro,[28] is the source of "logic, reason, the analytical workings of the mind" in *Wild Seed*. She has achieved her shape-shifting knowledge by careful, systematic inner quests, where she has studied herself down to the atoms. She learns what nature can provide—what foods are beneficial, which are poisonous—by ingesting small quantities and watching her bodily reactions. She can "clone" an animal or fish only after she has eaten some of it and studied within her its genetic makeup. She is both the scientist and the laboratory. Even then, she must consciously decide to shift her shape, and the process is painstaking as each part of her is absorbed or transformed.

Doro, on the other hand, is as much a life and death source as Anyanwu. He can be compared to the Nuban myth recounted by Frazer of the taboo person:

> The divine person who epitomizes the corporate life of his group is a source of danger as well as blessing; he must not only be guarded, he must be guarded against. . . . Accordingly the isolation of the man-god is quite as necessary for the safety of others as for his own. His magical virtue is in the strictest sense contagious; his divinity is a fire which, under proper restraints, confers endless blessings, but, if rashly touched or allowed to break bounds, burns and destroys what it touches.[29]

Doro is described as "a small sun" and seeks people who are "good prey," who will satisfy his appetite when he devours their life and assumes their body. He can exercise some control over his appetite if he has fed recently; otherwise his action is instinctual, irrational. He occupies the nearest body. Even his seemingly scientific quest for the right people for his selective breeding program is determined by his appetite for them—latent telepaths and people with other potential mental talents are "good prey." In fact, he began his breeding program originally as one would raise cattle—for food. He still uses his settlements for this, and the followers who love and fear him have come to accept the human sacrifices his appetite demands. Doro provides a frightening version of patriarchy; only the matriarchal balance which Anyanwu, whom he calls Sun Woman, chooses to provide him keeps Doro human in any way, as Isaac had predicted. It is from these roots that Mary eventually evolves, encompassing the ambiguities of both principles in herself and thereby giving birth to a society in which men and women can be equal.

Butler's archetypal frameworks allow us to see how seemingly insurmountable differences can be recognized as artificial polarizations of human qualities. By combining Afro-American, female, and science fiction patterns, she can reveal the past, the present, and a probable future in which differences can be seen as challenging and enriching rather than threatening and denigrating and in which power can be seen as an interdependence between the leader and those accepting that leadership, each accepting those limits on freedom that still allow for survival of the self. Within the archetypes, embodying them, are wise witches, black women willing to share their survival skills out of compassion and a sense of responsibility with those of us who are still willing to learn.

Notes

1. Quoted by Veronica Mixon in "Futurist Woman: Octavia Butler," *Essence* 15 (April 1979), p. 13.

2. Annis Pratt with Barbara White, Andrea Loewenstein, and Mary Wyer, *Archetypal Patterns in Women's Fiction* (Bloomington: Indiana University Press, 1981), p. 170.

3. Pratt, p. 173–74.

4. Pratt, p. 170.

5. Pratt, p. 33.

6. Frances Smith Foster, "Octavia Butler's Black Female Future Fiction," *Extrapolation*, 23: 1 (Spring 1982), p. 37.

7. Phyllis J. Day, "Earthmother/Witchmother: Feminism and Ecology Renewed," *Extrapolation*, 23: 1 (Spring 1982), p. 14.

8. *Mind of My Mind* (New York: Avon, 1977), pp. 220–21. Subsequent references are to this edition and will appear as page numbers in the text.

9. Pratt, p. 172.

10. Day, p. 14.

11. Quoted by Mixon, p. 12.

12. Quoted by Curtis C. Smith (ed.), *Twentieth Century Science-Fiction Writers* (New York: St. Martin's Press, 1981), p. 93.

13. Pratt, pp. 139–41.

14. Pratt, p. 142.

15. Pratt, p. 139.

16. Pratt, p. 140.

17. *Survivor* (rpt. 1978; New York: New American Library, 1979), p. 53. Subsequent references are to this edition and will appear as page numbers in the text.

18. "Science Fiction Myths and their Ambiguity," in *Science Fiction: Contemporary Mythology*, ed. by Patricia Warrick, Martin H. Greenberg, and Joseph Olander (New York: Harper & Row, 1978), pp. 6–7.

19. Quoted by Mixon, p. 12.

20. Pratt, p. 172.

21. *Kindred* (Garden City: Doubleday & Co., Inc., 1979), p. 246.

22. Beverly Friend, "Time Travel as a Feminist Didactic in Works by Phyllis Eisenstein, Marlys Millhiser, and Octavia Butler," *Extrapolation* 23:1 (Spring 1982), p. 55.

23. Day, p. 14.

24. Frazer, *The New Golden Bough*, edited by Dr. Theodor H. Gaster (New York: Criterion Books, 1959), p. 601.

25. *Wild Seed* (rpt. 1980; New York: Pocket Books, 1981), p. 120. Subsequent references are to this edition and will appear as page numbers in the text.

26. Aldous Huxley, *The Human Situation*, ed. Piero Ferruci (New York: Harper & Row, 1977), p. 200.

27. Scott Sanders, "Woman as Nature in Science Fiction," in *Future Females: A Critical Anthology*, ed. by Marleen S. Barr (Bowling Green, O.: State University Popular Press, 1981), p. 42.

28. Sanders, p. 53.

29. Frazer, p. 165.

13

"What It Is I Think She's Doing Anyhow": A Reading of Toni Cade Bambara's The Salt Eaters

GLORIA T. HULL

Although everyone knows instinctively that Toni Cade Bambara's first novel, *The Salt Eaters*,[1] is a book that he or she must read, many people have difficulty with it. They get stuck on page ninety-seven or give up after muddling through the first sixty-five pages twice with little comprehension. Some cannot get past chapter one. Lost and bewildered, students decide that it is "over their heads" and wonder what made their teacher assign it in the first place.

There are compelling reasons for studying the novel. It is a daringly brilliant work that accomplishes even better for the 1980s what *Native Son* did for the 1940s, *Invisible Man* for the 1950s, or *Song of Solomon* for the 1970s: It fixes our present and challenges the way to the future. Reading it deeply should result in personal transformation; teaching

A slightly different version of this essay appeared in *Home Girls: A Black Feminist Anthology*, ed. Barbara Smith (New York: Kitchen Table: Women of Color Press, 1983), pp. 124–42.

it well can be a political act. However, Toni Cade Bambara has not made our job easy. *Salt* is long, intricately written, trickily structured, full of learning, heavy with wisdom—is, altogether, what critics mean by a "large" book.

At its literal-metaphoric center, Velma Henry and Minnie Ransom sit on round white stools in the middle of the Southwest Community Infirmary. "The good woman Ransom," "fabled healer of the district," is taxing her formidable powers with Velma, who has lost her balance and attempted suicide. The novel radiates outward in ever-widening circles—to the Master's Mind, the ring of twelve who hum and pray with Minnie; to the music room cluttered with staff, visitors, and assorted onlookers; to the city of Claybourne surrounding the Infirmary walls—a community which itself is composed of clusters (The Academy of the Seven Arts, the cafe with its two round tables of patrons, La Salle Street, the park); to the overarching sky above and the earth beneath steadily spinning on its axis. From the center, the threads web out, holding a place and weaving links between everything and everybody. At the same time, this center is a nexus which pulls the outside in—setting up the dialectic of connectedness which is both meaning and structure of the book (see diagram).

Of the huge cast, certain characters stand out. There is M'Dear Sophie Heywood, Velma's godmother, who caught her at birth and has protected and praised her ever since. Now, she is so incensed with Velma's selfish nihilism that she has imposed silence upon herself and exited the circle/room, thinking back on her godchild as well as her deceased mate, Daddy Dolphy; on her son and Velma's almost-husband, Smitty, who was turned into an invalid by the police in a violent anti-war demonstration; and on her own bitter memories of being brutally beaten in jail by her neighbor, Portland Edgers, who had been forced to do so by guns and clubs. There is Fred Holt, the bus driver, "brimming over with rage and pain and loss" (and sour chili). Married as a youth to Wanda, who deserted him for the Nation of Islam, he now has a white wife Margie, who gives him nothing but her back. His misery is completed by the death of his best friend, Porter, a well-read conversationalist who was the only bright spot in Fred's days. Other important characters are Velma's husband Obie, whose "image of himself [is] coming apart"; Dr. Meadows, a conscientious young M.D. who is pulling together his "city" versus "country," his white westernized and ancient black selves; and a traveling troupe of Third World political performers called the Seven Sisters.

The rich cross section of variegated folks also includes less prominent characters such as Butch and Nadeen, two teenage parents-to-

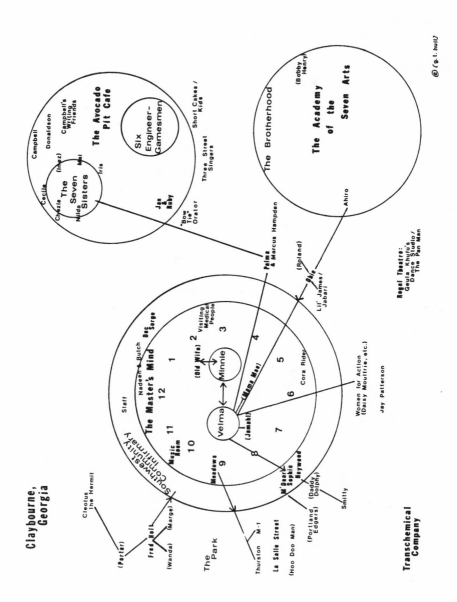

be; Jan and Ruby, activist women sharing a salad and organizing strategy; Donaldson, the inept FBI-CIA informant; and the list goes on. Some of these people appear onstage *in propria persona*; others are offstage fragments of memory. Some are quietly dead; others are roaming spirits. In many ways, these distinctions are false and immaterial, for everyone we meet takes up essential space, and there is no meaningful difference between their various states of corporeality/being/presence (a fact which confuses readers trying to keep the characters "straight"). Old Wife, Minnie's "Spirit Guide," is as "real" as Cora Rider grumbling in the music room. When Obie muses about his younger brother Roland, incarcerated in Rikers Island prison for raping a forty-six-year-old black woman, mother of four, Roland's voice and the woman's mopping up her own blood are as clear as Palma and Marcus hugging in the rain. And, like Velma, all of the major figures who need it undergo a healing change.

The healing that constitutes the central plot is a second consideration which dislocates some readers. Without addressing the issue of belief in healing or giving anyone else a chance to do so, Bambara posits its authenticity and describes it with the same faithful nonchalance that she accords to every other human activity. She gives us a picture of Minnie Ransom before her gift unfolded—"jumpy," "down on her knees eating dirt," "racing off to the woods," being called "batty, fixed, possessed, crossed, in deep trouble" (p. 51). And she tries to find a way to explain what Minnie does:

> She simply placed her left hand on the patient's spine and her right on the navel, then clearing the channels, putting herself aside, she became available to a healing force no one had yet, to her satisfaction, captured in a name . . . .On the stool or on the chair with this patient or that, Minnie could dance their dance and match their beat and echo their pitch and know their frequency as if her own . . . .Calcium or lymph or blood uncharged, congealed and blocked the flow, stopped the dance, notes running into each other in a pileup, the body out of tune, the melody jumped the track, discordant and strident. And she would lean her ear to the chest or place her hand at the base of the spine till her foot tapped and their heads bobbed, till it was melodious once more (p. 47–48).

But this is all music and metaphor, not intended to convince anyone of anything, but to say what can be said, leave us with it, and get on with the work. It is also interesting that Bambara shows "ordinary" people "tuning in" to what is actually happening. When Minnie—out-of-body—follows Old Wife to their "chapel," even Dr. Meadows, a skeptic, intuits that her "essential self [had] gone off" maybe to "a

secret rendezvous in the hills" (p. 57). And, at a later point, scary
Nadeen "saw something drop away from Mrs. Henry's face" (p. 101),
watched her wrist scars heal, and compared the miracle she was witnessing to the spurious healings of revival tents and spooky nighttime
sessions in the woods—all the while saying to herself, "This was the
real thing" (p. 113).

Bambara's handling of this healing stems from the fact that she
believes in "the spiritual arts"—that is, all those avenues of knowing/
being which are opposed to the "rational," "Western," "scientific"
mode: telepathy and other psychic phenomena; astrology; dream
analysis; numerology; colorology; the Tarot; past life glances and rein-
carnation; the Ouija board; reading auras, palms, tea leaves, cards,
and energy maps; throwing cowrie shells; herbal and folk medicine;
voices, visions, and signs; witches, loa, swamphags; saints, dinns,
and devas; the "ancient wisdoms"; the power of prayer; "root
men . . . conjure women . . . obeah folks"; divination; demons; and
so on. This material is incorporated throughout the text—sometimes
casually, at other times quite pointedly. Participants at the healing
are "visibly intent on decoding the flickering touch of mind on mind"
(p. 13). Travelers on the bus experience a "moment of correspondence—phenomena, noumena—when the glimpse of the life script
is called dream, déjà vu, clairvoyance, intuition, hysteria, hunger, or
called nothing at all" (p. 89). M'Dear instructs Velma about dreams:
"The dream is one piece, the correct picturing of impressions another.
Then interpretation, then action" (p. 219). Astrological references
abound.

Bambara struggles with the problem of finding words and ways to
communicate these forms of knowledge for which we, as yet, have
no adequate vocabulary. Readers most versed in these spiritual arts
(and in this new age, that number is growing) understand the work
most deeply. The fact that The Master's Mind wears yellow and white
works on a generally symbolic level, but resonates on other frequen-
cies if one considers that yellow is the hue of intellect and a saint's
nimbus and that white is the harmonious blending of all colors. The
basic meaning of the number twelve will be easily grasped; but everyone will not know to reduce the year 1871 (when the Infirmary was
built) and the 107 years it has been standing to their root "8," which
signifies worldly involvement and regeneration. Then, there is Cleo-
tus Brown, "The Hermit." Porter is planning to study with him when
he is killed; Doc Serge directs Butch to him for answers to his im-
pertinent questions; he himself appears incognito/in disguise to Jan
(with Ruby), eerily reminding her of something she should/does know
but cannot quite remember. He is the arcane figure from the Tarot

(which Jan reads), who symbolizes the right, initiatory path to real knowledge and truth. These three slight examples suggest how the entire novel can be annotated in this manner. Integrally related here, too, are the recurring symbols of mud, blood, salt, circles, mirrors, sight, water (rain), fire, snakes, and serpents.

Devising a vocabulary and symbology for communicating spiritual matters is only one aspect of Bambara's general quest for an adequate language and structure. She says: "I'm just trying to tell the truth and I think in order to do that we will have to invent, in addition to new forms, new modes and new idioms."[2] The process is an arduous one, beginning with the word, the first unit of meaning:

> I'm trying to break words open and get at the bones, deal with symbols as though they were atoms. I'm trying to find out not only how a word gains its meaning, but how a word gains its power.

It is further manifested in the overall composition of the book, Bambara's "avoidance of a linear thing in favor of a kind of jazz suite." Predictably, this approach results in a novel of extraordinary brilliance and density that swirls the reader through multiple layers of sound and sense.

The literal plot, which takes place in less than two hours, is almost negligible. However, while Velma and Minnie rock on their stools, other characters are proceeding with their lives. We follow first one and then another of them through the twelve chapters of the book. The effect is to recreate the discretely random, yet touching, simultaneity of everyday existence. A unifying focus—something shared in common by everyone—is the annual spring festival of celebration and rebirth. This basic structure, though, is complicated further by the near-seamless weaving in of flashbacks, flashforwards, dreams, and visions.

It is this dimension of the novel's technique that dismays many people and causes them to complain that they "can't tell what's *really* happening." In essence, this is a pointless lament, for, writing in this way, Bambara is attempting to convey that everything happening is real, occurring merely on different reality planes (some of which we have been taught to discount as immaterial). The characters slip easily in and out among these levels while Bambara solidly captures it all. Not surprisingly, this is the undifferentiated way that we remember the book. Porter's plunging his bus into the swamp, or Minnie's seducing Meadows on her porch while swinging her suedes and serving him tea—events that did not take place on this level—are no less distinct than Lil James bending from his bike to tie the laces of his

No. 13 sneakers or Guela Khufu nee Tina Mason dancing around her studio. What Bambara implies is that our dreams are as vivid as our waking activities—and just as real.

Tied in with this view of multiple reality planes is an equally complex conception of time. Time (synonymous with timelessness) is not fixed or one-dimensional or solely horological; instead, it exists in fluid manifestations of its various dimensions. Past, present, and future are convenient, this-plane designations which can, in fact, take place simultaneously. Even though this may be confusing, the novel demonstrates clearly how it works—in both simple and complex ways.

The subjective nature of time is perhaps the easiest idea to show. There are places where moments seem interminable, and others that telescope months and years. The short healing session, for instance, feels much longer. At one point, "several [bystanders] checked their watches, amazed that only five minutes of silence had ensued" (p. 106). Toward the end of *Salt*, events move swiftly. In the final chapter, scoring the transformations, Bambara strings passages together with the phrase, this-or-that character "would remember"/"would say," and with "by the fall of '83," "the summer of '84," etc. Commentators have criticized this section as a hasty tying up of loose ends.[3] It seems more important to see it as Bambara, once again, writing mimetically, here echoing the swiftness with which change occurs once the pivotal breakthrough has been won.

A less accessible notion of time (and being) governs the "she might have died" section of chapter 12 immediately prior to Velma's cure (pp. 271–76). It begins with Velma recalling possible ways she might have died earlier this lifetime—but did not. With only this sentence beginning, "And the assistants lifted her on the litter and carried her out of doors to the straw mat in the courtyard," it shifts to Velma, "some lives ago," having her return to health celebrated by her people with dancing and the reading of signs. "Be calm," Minnie croons next, in a paragraph of the present that pushes Velma "back into the cocoon of the shawl where she died again"—here, in a number of ways which range from the historical (being killed waiting in a six-block-long gas line) to the imaginary ("the taking of the food sheds or the Pentagon"). Then follows the horrible visions of the burial grounds and the young mutants—still couched in the past tense of "might have been." After the children's attack, Velma lies on her back in the ruined city street remembering her this-time childhood and thinking:

She did not regret the attack of the children. She regretted only as she lay on the straw mat, lay on the ground, pressed between the sacred rock, lying on her back under the initiation knife . . . , regretted only as . . . she bled [from the clitoridectomy] and the elder packed cobwebs and mud that would not dam the gush and she bled on as she'd dreamt she would.

In these sentences, Bambara slides without warning or guidepost into Velma's other lives and times. How she does this—coupled with her general ontological view—accounts, in large measure, for the original style and structure of *Salt*.

Its design is concomitantly determined by the deliberate way that "everything becomes a kind of metaphor for the whole."[4] Bambara herself explains it this way:

We have to put it all together . . . .The masseur, in my mind is the other half of the potter, in the sense that to raise the clay you've got to get the clay centered. The potter's wheel is part of the whole discussion of circles.

All of the images and symbols coalesce in this interlocking fashion.

Although Bambara has become a novelist with *Salt*, her "druthers as writer, reader, and teacher is the short story."[5] (In fact, *The Salt Eaters* originated as a story about a Mardi Gras society reenacting an old slave insurrection.) One of the principal vehicles she uses to make the stretch from short fiction to novel is her rhetoric. "An elaborator by nature,"[6] she joys in language and writes best when she feels free to pull out all the stops. In fact, she is similar to her character Buster, who can not rest until he has found the verbal "likes" (similes) to pin down a situation. Her penchant for drawn-out precision is very apparent in the "frozen moment" passages which "stop action" a scene, then exhaustively limn its every detail—for example, when Porter announces five minutes to Claybourne, or when the rumble of thunder is heard.

Another source of Bambara's rhetoric is her racial identity. No one writing today can beat her at capturing the black voice—Cora "reading"Anna's whist playing (pp. 108–109); Ruby loud-talking the "blood" in the Blues Brothers T-shirt (pp. 200–201); the "Black-say" of "How's your hammer hanging?"; the marvelous encomium to black musicians (p. 265) or Minnie "going off" on the wasteful bickering of the younger generation (p. 46). Everyone who has read the book can leaf to a favorite passage. Generally speaking Bambara is more rhetorical than lyrical. Yet, she can write the following:

They send a child to fetch Velma from her swoon and fetch a strong rope to bind the wind, to circle the world while they swell the sea with song. She is the child they sent. She is the song. (p. 273)

While it is not her usual mode, the poetic sensibility glistening here underlies the novel, giving it emotional appeal and beauty.

Form and rhetoric become even more important for Bambara because they enable her to talk about the spiritual-political dichotomy that is the critical equation in *Salt*. She explains this novelistic intention:

> . . . there is a split between the spiritual, psychic, and political forces in my community . . . . It is a wasteful and dangerous split. The novel grew out of my attempt to fuse the seemingly separate frames of reference of the camps; it grew out of an interest in identifying bridges; it grew out of a compulsion to understand how the energies of this period will manifest themselves in the next decade.[7]

Often this schism is referred to explicitly—for example, as "the two camps of adepts still wary of the other's way." One side complains: "Causes and issues. They're vibrating at the mundane level." The other counters: "Spirit this and psychic that. Escapism. Irresponsible, given the objective conditions" (p. 293). It is embodied in the verbal skirmishes between Ruby, a 1960s-vintage politico, and Jan, an astrologist, and kept constantly to the fore in the ubiquitous images of split and wholeness. The point is that we contain both of these sides (as Sophie says, "We're all clairvoyant if we'd only know it"[p. 13]) and that this enervating schizophrenia must be healed individually and collectively.

This is the hard-learned lesson which Velma objectifies. She breaks down being solely political and relentlessly logical, and gets well when she comes into conscious possession of her spiritual being. As a young girl, Velma's search for the missing something in her life begins when she runs from church to tunnel her way to China in the rain. She matured into a truly dedicated civil rights worker, committed even to the dirty and thankless behind-the-scenes toil. One march (later the subject of bitter memories) she completes swollen-footed and beginning her menstrual period with a raggedy tampon in a filthy gas station toilet, while "The Leader" steps cool, pressed, and superficial from his air-conditioned limousine. Married to Obie, Velma keeps her life on the line—adopting a baby after she miscarries, filling jobs as a computer programmer (and being interrogated for security leaks), playing piano for the Seven Sisters, and working so hard at the Academy that it takes "[Obie], Jan, Marcus (when he was in town), Daisy

Moultrie and her mother (when they could afford to pay them), the treasurer of the board, and two student interns to replace" her (p. 93). In addition, she somehow manages to hold together the various factions, keeping things "all of a piece."

Immediately prior to her breakdown, she cannot relax, frightens Obie, upsets their son, goes on walking/talking jags, disappears, has an affair after Obie begins sleeping around, and gets described as a "crackpot." The most telling detail is when she "had come to the table stiff-necked and silent and bitten right through her juice glass" (p. 140). Ruby describes her as being guarded, defended; Obie begs her to let go of old pains. But Velma, who had thought herself immune to the sting of the serpent, succumbs—slits her wrists and thrusts her head into a gas oven hunting for inviolable stillness, "to be that un-available at last, sealed in and the noise of the world, the garbage, locked out" (p. 19). It is the price she pays for blotting out the mud mothers as a child, for seeking at the swamp with a willful spirit, and, finally, for running from the answer when it stares her in the face:

> Something crucial had been missing from the political/economic/social/ cultural/aesthetic/military/psychosocial/psychosexual mix. And what could it be? And what should she do? She'd been asking it aloud one morning combing her hair, and the answer had almost come tumbling out of the mirror naked with serrated teeth and hair alive, birds and insects peeping out at her from the mud-heavy hanks of the ancient mothers' hair. And she had fled feverish and agitated from the room, . . . fled lest she be ensorceled, fled finally into a sharp and pierc-ing world, fled into the carbon cave. (p. 259)

Velma is fleeing from her own reflection; from wisdom which is primitive, intuitive, unconscious; from thought, imagination, magic, self-contemplation, change, ambivalence, past memories and images, the multiple possibilities of her soul, passage to "the other side"—all symbolized by the mud mothers and the mirror. Spiraling upward from her dangerous descent, she makes these connections, calling Minnie's jugs and bowls by their right names of *govi* and *zin* that she did not even know she knew, seeing for the first time the "silvery tendrils" of auric light and energy extending about her. Only then does she rise on steady legs, throwing "off the shawl that drops down on the stool a burst cocoon" (p. 295). In a less dramatic fashion, this is the spiritual breakthrough achieved by other characters, with vary-ing degrees of import and transformation—Nadeen becomes a woman, Fred sees Porter in the streets, Meadows vows to give the Hippocratic oath some real meaning in his life.

Actually, however, undergirding this emphasis on spiritual unification is Bambara's belief (shared by geniuses and mystics) that all knowledge systems are really one system and that "everything is everything," that the traditional divisions are artificial and merely provide the means for alienating schisms. This basic epistemology is one reason why *The Salt Eaters* is such a "heavy" book. With its universal scope, it demands our intelligent participation in disciplines and discourse other than our narrowly conceived own—ancient and modern history, world literature, anthropology, mythology, music, astronomy, physics, biology, mathematics, medicine, political theory, chemistry, philosophy, and engineering. Allusions to everything from space-age technology through Persian folklore to black American blues comfortably jostle each other (and the reader—but perhaps not so comfortably).

The prodigy-journalist Campbell flashes on the truth about the oneness of knowledge,

> Knew in a glowing moment that all the systems were the same at base— voodoo, thermodynamics, I Ching, astrology, numerology, alchemy, metaphysics, everybody's ancient myths—they were interchangeable, not at all separate much less conflicting. (p. 210)

Knowing this, he is able "to discuss fission in terms of billiards, to couch principles of thermonuclear dynamics in the language of down-home Bible-quoting folks" (p. 210). And he can ultimately write with assurance:

> Damballah [a popular voodoo deity, associated with water, lightning, and the serpent-snake] is the first law of thermodynamics and is the Biblical wisdom and is the law of time and is . . . everything that is now has been before and will be again in a new way, in a changed form, in a timeless time. (p. 249)

Amen. Campbell is a projection of the author's own incredibly associative mind. She keeps us alert with her constant yoking together of far-flung, but perfectly matched, bits of information—as when she refers to today's "screw-thy-neighbor paperbacks" as "the modern grimoires of the passing age" (p. 264), making an ironically appropriate comparison between our sex and selfishness "manuals," and the old textbooks of instructions for summoning the devil and performing other darkly magical feats.

Just as Bambara stresses unity throughout, so too is the political vision she screens in *Salt* a holistic one—an analysis that tries to be both total and coherent. The best example of how lifesaving connections among issues are made is this pointed exchange between Jan and Ruby:

> "All this doomsday mushroom-cloud end-of-planet numbah is past my brain. Just give me the good ole-fashioned honky-nigger shit. I think all this ecology stuff is a diversion."
> "They're connected. Whose community do you think they ship radioactive waste through . . . .What parts of the world do they test-blast in? And all them illegal uranium mines dug up on Navajo turf—the crops dying, the sheep dying, the horses, water, cancer . . . . And the plant on the Harlem River and—Ruby, don't get stupid on me." (p. 242)

The tacit reproof is that neither should we, the readers, opt for a reductionist and divisive theory. All revolutionary causes and movements must be addressed if we are to "rescue the planet" and redefine power as "the human responsibility to define, transform, and develop."[8]

This message (for community organizers, especially) goes out in what Bambara conceptualizes as a "call" to bridge the gap between "artists and activists, materialists and spiritualists, old and young, and of course the communities of color."[9] This task (embodied in the Seven Sisters) is particularly timely now when many seasoned political workers are beginning to devote themselves more exclusively to their art or to seemingly privatistic personal development. In specific terms, Bambara shows "Women for Action" breaking away from sexist black politicians and independently tackling the problems of "drugs, prisons, alcohol, the schools, rape, battered women, abused children . . . the nuclear power issue" (p. 198). M'Dear Sophie even feeds her boarders "natural growth," no "food in tin cans on shelves for months and months and aged meat developing in people's system an affinity for killed and old and dead things" (p. 152)—although Cecile is allowed to wisecrack about "plant-life sandwiches with cobwebs" (p. 141).

The movement which is least concretely handled in the novel is lesbian and homosexual rights. "Gays" are cataloged in one or two lists; a joke of sorts is made about Ahiro "hitting on" Obie; and there is a surreal encounter between Meadows and a group of wacky male cross-dressers whose sexuality is left in doubt (who legitimately symbolize the confusion, chaos, and social inversion of carnival). This scant and indirect attention—especially in such a panoramic work which so wonderfully treats everything else—is unrealistic and all the more glaring. It indicates, perhaps, that for the black community at the heart of the novel, unabashed recognition of its lesbian and homo-sexual members and participation in their political struggle is, in a very real sense, the final frontier.

For—her cosmopolitan inclusiveness notwithstanding—the Afro-American community is clearly Bambara's main concern. She is ask-ing: Where are we now? Where should we be heading? How do we get there? Above all, she wants black people to "get it together." This is crisis time, but the beginning of a new age, the last quarter, the end of the twentieth jumping into the twenty-first century. *The Salt Eaters* is about love and change. It challenges: "When did it begin for you?"—when the future was ushered in with a thunderbolt that trans-fixed people, opening up the Third Eye and clearing the way for useful visionary action in this world. The question feels almost apocalyptic, and resounds with the fervor of Minnie's "Don't they know we on the rise?" (p. 46). "On the subject of Black anything," the wisdom remains the same:

> Dispossessed, landless, this and that-less and free, therefore to go any-where and say anything and be everything if we'd only know it once and for all. Simply slip into the power, into the powerful power hanging unrecognized in the back-hall closet. (p. 265)

Two versions of the future are given. One is an in-process sketch of a humanitarian society newly evolving from the death of "the au-thoritarian age" (p. 248). The other is a nightmarish glimpse of "every-one not white, male and of wealth" fighting for burial grounds, of radioactively mutant kids roaming the stockaded streets killing "for the prize of . . . gum boots, mask and bubble suit" needed to breathe the contaminated air (p. 274). Yes, there are "choices to be noted. Decisions to be made" (p. 248). This ultimatum is the burden of the question that Minnie repeatedly puts to Velma: "Are you sure, sweet-heart, that you want to be well?"—for health entails taking respon-sibility for the self and the world we live in. Years after her healing, Velma "would laugh remembering she'd thought *that* was an ordeal. She didn't know the half of it. Of what awaited her in years to come" (p. 278).

Concern for a viable future explains the emphasis which Bambara places upon children, the succeeding generations. Unfortunately, they, too, are suffering from the vacuity of the age:

> . . . there was no charge, no tension, no stuff in these young people's

passage. They walked by you and there was no breeze of merit, no vibes. Open them up and you might find a skate key, or a peach pit, or a Mary Jane wrapper, or a slinky, but that would be about all. (p. 135)

They want a sweet, easy life, and they fight each other. Like their elders, they, too, have to be saved from and for themselves, for, as Old Wife declares, "The chirren are our glory" (p. 47).

As a self-described "Pan-Africanist-socialist-feminist,"[10] Bambara not only cares about children, but manifests a political consciousness which makes her a socially committed writer. It was quite some time, she says, before she "began to realize that this [writing] was a perfectly legitimate way to participate in struggle."[11] Now she fulfills what Kalamu ya Salaam defines as the "responsibility of *revolutionary* Third World writers": "to cut through this [mass media] crap, to expose the cover-ups and ideological/material interests inherent in these presentations, and . . . to offer analysis, inspiration, information and ideas which . . . work in the best interest of Third World defense and development."

Her life experiences have provided ground for this mission, beginning, no doubt, even before 1948 when, in her words, "my first friend, teacher, map maker, landscape aide Mama Helen . . . , having come upon me daydreaming in the middle of the kitchen floor, mopped around me."[12] Born and bred in New York City, she took a 1959 B.A. from Queens College in Theater Arts/English Literature, and a 1963 M.A. from the City College of New York in Modern American Literature. In the arts, her training has included traditional and modern dance, trapeze, theater, mime, film, weaving, pottery, watercolor, acrylics, oils, and basketry. She has worked as a welfare investigator, community center program director, university English professor, and artist-in-residence, while consulting for various organizations and rendering service to such institutional and community groups as the Gowanus Neighborhood Houses and the Livingston College Black Studies Curriculum Committee. Lectures; workshops on black women, black literature, and writing; television, radio, and tape programs; book reviews and articles; and, of course, her fiction writing have all occupied her. From 1968 to the present, she has "read prose works at high schools, elementary schools, college campuses, factories, in prisons, over radio, at bookstores, at conferences, at rallies." Ultimately, one suspects that Velma's spiritual journey echoes the author's own, and that more than a little of the novel is autobiographically generated.

Bambara's outlook—and this is one of her greatest strengths—is consistently *positive*. She will have none of the despair and negativity which is always being passed around:

> As for my own writing, I prefer the upbeat. It pleases me to blow three or four choruses of just sheer energetic fun and optimism, even in the teeth of rats, racists, repressive cops, bomb lovers, irresponsibles, murderers. I am convinced, I guess, that everything will be all right.[13]

But her optimism is not blind. One of the ways she uses its reality is in the portraiture of her characters. To a certain extent, the "together" ones are larger-than-life super people—Doc Serge, for instance (in some ways a questionable personality), who can manage smoothly anything from a "stable" of prostitutes to a community hospital. His outrageous paean of self-praise is not simply "fun," but the revelation of a mighty secret: "that self-love produces the gods and the gods are genius" (p. 137).

The Seven Sisters provide another example. They are simultaneously engaged in myriad projects, always thinking and doing, being political and creative, smart and hip, all at the same time. On Porter's bus, making him nervous with their "unbridled bosoms," "bossy T-shirts," and "baffling" talk, they do everything from argue Marx to write a skit on John Henry and Kwan Cheong, to overhaul their cameras and tape recorders. Through such characters, the novel presents models to strive toward. True, they are ideals of sorts, but they are near enough in contour to familiar prototypes to function as possible, actualized versions of our daily existence. Thus, through them, too, we apprehend the truth of the street exhorter's cry: "The dream is real, my friends. The failure to make it work is the unreality" (p. 126).

Bambara is also creating from her identity as a woman writer. Demonstrably, women are at the novel's center. Other aspects of it, too, are very *female*—references to "the moony womb," "the shedding of skin on schedule," and the synchrony of Palma's and Velma's menstrual clocks; the sister love between Nilda and Cecile who wear each other's hats; Obie's precise description of Velma's orgasm as "the particular spasm . . . the tremor begin[ning] at the tip of his joint" which it had taken him two years living with her to recognize; M'Dear's teaching that the "master brain" was in the "uterus, where all ideas sprung from and were nurtured and released to the lesser brain in the head" (p. 271). Such intimate attention parallels Bambara's larger interest in "Black women and other women, particularly young women," in "that particular voice and stance that they're trying to find":

I think they have a really tremendous contribution to make because no one else has their vantage point. No one moves in the universe in quite that way, in all the silences that have operated in the name of I don't know what: "peace," "unity," and some other kinds of bogus and ingratiating thing.[14]

Like them, Bambara searches for a "new vocabulary of images" which, when found, is "stunning . . . very stunning."

First at the beginning, and then finally at the end, of studying the novel, one must reckon with its initially strange name. Of the three working titles which Bambara used to help her stay focused—"In the Last Quarter," "The Seven Sisters," and "The Salt Eaters"—this is the one she retained. Her explanation of its meaning suggests two applications:

Salt is a partial antidote for snakebite. . . . To struggle, to develop, one needs to master ways to neutralize poisons. "Salt" also keeps the parable of Lot's Wife to the fore. Without a belief in the capacity for transformation, one can become ossified.[15]

This title also calls into the subconscious images related to the folk concepts of "swallowing a bitter pill" and "breaking bread together." There are many allusions to salt in the novel, but they are not as numerous as references to some of the other major symbols. While the image of "The Salt Eaters" condenses the essence of this grand work, it does not reverberate all of its colors.

Providing the exegetical glossing to thoroughly illuminate *The Salt Eaters* would require multiple volumes. Because the book is such a mind-expanding experience, it must, ultimately, be read and reread. Bambara says that she "came to the novel with a sense that everything is possible."[16] We leave it feeling that yes, indeed, everything *is*.

Notes

1. *The Salt Eaters* (New York: Random House, 1980). Page numbers for the novel are given in parentheses within the text.

2. This quote and the two following come from "Searching for the Mother Tongue," an interview with Toni Cade Bambara by Kalamu ya Salaam in *First World* 2:4 (1980), pp. 48, 50.

3. An example in print is Susan Lardner's article, "Third Eye Open," *The New Yorker* 56 (May 5, 1980), p. 173.

4. This quote and the subsequent one are taken from "Searching for the Mother Tongue," p. 50.

5. "What It Is I Think I'm Doing Anyhow," *The Writer on Her Work*, ed. Janet Sternburg (New York and London: W. W. Norton & Co., 1980), p. 174. Bambara speaks briefly about the novel's origins in "Searching for the Mother Tongue," p. 49.

6. Susan Lardner, p. 173.

7. "What It Is I Think I'm Doing Anyhow," p. 165.

8. *Ibid.*, p. 153.

9. "Searching for the Mother Tongue," p. 50. "What It Is I Think I'm Doing Anyhow," p. 165.

10. "What It Is I Think I'm Doing Anyhow," p. 154.

11. "Searching for the Mother Tongue," p. 51. Kalamu ya Salaam's remarks occur as a "Commentary" on the interview, p. 53.

12. Dedicatory page, *The Salt Eaters*. Other biographical information is taken from Bambara's "Vitae."

13. "What It Is I Think I'm Doing Anyhow," p. 158.

14. "Searching for the Mother Tongue," p. 51.

15. "What It Is I Think I'm Doing Anyhow," p. 166.

16. *Ibid.*, p. 168.

14

Trajectories of Self-Definition: Placing Contemporary Afro-American Women's Fiction

BARBARA CHRISTIAN

1

> I see a greater and greater commitment among
> black women writers to understand self, multiplied
> in terms of the community, the community multiplied
> in terms of the nation, and the nation multiplied
> in terms of the world. You have to understand what
> your place as an individual is and the place of the
> person who is close to you. You have to understand
> the space between you before you can understand
> more complex or larger groups.[1]

In this straightforward statement, Alexis DeVeau alludes to a dominant theme in Afro-American women's fiction of the last decade, as
well as to the historical tension from which that theme has emerged.
Of course, many literate persons might say that the commitment to
self-understanding and how that self is related to the world within
which it is situated is at the core of good fiction, and that this statement
is hardly a dramatic one. Yet, for Afro-American women writers, such
an overtly self-centered point of view has been difficult to maintain

because of the way they have been conceptualized by black as well as white society. The extent to which Afro-American women writers in the seventies and eighties have been able to make a commitment to an exploration of self, as central rather than marginal, is a tribute to the insights they have culled in a century or so of literary activity. For Afro-American women writers today are no longer marginal to literature in this country; some of them are its finest practitioners.

But in order to really understand the remarkable achievement of a Toni Morrison, an Alice Walker, or a Paule Marshall or the budding creativity of a Gloria Naylor or an Alexis DeVeau, one must appreciate the tradition from which they have come and the conflict of images with which their foremothers have had to contend. For what Afro-American women have been permitted to express, in fact to contemplate, as part of the self, is gravely affected by other complex issues. The development of Afro-American women's fiction is, in many instances, a mirror image of the intensity of the relationship between sexism and racism in this country. And while many of us may grasp this fact in terms of economics or social status, we often forget the toll it takes in terms of self-expression and therefore self-empowerment. To be able to use the range of one's voice, to attempt to express the totality of self, is a recurring struggle in the tradition of these writers from the nineteenth century to the present. Although this essay could hardly survey the scope of such an inquiry, I am interested in showing some measure of the extent to which the tradition has developed to the point where Alexis DeVeau can make the claim she does, and how that claim has resulted in the range of expression that marks the fiction of the seventies and eighties.

Early Afro-American women novelists indicate, through their stated intentions, their primary reasons for writing their works. Frances Harper, for example, in her preface to *Iola Leroy*, made clear her purpose when she wrote that "her story's mission would not be in vain if it awaken in the hearts of our countrymen a stronger sense of justice and a more Christian-like humanity."[2] Harper was pleading for the justice due Afro-Americans, who, in the 1890s, were being lynched, burned out, raped, and deprived of their rights as citizens in the wake of the failure of Reconstruction. Iola Leroy, Harper's major character, does not attempt to understand either herself as an individual or black women as a group. Rather, Iola Leroy is a version of the "lady" Americans were expected to respect and honor, even though she is black. By creating a respectable ideal heroine, according to the norms of the time, Harper was addressing not herself, black women, or black people, but her (white) countrymen.

Audience was a consideration, as well, for Jessie Fauset, the most published Afro-American woman novelist of the Harlem Renaissance. She, together with Nella Larsen, wanted to correct the impression most white people had that all black people lived in Harlem dives or in picturesque, abject poverty.[3] In her preface to *The Chinaberry Tree* (1931) she tells us why she chose to create the heroines she did. Beginning with the disclaimer that she does not write to establish a thesis, she goes on to point out that the novel is about "those breathing spells in-between spaces where colored men and women work and live and go their ways in no thought of the problem. What are they like then? So few of the other Americans know."[4] And she concludes her preface by identifying the class to which her characters belong: the Negro who speaks of "his old Boston families," "old Philadelphians," "old Charlestonians."[5]

Both Harper and Fauset were certainly aware of the images, primarily negative, of black people that predominated in the minds of white Americans. They constructed their heroines to refute those images, as their way of contributing to the struggle of black people for full citizenship in this country. Of necessity their language was outer-directed rather than inwardly searching, for their characters were addressed to "the other Americans" who blocked group development. To white American readers, self-understanding for black characters might have seemed a luxury. To the extent that their writers emphasized the gender as well as the race of their heroines they were appealing to a white female audience that understood the universal trials of womanhood. These writers' creations, then, were conditioned by the need to establish "positive" images of black people; hence, the exploration of self, in all its complexity, could hardly be attempted.

To a large extent, and necessarily so until the 1940s, most black women fiction writers directed their conscious intention toward a refutation of the negative images imposed upon all black women, images decidedly "masculine" according to the norm of the times.[6] Nonetheless, from *Iola Leroy* (1892) to Dorothy West's *The Living Is Easy* (1948), there is an incredible tension between the "femininity" of the heroines and their actual behavior. On the one hand, the writers try to prove that black women *are* women, that they achieve the ideal of other American women of their time. That is, that they are beautiful (fair), pure, upper class, and would be nonaggressive, dependent beings, if only racism did not exist. At the same time, they appear to believe that if Afro-American women were to achieve the norm, they would lose important aspects of themselves. The novels, especially those about passing, embody this tension. But even in the novels that do not focus on this theme, the writers emphasize the self-directedness of their heroines, as well as their light-skinned beauty and Christian morality. Thus Iola Leroy believes that women should work; Pauline Hopkins's heroine in *Contending Forces* (1900) wants to advance the race; Fauset's characters, though class-bound, have ambition to an unfeminine degree; Larsen's heroine Helga Crane in *Quicksand* (1928), though restricted by conventional morality, senses the power of her sensuality and the lie the image of the lady represents.

The tension between the femininity of these heroines and their "contrary instincts"[7] has its roots, in part, in the fact that Afro-American women, contrary to the norm, could not survive unless they generated some measure of self-definition. If they tried to live by the female version of The American Dream, as pure, refined, protected, and well-provided for, they were often destroyed, as is Lutie Johnson, Ann Petry's heroine in *The Street* (1946). And even if they secured a measure of the Dream, some like Cleo in West's *The Living Is Easy* became destructive, frustrated, alienated from self.

One notable exception to this trend in early Afro-American women writers' works is Zora Neale Hurston's *Their Eyes Were Watching God* (1937). For in this work Hurston portrays the development of Janie Stark as a black woman who achieves self-fulfillment and understanding. It is interesting to note, however, that Hurston was obviously aware that the literature of that time focused on the black woman's drive toward economic stability and "feminine" ideals. She constructs the novel so that Janie moves through three stages that embody different views of black women: in her relationship with her first husband, Logan Killicks, Janie is treated like a mule; she is rescued from that state by marrying Jody Starks, who wants her to become a lady, "The Queen of the Porch."[8] But Hurston critiques the achievement of economic stability through feminine submission in marriage as *the* desirable goal for the black woman. She portrays the disastrous consequences of this goal on Janie—that she becomes, in this situation, a piece of desirable property, cut off from her community and languishing in the repression of her natural desire to be herself. Though Janie's relationship with Tea Cake is not ideal, Hurston does present us with a vision of possibility in terms of some parity in a relationship between a woman and a man, based not on material gain or ownership of property but on their desire to know one another.

It is significant, I believe, that Hurston characterizes this relationship as play, pleasure, sensuality, which is for her the essential nature of nature itself, as symbolized by the image of the pear tree that pervades the novel. It is also critical to an appreciation of Hurston's radical effect on the tradition of Afro-American women's fiction that her language is so different from the language of the "conventional" novel of the times. Rooted in black English, Hurston uses metaphors derived from nature's play to emphasize the connection between the natural world and the possibilities of a harmonious social order. And in keeping with her choice of language, she structures her novel as a circle, in which the returning Janie explores her own development by telling her story to Pheoby, whose name means "the moon," and who is her best friend and the symbolic representative of the community.

In its radical envisioning of the self as central, and in its use of language as a means of exploring the self as female and black, *Their Eyes Were Watching God* is a forerunner of the fiction of the seventies and eighties. In general, though, most novels published before the 1950s embodied the tension between the writers' apparent acceptance of an ideal of woman derived from white upper-class society and the reality with which their protagonists had to contend. And most seemed to be written for an audience that excluded even the writers themselves.

But the attempt to present "positive" images of the black woman, to restrict her characterization to a prescribed ideal, did not result in any improvement in her image or in her condition. Rather, the refutation of negative images created a series of contradictions between the image that black women could not attain, though which they sometimes internalized, and the reality of their existence. That tension increased throughout the first half of the century, until in the 1940s the destruction it created becomes apparent in the fiction written by black women. The heroines of this period, Lutie Johnson in *The Street* and Cleo Judson in *The Living Is Easy*, are defeated both by social reality and by their lack of self-knowledge. Self-knowledge was critical if black women were to develop the inner resources they would need in order to cope with larger social forces.

2

Beginning with Gwendolyn Brooks's *Maud Martha* (1953), we can observe a definite shift in the fiction of Afro-American women, a shift in point of view and intention that still characterizes the novels written today. And that is that Afro-American women writers are, as Alexis DeVeau noted, putting more emphasis on reflecting the process of self-definition and understanding women have always had to be engaged in, rather than refuting the general society's definition of them. The shift is, of course, not a sudden or totally complete one; there are many phases in the process.

The first phase focused on portraying what the early literature tended to omit, namely, the complex existence of the ordinary, dark-skinned woman, who is neither an upper-class matron committed to an ideal of woman that few could attain, as in the novels of the Harlem Renaissance, nor a downtrodden victim, totally at the mercy of a hostile society, as in Ann Petry's *The Street*.

Gwendolyn Brooks claims that her intention in writing *Maud Martha* was to paint a portrait of an *ordinary* black woman, first as daughter, then as mother, and to show what she makes of her "little life."[9] What Brooks emphasizes in the novel is Maud Martha's *awareness* that she is seen as common (and therefore as unimportant), and that there is so much more in her than her "little life" will allow her to be. Yet, because Maud Martha constructs her own standards, she manages to transform that "little life" into so much more despite the limits set on her by her family, her husband, her race, her class, whites, American society. Maud Martha emerges neither crushed nor triumphant. She manages, though barely, to be her own creator. Her sense of her own integrity is rooted mostly in her own imagination—in her internal language as metaphors derived from women's experience, metaphors which society usually trivializes but which Brooks presents as the vehicles of insight. Though Maud Martha certainly does not articulate a language (or life) of overt resistance, she does prepare the way for such a language in that she sees the contradiction between her real value as a black woman and how she is valued by those around her.

Perhaps because *Maud Martha* was such a departure from the usual characterizations of Afro-American women in previous fiction, the novel went out of print almost immediately after it appeared. Nonetheless, it was to influence Paule Marshall, whose *Browngirl, Brownstones* (1959) is a definite touchstone in contemporary Afro-American women's fiction. In a lecture she gave in 1968, Marshall pointed to *Maud Martha* as "the finest portrayal of an Afro-American woman in the novel"[10] to date and as a decided influence on her work. And in characterizing Brooks's protagonist, Marshall noted Maud Martha's process of self-exploration: "In her daily life, Maud Martha functions as an artist; in that way, this novel carries on the African tradition that the ordinary rituals of daily life are what must be made into art."[11] The elements Marshall noted in *Maud Martha*—a focus on the complexity of women characters, who are central rather than marginal to the world, and the significance of daily rituals through which these women situate themselves in the context of their specific community and culture—are dominant characteristics of her own novels.

Like *Maud Martha*, the emphasis in *Browngirl, Brownstones* is on the black woman as mother and daughter. In an interview with Alexis DeVeau in 1980, Marshall recalls that she wrote her first novel in the late fifties as a relief from a tedious job. She wrote the novel not primarily for publication but as a process of understanding, critiquing, and celebrating her own personal history.[12] In understanding "the talking women," who were the most vivid memories of her youth, Marshall also demonstrates through her portrayal of Silla Boyce how the role of *mother* for this black woman is in conflict with her role as *wife*, because of the racism that embattles her and her community. Marshall's novel, as well as Brooks's, was certainly affected by society's attitude that black women were matriarchs, domineering mothers who distorted their children who in turn disrupted society—a vortex of attitudes that culminated in the Moynihan Report. In attempting to understand her maternal ancestors, then, Marshall had to penetrate the social stereotypes that distorted their lives.

Few early Afro-American women's novels focused on the black woman's role as mother, because of the negative stereotype of the black woman as mammy that pervaded American society. But instead of de-emphasizing the black woman's role as mother, Marshall probes its complexity. She portrays Silla Boyce as an embittered woman caught between her own personality and desires, and the life imposed on her as a mother who must destroy her unorthodox husband in order to have a stable family (as symbolized by the brownstone). This analysis of the black mother prefigures other analyses of this theme in the 1970s, especially Toni Morrison's *Sula* and Alice Walker's *Meridian*. And Marshall shows that racist and sexist ideology is intertwined, for Silla's and Deighton Boyce's internalization of the American definition of woman and man runs counter to their own beings and to their situation as black people in American society, and precipitates the tragedy that their relationship becomes.

Silla, however, is not an internal being like Maud Martha. She fights, supported by her women friends who use their own language to penetrate illusion and verbally construct their own definitions in order to wage their battle. As a result, Selina, Silla's daughter, will, by the end of the novel, have some basis for the journey to self-knowledge upon which she embarks, fully appreciating the dilemma which her mother and father could not solve.

Like Brooks's novel, *Browngirl, Brownstones* emphasizes how the black community, its customs and mores, affects the process of the black woman's exploration of self. But Marshall's novel also stresses the importance of culture and language as contexts for understanding *society's* definitions of man and woman. She veers sharply away from much of the preceding literature, which emphasized advancement for black women in terms of white American values. She portrays the Barbadian-American community both as a rock her characters can stand on, and as the obstacle against which they must struggle in order to understand and develop their own individuality. Finally, though, Selina's decision to return to the Caribbean is her attempt to claim her own history as a means of acquiring self-consciousness. In *Browngirl, Brownstones*, an appreciation of ethnic and racial community becomes necessary for black women in their commitment to self-development.

The emphasis on community and culture in *Maud Martha* and *Browngirl, Brownstones*, as a prerequisite for self-understanding, reflected a growing sense among Afro-Americans in the late fifties and sixties of their unique cultural identity. But by 1970, when Toni Morrison's *The Bluest Eye* and Alice Walker's *The Third Life of Grange Copeland* were published, black women writers' stance toward their communities had begun to change. The ideology of the sixties had stressed the necessity for Afro-Americans to rediscover their blackness, their unity in their blackness. As positive as that position was to the group's attempt to empower itself, one side effect was the tendency to idealize the relationship between black men and women, to blame sexism in the black community solely on racism or to justify a position that black men were superior to women.

During the sixties few novels by Afro-American women were published; rather, poetry and drama dominated the literature perhaps because of the immediacy of these forms and because of the conviction that literature should be as accessible as possible to black communities. The result of that change in perception about audience was that Afro-American writers consciously began to view their communities as the group to which they were writing. Black communities are clearly one of the many audiences to which Morrison and Walker addressed their first novels, for both works critique those communities and insist that they have deeply internalized racist stereotypes that radically affect their definitions of woman and man. In both novels, the community is directly responsible for the tragedies of the major characters—for the madness of Pecola Breedlove, for the suicide of Margaret Copeland, and for the murder of Mem Copeland by her husband. In *The Bluest Eye*, Morrison emphasizes the women's view of themselves. In *Grange Copeland*, Walker stresses the men's view. In these novels it is not only that an individual heroine accepts the sexist and racist definitions of herself, but that the entire black community, men and women, accept this construct—resulting in the destruction of many black women.

This fiction in the early seventies represents a second phase, one in which the black community itself becomes a major threat to the survival and empowerment of women. Women must struggle against the definitions of gender. The language of this fiction therefore becomes a language of protest, as Afro-American women writers vividly depict the victimization of their protagonists. Morrison, Walker, Gayl Jones, and Toni Cade Bambara all expose sexism and sexist violence in their own communities. But it is not so much that they depict an altered consciousness in their protagonists; rather, it is that their attitudes toward their material, and the audience to which they address their protest, has changed since the novels of the 1940s with their emphasis on oppression from outside the black community. In the novels of the early seventies, there is always someone who learns not only that white society must change, but also that the black community's attitudes toward women must be revealed and revised. Interestingly, in *The Bluest Eye* it is Claudia McJeer, Pecola's peer and friend, who undergoes this education, while in *The Third Life* it is the grandfather, Grange, who must kill his son, the fruit of his initial self-hatred, in order to save his granddaughter Ruth. Both Claudia and Ruth possess the possibility of constructing their own self-definitions and affecting the direction of their communities, because they have witnessed the destruction of women in the wake of prevailing attitudes.

By the mid-1970s, the fiction makes a visionary leap. In novels like *Sula* and *Meridian*, the woman is not thrust outside her community. To one degree or another, she chooses to stand outside it, to define herself as in revolt against it. In some ways, Sula is the most radical of the characters of seventies fiction, for she overturns the conventional definition of good and evil in relation to women by insisting that she exists primarily as and for herself—not to be a mother or to be the lover of men. In other ways, Meridian is more radical in that she takes a revolutionary stance by joining a social movement, the Civil Rights movement that might have redefined American definitions of both race *and* gender. Sula stands alone as a rebel; Meridian gradually creates a community of support. It is important that both of these women claim their heritage. Sula and Meridian are who they are because of their *maternal* ancestry and their knowledge of that ancestry; and it is from their mothers that they acquire their language. This is also true of Merle Kimbona in Marshall's second novel, *The Chosen Place, The Timeless People*. Though published in 1969, this novel depicts a black woman as both outside and inside the black world, as both outside and inside the West. As such, Merle becomes a spokesperson for her people, both female and male, who do not always understand their own dilemmas.

The heroines of the mid-1970s are socio-political actors in the world. Their stance is rebellious; their consciousness has been altered, precisely because of the supposed crimes they are perceived as having committed against Motherhood, and beyond the constraints society imposes on female sexuality. Yet they are wounded heroines, partly because their communities are deeply entrenched in their view of woman as essentially a mother or as the lover of a man. But although these characters are critical of their own communities, they come back to them and work out their resistance in that territory. Marshall and Walker both extend their analyses to the ways in which white women are also affected by definitions of sex and race. Essentially, though, it is within the context of black communities, rather than in the world of women, that they struggle.

By the mid-seventies, Afro-American women fiction writers, like Paule Marshall, Toni Morrison, Alice Walker, Toni Cade Bambara, and Gayl Jones had not only defined their cultural context as a distinctly Afro-American one, but they had also probed many facets of the interrelationship of sexism and racism in their society. Not only had they demonstrated the fact that sexism existed in black communities, but they had also challenged the prevailing definition of woman in American society, especially in relation to motherhood and sexuality. And they had insisted not only on the centrality of black women to Afro-American history, but also on their pivotal significance to present-day social and political developments in America.

3

The novels of the late seventies and the eighties continue to explore these themes—that sexism must be struggled against in black communities and that sexism is integrally connected to racism. The fiction of this period—Morrison's *Song of Solomon* (1978) and *Tar Baby* (1980), Gloria Naylor's *The Women of Brewster Place* (1980), Toni Cade Bambara's *The Salt Eaters* (1980), Alice Walker's *You Can't Keep a Good Woman Down* (1981) and *The Color Purple* (1982), Joyce Carol Thomas's *Marked by Fire* (1982), Ntozake Shange's *Sassafrass, Cypress and Indigo* (1982), Audre Lorde's *Zami* (1982), and Paule Marshall's *Praisesong for the Widow* (1983)—cannot be treated collectively, for it reflects a great deal of difference. Yet all of these novels look at ways in which the quality of black women's lives is affected by the interrelationship of sexism and racism. And many of them go a step further. They pose the question concerning to what community black women must belong in order to understand themselves most effectively in their totality as blacks *and* women.

Morrison's novels, of those of the major writers, have moved furthest away from the rebellious-woman stance of the mid-seventies, for she has focused, in her last two books, on men as much as women. Still she makes an attempt in both novels to figure out the possibilities of healing and community for her women characters. In *Song of Solomon* Pilate is such a character, although she derives her accumulated wisdom from her father and primarily benefits Milkman, her nephew, rather than any other woman in the novel. Jadine in *Tar Baby* is portrayed as the woman who has taken a position so far removed from her community that she becomes a part of the West. In her search for self, she becomes selfish; in her desire for power, she loses essential parts of herself. Thus Morrison has moved full circle from Pecola, who is destroyed by her community, to Jadine, who destroys any relationship to community in herself.

On the other end of the spectrum, Walker's Celie comes close to liberating herself through the community of her black sisters, Nettie, Sophie, and Shug, and is able to affect the men of her world positively. The motif of liberation through one's sisters is repeated in Shange's *Sassafrass*, in which the healing circle is that of black women: three sisters and their mother. In contrast to the novels of the early seventies because of the presence of a strong woman's community, the major protagonists do survive, some with the possibility of wholeness. Ironically, the lush *Tar Baby* is the most pessimistic; the spare *Color Purple*, the most optimistic. For Morrison sees no practical way out of the morass of sexism, racism, and class privilege in the Western world, as it is presently constructed, for anyone, black or white, female or male. Walker, however, sees the possibility of empowerment for black women if they create a community of sisters which can alter the present-day unnatural definitions of woman and man.

Between these two ends of the spectrum, other novelists propose paths to empowerment. In Marshall's most recent novel, *Praisesong for the Widow* (1983), Avey Johnson must discard her American value of obsessive materialism, must return to her source, must remember the ancient wisdom of African culture—that the body and spirit are one, that harmony cannot be achieved unless there is a reciprocal relationship between the individual and the community—if she is to define herself as a black woman. Her journey through myth and ritual, precipitated by the dream of her old great-aunt, takes her back in time and space as she prepares to move forward in consciousness. So too with Audre Lorde's *Zami* (1982) in that she probes the cosmology of her black maternal ancestors in order to place herself. Lorde focuses more specifically than Marshall on a community of women who live, love, and work together as the basis for the creation of a community that might effect the empowerment of Afro-American women. These fictional works are similar, however, in that the source for a unity of self takes these women to the Caribbean and ultimately to Africa.

In fact, in many of these novels, Africa and African women become important motifs for trying out different standards of new woman-hood. In *Tar Baby*, Toni Morrison uses the image of the African woman in the yellow dress as a symbol for the authenticity that the jaded Jadine lacks. It is this woman's inner strength, beauty, and pride, manifested in the defiant stance of her body, that haunts Jadine's dreams and throws her into such a state of confusion that she flees her Parisian husband-to-be and retreats to the Isle de Chevaliers in the Caribbean. In contrast, Alice Walker reminds us in *The Color Purple*, one-third of which is set in Africa, that "black women have been the mule of the world there, and the mule of the world here,"[13] and that sexism flourishes in Africa. Audre Lorde begins *Zami* by describing her foremothers in Grenada: "There is a softer edge of African sharpness upon these women, and they swing through the rain-warm streets with an arrogant gentleness that I remember in strength and vulnerability."[14] Like Lorde, Marshall recalls in *Praisesong for the Widow* the uniquely African quality of the women she encounters in her Caribbean sojourn on Carriacou, an Africanness that reminds her of her Great Aunt Cuney who lived in Tatum, South Carolina. The recurring motif of *Praisesong*, itself a distinctly African form, is "her body she always usta say might be in Tatum but her mind, her mind was long gone with the Ibo's."[15] Marshall concentrates, more than any of the other novelists of this period, on delineating the essential African wisdom still alive in New World black communities. Ntozake Shange, too, uses African motifs in *Sassafrass*, focusing on their centrality in U.S. southern culture and especially on the development of sensuality in her three sister protagonists. She quite consciously links African rhythms, dance, and style to a uniquely Afro-American woman culture which is at the core of this book's intentions, and connects it to the style and rhythms of other Third World American women.

What is particularly interesting about these novelists' use of African elements in relation to the concept of woman is their sense of concreteness rather than abstraction. All of the major characters in the books I've just mentioned have moved from one place to another and have encountered other worlds distinctly different from their own. Mobility of black women is a new quality in these books of the early eighties, for black women, in much of the previous literature, were restricted in space by their condition. This mobility is not cosmetic. It means that there is increased interaction between black women from the United States, the Caribbean, and Africa, as well as other women of color. And often it is the movement of the major characters from one place to another (*Tar Baby*'s Jadine from Paris to the Caribbean to the United States; *Praisesong*'s Avey Johnson from White Plains to Grenada; *Sassafrass*'s Cypress from San Francisco to New York; *Color Purple*'s Nettie from the U.S. South to Africa) that enlarges and sharpens their vision.

Not only is mobility through space a quality of present-day fiction, so also is mobility from one class to another. In contrast to the novels of the twenties which focused on upper-middle-class black women, novels of the forties which tended to emphasize proletarian women, or novels of the seventies which featured lower-middle-class women, many of the novels of this period present the development of black women who have moved from one class to another as a major theme of the work. Thus Jadine in *Tar Baby*, Celie in *Color Purple*, and Avey Johnson in *Praisesong* have all known poverty and have moved to a point where they have more material security. Still there are many variations in these authors' analysis of such a movement.

In *Tar Baby*, Jadine is able to reap the material benefits of her aunt's and uncle's relationship to Valerian, their wealthy white employer, and becomes, in some ways, an Afro-American princess. Morrison's analysis of Jadine's focus on security and comfort emphasizes the danger that obsession with material things might have for the ambitious black woman. In pursuing her own desire to "make it," Jadine forgets how to nurture those who have made it impossible for her to be successful. She forgets her "ancient properties"[16] as Therese, the Caribbean sage points out, and succumbs to the decadent Western view of woman. Paule Marshall also focuses on the dangers of materialism, on how the fear of poverty and failure has affected Avey's and Jay Johnson's marriage—and their sense of themselves as black—to such an extent that they do not even recognize their own faces. *Praisesong* has, as one of its major themes, middle-aged, middle-class Avey Johnson's journey back to herself, an essential part of which is the African wisdom still alive in the rituals of black societies in the West. While Morrison warns us that our ancient properties can be easily eroded by the materialism of the West, Marshall emphasizes the seemingly irrational ways in which the collective memory of black people has a hold even on the Avey Johnsons of America. Alice Walker approaches the element of class mobility in another way. Celie does not lose her sense of community or her spiritual center as she moves from dire poverty and deprivation to a more humane way of living, perhaps because she comes to that improvement in her life through inner growth and through the support of her sisters.

One effect of such a variety of themes and characters in the fiction of the early eighties is not only black women writers' analysis of the intersection of class, race, and gender, but also their presentation of many styles of life, many different ways of approaching the issues that confront them as blacks, as women, as individual selves.

This expression of a range of experience is nowhere more apparent than in these authors' treatment of their characters' sexuality. One radical change in the fiction of the 1980s is the overt exploration of lesbian relationships among black women and how these relationships are viewed by black communities. This exploration is not, I believe, to be confused with the emphasis on friendship among black women that is a major theme in earlier literature. This new development may have a profound effect on present-day attitudes about the relationship between sex and race, and about the nature of women. The beginning of this exploration has already shown that lesbianism is a complex subject, for sexual relationships between women are treated differently in *The Color Purple, The Women of Brewster Place, Sassafrass,* and *Zami.*

In *The Color Purple,* the love/sex relationship between Celie and Shug is at the center of the novel, and is presented as a natural, strengthening process through which both women, as well as the people around them, grow. Walker also seems to be influenced by Zora Neale Hurston's use of language in *Their Eyes Are Watching God,* a book that she greatly admires. For the lesbian relationship between Celie and Shug is expressed through the metaphors of nature and in the form of black English. In a sense, in *The Color Purple* Walker does for the sexual relationships between black women what Hurston in *Their Eyes Were Watching God* did for sexual relationships between black women and men. In contrast, Gloria Naylor, in *The Women of Brewster Place,* places more emphasis on the reactions of the small community to which the lovers belong, as well as their own internalization of social views about lesbianism. There is more concentration in this novel on the oppression that black lesbians experience. Appropriately Naylor uses metaphors of endurance rooted in Afro-American folk speech. In Shange's *Sassafrass,* the sexual relationship between Cypress and her lover is a part of a community of lesbian women who, while affirming themselves, are also sometimes hostile to one another as the outer world might be. *Sassafrass's* lesbian community is an imperfect one, and Cypress's sexual love for another woman is but part of a continuum of sexual love that includes her involvement with men.

In *Zami,* however, the definition of a lesbian relationship is extended, since Lorde beautifully demonstrates how the heritage of her Grenadian mother is integrally connected to her development as a

woman-identified woman. In using the word *Zami* as a title, a word
which means "women who live, love and work together,"[17] Lorde
searches for the connections between myth, poetry, and history that
might shift the focus of the definition of humankind, particularly black
humankind, from one that is predominantly male. One question
which these novels leave unanswered is whether the bond between
women might be so strong that it might transcend the racial and class
divisions among women in America, and make possible a powerful
women's community that might effect significant change.

utopian?

   The emphasis on the culture of women as a means to self-understanding and growth is not only treated thematically in this new fiction, but it is also organic to the writers' forms. Increasingly, the
language and forms of black women's fiction are derived from wom-
en's experiences as well as from Afro-American culture. The most
revolutionary transformation of the novel's form is Alice Walker's *The
Color Purple*. It is written entirely in letters, a form which (along with
diaries) was the only one allowed women to record their everyday
lives and feelings, their "herstory." And of equal importance, Walker
explores the richness and clarity of black folk English in such a way
that the reader understands that the inner core of a person cannot be
truly known except through her own language. Like Walker, Ntozake
Shange consciously uses a potpourri of forms primarily associated
with women: recipes, potions, letters, as well as poetry and dance
rhythms, to construct her novel. In *Song of Solomon* and *Tar Baby*
Morrison continues to explore Afro-American folktales and folklore,
the oral tradition of black people, which as Marshall reminds us in
Praisesong for the Widow is often passed on from one generation to the
next by women. Marshall also uses dream, ritual, and hallucination,
using the metaphors of women's experience in composing the ritualistic process of *Praisesong*. This exploration of new forms based on
the black woman's culture and her story has, from my perspective,
revitalized the American novel and has opened up new avenues of
expression, indelibly altering our sense of novelistic process.

   Thematically and stylistically, the tone of the fiction of the early
eighties communicates the sense that women of color can no longer
be perceived as marginal to the empowerment of all American women
and that an understanding of their reality and imagination is essential
to the process of change that the entire society must undergo in order
to transform itself. Most importantly, black women writers project
the belief, as Alexis DeVeau pointed out, that commitment to an
understanding of self is as wide as the world is wide. This new fiction
explores in a multiplicity of ways Alice Walker's statement in a recent
interview:

Writing to me is not about audience exactly. It's about living. It's about expanding myself as much as I can and seeing myself in as many roles and situations as possible. Let me put it this way. If I could live as a tree, as a river, as the moon, as the sun, as a star, as the earth, as a rock, I would. Writing permits me to be more than I am. Writing permits me to experience life as any number of strange creations.[18]

Notes

1. Claudia Tate, ed., *Black Women Writers At Work*, (New York: Continuum Publishing Co., 1983), p. 55.

2. Frances Harper, *Iola LeRoy, Shadows Uplifted*, 3rd ed. (Boston: James H. Earle, 1895), p. 281.

3. Hiroko Sato, "Under that Harlem Shadow: A Study of Jessie Fauset and Nella Larsen," *The Harlem Renaissance Remembered*, ed. Arna Bontemps (New York: Dodd Mead and Co., 1972), p. 67.

4. Jessie Redmon Fauset, Foreword to *The Chinaberry Tree* (New York: Frederick A. Stokes Co., 1931), p. ix.

5. *Ibid.*, p. ix.

6. For a discussion of this question see *Black Women Novelists, The Development of a Tradition*, Barbara T. Christian (Westport, Conn.: Greenwood Press, 1980).

7. Alice Walker uses this phrase most effectively in her essay "In Our Mothers' Gardens," *Ms.* 2:11 (May 1974), p. 71.

8. Zora Neale Hurston, *Their Eyes Were Watching God* (Greenwich, Conn.: Fawcett Publishing Co., Inc. [1965 edition]; first printed by Philadelphia: Lippincott Co., 1937), p. 42.

9. Gwendolyn Brooks, *Report from Part I* (Detroit: Broadside Press, 1972), p. 162.

10. Paule Marshall, tape of lecture at conference "The Negro Woman Writer," Howard University, 1968.

11. Mary Helen Washington, "Book Review of Barbara Christian's *Black Women Novelists*," *Signs: Journal of Women in Culture and Society* 8:1 (August 1982), p. 179.

12. Alexis DeVeau, "Paule Marshall—in celebration of Our Triumph," *Essence* 10:1 (May 1980), p. 96.

13. Gloria Steinem, "Do You Know This Woman, She Knows You—A Profile of Alice Walker," *Ms.* 10:1 (June 1982), p. 193.

14. Audre Lorde, *Zami: a new spelling of my name* (Watertown, Mass.: Persephone Press, Inc., 1982), p. 9.

15. Paule Marshall, *Praisesong for the Widow* (New York: G. P. Putnam's Sons, 1983), p. 39.

16. Toni Morrison, *Tar Baby* (New York: Alfred A. Knopf, 1981), p. 305.

17. Audre Lorde, *Zami*, p. 255.

18. Claudia Tate, ed., *Black Women at Work*, p. 185.

Afterword

Cross-Currents, Discontinuities: Black Women's Fiction

HORTENSE J. SPILLERS

To elaborate a point that Marjorie Pryse makes in the introduction to this volume, the community of black women writing in the United States now can be regarded as a vivid new fact of national life. I deliberately substitute the participle for the noun to suggest not only the palpable and continuing urgency of black women writing themselves into history, but also to convey the variety of aims that accompany their project. This community of cultural workers has no simple centrality inasmuch as it is comprised of fiction writers as well as writers of criticism, who are also teachers of literature, with all the descriptive categories occasionally overlapping. Some of the fiction writers whose works are discussed here are (or were) also teachers in the academy, just as the critics are, so that the site of the institution becomes as crucial an aspect of the whole discussion as the audience toward which this volume of essays is aimed. We are called upon to witness, then, the formation of relatively new social and political arrangements that articulate fruitful contradictions. The American academy, despite itself, is one of the enabling postulates of black women's literary community simply because it is not only a source of income for certain individual writers, but also a point of dissemination and inquiry for their work. This development, in perspective with the generation of Jessie Fauset and Zora Neale Hurston, seems relatively unprecedented as it also lends special character to this period of lit-

good ups in back. insightful readings of texts which give a sense of historical progression of blk women's fiction + place this fiction in the context of community consciousness (1940's-1980's)

erary and *lived* history. In short, the image of black women writing
in isolation, across time and space, is conduced toward radical revi-
sion. The room of one's own explodes its four walls to embrace the
classroom, the library, and the various mechanisms of institutional
and media life, including conferences, the lecture platform, the television talk show, the publishing house, the "best seller," and collections of critical essays. These new arrangements, when perceived
against the background of the Black Nationalist Movement and the
most recent phase of the Women's Movement in the United States,
give us striking insight into the situations of "tradition." The latter
arises not only because there are writers there to make it, but also
because there is a strategic audience of heightened consciousness prepared to read and interpret the work as such. Traditions are not born.
They are made. We would add that they are not, like objects of nature,
here to stay, but survive as *created social events* only to the extent that
an audience cares to intersect them.

One of the most exciting aspects of the new reality is its appeal as
a community conscious of itself. The various writers represented here
share a broadly thematic synonymity: Each of them specifically addresses the multiplicity of life issues that converge with black American women's historic and coeval experience. That thematic alignment
becomes the implicit assumption of a single volume of interviews,
Claudia Tate's *Black Women Writers at Work*; a book of theory, Barbara
Christian's *Black Women Novelists: The Development of a Tradition, 1892–
1976*; and two fairly recent anthologies of short fiction, Mary Helen
Washington's *Black-Eyed Susans* and *Midnight Birds*,[1] that all complement an initial impression: The reader, having recognized before now
the outlines of a tradition, gains, with this era of black women writing,
a sharper sense of contours, of more precisely differentiated markings,
from the publication of Margaret Walker's *Jubilee* (1965) through Gloria
Naylor's *Women of Brewster Place*, Alice Walker's *Color Purple*, Paule
Marshall's *Praisesong for the Widow*, and Ntozake Shange's *Sassafrass,
Cypress, and Indigo*,[2] all published within the last three years. No doubt
that as I am writing this piece and well before this volume becomes
a fact of publication and a reality of the marketplace, other works by
black women will have found their distinguished place in the women's
library. Marita Golden's *Migrations of the Heart: A Personal Odyssey* and
Audre Lorde's *Zami: A New Spelling of My Name*[3] are among the new
harvest, and in the case of Lorde's book, there is more than subtle
hint that the publishing center of gravity is shaking loose from its
customary moorings as the marginal women's press begins to redes-
cribe the lines of disseminative power.

It would appear that books, like the genetic parents, beget books, and that the sheer proliferation of the work, if nothing else, inscribes an impression point at which the makers and patrons of the traditional canon of American literature and the very structure of values that decides the *permissible* must now stop and rethink their work. Reading against the canon, intruding into it a configuration of symbolic values with which critics and audiences must contend, the work of black women's writing community not only redefines tradition, but also disarms it by suggesting that the term itself is a critical fable intended to encode and circumscribe an inner and licit circle of empowered texts. I have been prepared by my collective and individual history to stand outside that circle and, in fact, to try to *choose* this standing-apart-from as the locus of a radical dissent and critique that the collective and individual "I" must keep alive for the duration. Wanting to do so, I would claim for black women writers the widest possible application of the term at the same time that I would employ it as a working word to differentiate the literature that speaks to a particular historical order as a *counter*–tradition, a *counter*-myth. In the closing words of this volume, I would want to say that "tradition" for black women's writing community is a matrix of literary *discontinuities* that partially articulate various periods of consciousness in the history of an African-American people. This point of paradox not only opens the future to the work to come, but also reminds us that *symbolic discontinuity* is the single rule of terministic behavior that our national literature has still to pursue. The day it does so, the reader and writer both will have laid sight on a territory of the literary landscape that we barely knew was possible.

As it is now, the year 1929, for instance, is remarkable for more than one kind of explosion, even though we generally note only a single phase of it. Grafted onto the national memory like a vivid chancre, 1929 marks the economic downslide of the affluent classes in America and intercepts the "Harlem Renaissance," the historians say, and, along with it, a stage of "affirmative-action publishing" in the country. That Faulkner's *Sound and Fury* shares the same publishing year as Nella Larsen's *Passing* (as his *Sanctuary* and Jessie Fauset's *Chinaberry Tree* both appear in 1931) is less interesting as a piece of suppressed literary history than it is as a silenced clue into the rhetorical fortunes of "race" as thematic material of an era. This unfinished chapter of literary history once reconstructed might show us the deep matter of American race locking several writers (across gender, race, and region) in deadly combat with private conscience as the latter confronts coeval literary practice and the symbolic will to power.

The national totem of race invoked by these three writers conceals a deeper problematic in their respective work. The comparison is not at all ludicrous when we recall Faulkner's Joe Christmas (*Light in August*) and Charles Bond (*Absalom, Absalom!*), Larsen's Irene Redfield and Clare Kendry (*Passing*), and Fauset's Strange women (*Chinaberry Tree*), all stranded in some region of a terrible ambiguity. From their widely divergent points of view, Jessie Fauset, Nella Larsen, and William Faulkner (an unlikely ménage à trois at any rate) take on questions of guilt with varying degrees of emphasis and success. Faulkner finds his formula on the basis of a reified South that essentially replicates the notions of myth—a reanimation of the paradox of motion—so that the economics of sacrifice and the theme of racial victimage are a perfectly conforming instance. It appears that all three writers are searching for the terms of tragedy that would fit an age nowhere remotely close, in any sense, to the overgrown proportions of the classically tragic scene. Fauset, for instance, understands dreadfulness and the mechanisms of guilt and contamination as they operate in the life of her mulatto figure, Laurentine Strange, and her mother Sal, black woman fallen among the gentiles. In trying to locate an explicit metaphor for *tragic guilt*, Fauset engages notions of racist ideology in isolation from a solid base of other grammars of experience. The outcome in *Chinaberry Tree* is as warped as the word *mulatto* is false and exotic naming—both an exaggeration of terms that have not yet located modulation and perspective. I believe that the same lack of mediation might be adopted as a general descriptive formula for Larsen's *Quicksand* (1928) and *Passing*, even though both writers achieve certain powerful effects in their attempt to portray the very origins of "race" as the site of a *transformation* in the classical patterns of marking and victimage.[4]

The theme of "passing" passes, as it is neither clear why, nor regrettable to us that, it does. We pause nonetheless because the theme specifies a rupture in the table of fictional content and a radical departure in sensibility and the syntax that demarcates it, both in the very short distance (same decade) between Fauset's and Larsen's work and Hurston's *Their Eyes Were Watching God*.[5]

It is as though Hurston never heard of either, let alone read and studied their work. Between *Chinaberry Tree* and the tale of Janie Starks, we cross six short years, but the differences between the texts create so sharp a rift on the literary surface that from the angle even of the late thirties, Larsen and Fauset have already become signs of a reliquary, whose objects, no longer ready to hand, are now delicate and bizarre curiosities. Janie Starks's "light skin" and "long hair" are carefully domesticated objects of sense that belong unmistakably to the same vocabulary of feeling that subsumes the work of Larsen and

Fauset, but the terms of their apprehension have just as decisively shifted. There is no question concerning Janie's racial affiliation and allegiance; the novel doesn't even broach the matter, except that the begetting of Leafy—Janie's mother—rehearses the typology of the master/slave relationship in its sexual and genetic manifestations. Quite simply, Janie's grandmother is the forced paramour and rape victim of her owner and must flee the wrath of the mistress shortly before the Civil War South is overcome by Union military forces. Because Janie's biography *absorbs* the question of racial origin, Janie is therefore liberated to an existential quest whose inspiration is *inner-directed*, rather than imposed by an outer means or force.

By contrast, Larsen's and Fauset's agents are put in motion through a material scene by the prerogatives of a determinism that we could variously name, but the point is that the strategy of complication or dramatic movement in their case is imposed on them with tenacious blindness by an outer agency. Their names do not matter because any actor in their place would be forced to the same nausea of recognition, the same acts and practices of ambivalence that point the marked or victimized agent. To that extent, the determining force appears to be ahistorical, or a symptom of Necessity that falls on any subject that stands in its way. "Race" becomes, in this order of things, an extension of scene or background. It is a "god-term," or a capital term of human existence that is imbued with authority as from a divine source.[6] Not amenable to human history, "race," as the fiction writers deployed it, is roughly the equivalent of "environment" (in the case of Richard Wright's *Native Son*), or the principle of Necessity that stands in for "God," or in the place of "God." According to this reading, Larsen and Fauset may be said to privilege a notion of Necessity, or of *scene*, as opposed to *agent*, but the saying so does not, by any means, exhaust their fiction.

Hurston, on the other hand, moves *agent* (or actor) into the foreground as Janie Starks becomes the individualized subject of her own experience. It does matter that she is named *Janie* and that her naming differentiates her from a *type*, whose life possibilities have already been circumscribed and prescribed by preconditions that remain essentially faceless and out of time. (The effect is much like a world series, we might imagine, whose outcome is established before the players and spectators arrive on the scene.) This shift in epistemic procedure dictates the habits of style that distinguish the tale of Janie Starks. Her interior life, her "cosmic" dreaming, her storytelling strategies to Pheoby Watson are seen under the auspices of an individualized agency no longer haunted in the woman's text by a Presence that neither identifies itself nor goes away. In short, Janie is free to do what she can, just as she must contend with the forces of circumstance (primarily, other human beings just as willful as herself) that meet and balance her own efforts. An agent endowed with the possibilities of action, or who can *make* her world, just as she is *made* by it, is the crucial dialectical motion that is missing in deterministic fictions.[7] I certainly do not mean to say that all an agent in life and literature has to do is act and everything will be fine, but, rather, that an agent must be seen in perspective with background in order to be seen at all, for act to have symbolic meaning at all.

An attempted archaeology of narrative strategies between Fauset and Hurston's era of work would not ignore the overwhelming influence of Dreiser's naturalistic fiction on American literature from c. 1900 to the publication of *Native Son* (1942). But it is more than intriguing that the influence of naturalism, or an ideology of the environment, is not pronounced among black American women writers until relatively late in this volume's survey, notably Ann Petry's *The Street* (1946).[8] Not only is the latter novel discontinuous with *Their Eyes Were Watching God*, but also markedly contrastive with Petry's own *Country Place*, published twelve months later. Lutie Johnson of *The Street* resembles the mulatto heroines of the preceding literary era only in her creator's insistence on the maleficence of background as the primary and controlling agency of human action. But this single basis of a structural alignment is enough to juxtapose Petry and the past, except that the voice of Hurston intrudes itself forcefully enough to create a break whose particular features demolish any notions of immediate linear continuity or "influence." Furthermore, Petry's ideology of the environment—one of the strains of a materialist philosophy—is so sharply divergent from Larsen and Fauset's genetic determinism that these apparently comparable philosophies of ascription occupy, in fact, quite different orbits of the literary universe.

Lutie Johnson, in short, has been stripped of the decorative object, or the ornament of fashion, that constitutes an entire repertoire of traits in the work of the earlier generation of writers. Lutie's new class affiliation for literary character appears to be an effect of an altered perspective rather than a cause, as Bigger Thomas's impoverishment is a physical sign of his spiritual and psychic degradation. These elements of *lumpen proletariat*, the urban dispossessed, are mobilized on the literary landscape with a specificity that rivals the concretely delineated products of a new civic order—Norris's and Faulkner's trains; Dreiser's cities and hotels; Wright's skyscrapers and airplanes. These powerful signs of plenitude assume the character of a prohibition, mark off a territory of the sacred, which the pariah, coexistent with it, can either not approach at all or only inchoately understand. To

Lutie's mind, the "street," for instance, becomes an undifferentiated spatial progression that oppresses her as in an endless nightmare, retrogressively involving into itself. This horrible absence of closure for the naturalistic agent identifies precisely the vacuum that action would fill up, since the character is impeded by an antagonism infinitely more potent than itself and is anaesthetized by it. To be stripped on such a background is not only degradation. It is death to the agent. The naturalized scene, as a result, is a proliferation of antinomous meanings—ruined bare rooms over and against the tangible manifestations of power. Their binary evocation is meant to seal the exacting rule of destiny, whose latest disguise calls itself "environment."

Larsen's characters in *Passing*, on the contrary, are allowed to handle fine exquisite things, such as Irene Redfield's lacquered black cigarette box or Clare Kendry's golden bowl of a hat, so that the material object is made to stand in an "objective correlative" relationship to the nuances of dramatic action. The "objective correlative" slides into its future, changes names, attaches to filmic discourse, and we call it, after Roman Jakobson, the "metonymic close-up." For instance, Irene Redfield never says to anyone that she knows that Clare Kendry is stealing her husband Brian, but we know she knows when she drops a piece of crystal that shatters on the carpet. A precisely choreographed gesture displaces the verbal sign in expressing a critical change in dramatic and narrative development. It is the sort of displacement that moviegoers—some twenty years later—will become accustomed to in "overhearing" clues that no one has uttered. The gain in subtlety and visual richness cannot be overemphasized, as the object is not simply a small geometrical intrusion, but a means of stage direction that moves the agents from one moment of plot to another. The vocabulary of objects in a relationship to character introduces to Fauset's and Larsen's genetic determinism an oddly disjunctive (and relieving!) quality, as though the writers had two simultaneous, but incompatible, purposes in mind at once. Naturalistic strategies heal the breach by doing away with objects of intimacy and possession altogether so that a Lutie Johnson is the unnuanced, unaccommodated subject who simply answers the logic of a syllogism.

Alice Walker's first novel, *The Third Life of Grange Copeland* (1970),[9] insinuates a similar structure of figural elaborations, but it is important to observe that this apprentice novel is a monument to the late Civil Rights era and has in view, consequently, a lesson in the redemption of black American manhood. The tale of the reconstructed life of Grange Copeland actually interlards a rhetoric of determinism and a Christian metaphysics that we discern in the novel's well-disguised sacrificial theme. Grange Copeland, as the biological father of Brownfield, is also the spiritual father of his son. The inaugural scenes of Grange's sodden misery anticipate Brownfield's "fall" so that we perceive not only an analogy here on ancestral guilt and its transference across the generations, but also a contemporary reading on "original sin." Ancestral guilt and "original sin" are one and the same. An order of substitution is appropriate—Grange is to the Copeland bloodline what Adam is to the human family, and just as we discern dimensions of allegory in the creation myth, we note similar allegorical purposes in Walker. Scenes of humiliation unfold with such avid pageantry that one recalls Lewis's *Jungle* as a closely comparable fiction. Walker's traffic in scenes of degradation, pursued with homiletic commitment, leads to an ending that opens out into the brave new world. The returned father will give his life for his granddaughter Ruth in a scene reminiscent of Jonathan Jackson's assault on "justice" in the now-famous confrontation at Marin County Courthouse. The return of Grange with his "act together," so to speak, introduces the theme of forgiveness and resurrection as Grange is born into new life; at the same time, he transcends his guilt, taking up the implements and weapons of love for the third generation.

That Walker embraces in the 1970s fictional moves that appear historically bound to an earlier contemporaneity cannot be easily explained, if at all. We can only repeat the obvious: (1) The cause of redeemed personhood seems to evoke its own rhetorical means—a context of confrontational hostility between an agent and an unyielding world must be so inevitably and solidly structured that its interruption divides the time of the agent into a "before" and "after." What Walker adds to the scenic apparatus of the "environment" is the dynamic of willful sacrifice and "overcoming," which thematic feature is missing in the tale of Lutie Johnson. Interestingly enough, the agents of naturalism do not, as a rule, survive; Grange Copeland, therefore, belongs to the same class of literary/cultural agents as Bigger Thomas, many years before him, with a decisive difference: Grange, as Walker's chief heuristic model, must have reasons for continuity now which his granddaughter provides and pointedly provides in an era of racial rebirth and renewal. (2) In order to make her point, Alice Walker reaches behind her most immediate writing predecessor, Margaret Walker, and reclaims the tendentious rhetorical strategies of writers decades before. Strategically, my argument is intended to illustrate the jagged career of deterministic rhetoric among black women writers as a single example of unpredictable rupture on the surface of literary events that worries significantly our agreement to order and succession as the law of symbolic behavior.

One is startled by a chronological scheme that yields the following juxtaposed points of contact:

> *Jubilee* (1965)
> *Chosen Place, Timeless People* (1969)
> *The Bluest Eye* (1970)
> *The Third Life of Grange Copeland* (1970)
> *Sula* (1973)
> *Corregidora* and *Eva's Man* (1975; 1976)
> *Meridian* (1976)
> *Song of Solomon* (1977)
> *The Salt Eaters* (1980)
> *Tar Baby* (1981)
> *Sassafrass, Cypress, and Indigo* (1982)
> *Color Purple* (1982)
> *Women of Brewster Place* (1982)
> *Praisesong for the Widow* (1983)

This listing is no attempt to exhaust even the titles of fictions by black American women in the last twenty years, but if we extended it, I believe we might confirm a point I am driving at in the preceding analyses. The single thread of most persistent comparison among these novels is their shared point of historical reference. *Jubilee, Chosen Place,* and *The Bluest Eye,* for instance, show temporal proximity, but are as divergent in their vocabularies of feeling, orders of meaning, and tendencies of belief as the writers are different. *The Salt Eaters, Tar Baby,* and *Sassafrass,* for another example, exhibit similar temporal closeness, but the tale of Velma Henry (*The Salt Eaters*), articulated through a seamless web of a combined narration of central intelligence and stream-of-consciousness, is worlds apart from the omniscient and concealed-narrative points of view deployed in *Tar Baby* and *Sassafrass.* Again, the narrative stage of *Jubilee* and *Timeless People* is immense. The natural historical progression of Africans in the Diaspora is, in both cases, a crucial aspect of exposition and argument, but Walker's vision of human history as an extension of Divine Will stands in antipodal thematic opposition to Paule Marshall's completely secularized mediations of a particular historical order. The uses to which history is put in *Corregidora* are sharpened to a point of ontological specificity that might be compared with *Song of Solomon* and *Praisesong for the Widow,* as all three novels carve out a single figure against a field. *Sula* touches historical function only around the edges. Morrison's chapter titles, adopted from certain important annual dates, suggest that her character has not come into this world full-blown, even if we regard Sula's ad hoc moral stance as disruptive of the very notion of order and degree.

This rough and sporadic calendar of fictions and brief speculations concerning them cannot be considered anything more than a preliminary brainstorming toward a totalization, whose work belongs to our common future, as the essays in this volume anticipate. What these breaks and interstices in the pattern of woman-making would argue is that these writers engage no allegiance to a hierarchy of dynastic meanings that unfolds in linear succession and according to our customary sense of "influence."[10] Critics are called upon, then, to try these literary relationships in their serial array, wherein contradiction and rupture appear as a structural thematics against the general background of African-American life and thought. We specifically wish to know the points at which experience and discourse about it contrast and intercept each other since we realize that the writer is not providing for us a transcript of a courtroom procedure, but illuminations that borrow their plenitude from the time/space continuum that we call "real"—four-dimensional. We have yet to place this community of writers in perspective with writing communities that run parallel to it—black American men's; Anglo-American women's and men's; communities of genres contemporaneous with it—the poetry, drama, autobiographies, and other nonfictional writings of black American women; the gynocritical themes of recent feminist inquiry;[11] the codes of the "objective" text; or those writings whose chief display is the play of "logology," those texts whose basic unit of composition moves toward the lexical and the syllabic in counter and contrastive currency to *story*. Then there is the work of discovering the elaborate and submerged particularities of the texts from writer to writer and within a writer's own career. For lack of a better word, we could call this project the "archaeological" since it questions matters of lexis, syntax, and semantics and tries to decide from what common fund of rhetorical legacies (and betrayals?) writers across time and in the same time were drawing.

Such perspective is entirely appropriate because our primary aim as audience is to understand how symbolic behavior works as its own integrity and in relationship to a whole world of cultural subjects and objects. The emergent community of lesbian thinkers and writers demands that we now consider our shared symbolic economies in light of patriarchist *and* heterosexual hegemony.[12] In short, the critical work of the future requires, I believe, our constant vigilance and responsiveness to this community of writers in their total and dynamic historical situatedness.

In various literature courses that I have taught between 1973 and the present, one of the ways that I often distinguish between fiction written before 1925 and that written after that time in English–speaking traditions is to say that the latter tends to be a fiction of the classroom. This oversimplification actually works quite well until we get down to specific and refining cases. Nevertheless, the rule is handy in pointing an inclination, which also explains the lively critical enterprise of the "variorum" text, the "tour guides" to writers whose very *goal* is obfuscation, the sometimes impressive and playful new (and short!) critical pieces, and the rich proliferations of symbologies that threaten to enclose the literary/critical universe in a space of exclusionary and hieratic practices. This literature, which teachers tend to privilege because it supports and reenforces the myth of "complexity," the figures of irony, and our virtually religious predisposition to "ambiguity" as the law of the new world, is, at the moment, the ascendant literature of the classroom, and the process feeds on itself, we suppose. Students become adult readers sometimes who expect their learned values to be flattered and, in turn, valorize (and buy) that literature which they have been taught to value as "hard" and "really good." (It might be interesting to study, though, to what extent the *permissible* culture is undermined among undergraduate populations by "soap opera" forms, or Every Intelligent Person's "Nancy Drew" fiction that she/he hides between the covers of the infamous brown paper bag.) Those of us trained in the graduate academy since the coronation of "close reading" in the fifties were taught the same way, and nothing appears drastically out of place since my tenure at Brandeis University as a graduate student in English during the late sixties–early seventies.

But not so slowly, the literature of the American classroom changes, and only in some communities are "the people" not reading novels any more since novels abandoned "plain-speaking," bound for *explication de texte*, about sixty years ago. It appears that women's fictional work maintains, as a general rule, not only an allegiance to "power to the people," but also "talking" to "the people" in the now-familiar accents of representation and mimesis. The work of black women writers is specifically notable in this regard.

The day will come, I would dare to predict, when the black American women's writing community will reflect the currents both of the new new critical procedures and the various literatures concurrent with them. (*The Salt Eaters*, I believe, already anticipates some of the future moves, as *Song of Solomon* and *One Hundred Years of Solitude* bear more than superficial resemblance, my new fall line for Haverford's English 261 conjectures.) More than that, this literature of the future, as far as we can know it and as far as it must require of reader and writer a widened critical awareness, might not renounce, either, its inexorable ties to the drama of the "tremendous strivings" of a people.[13] If that happens, then the academy meets life, and life the academy, in a situation of emphases neither of whose resonance and value we can afford to deny in our own small strivings. "Tradition," as I would mean it, then, is an active verb, rather than a retired nominative, and we now are its subjects and objects. Quite correctly, "tradition" under the head of a polyvalent grammar—the language of learning woven into the tongue of the mother—is the rare union of bliss toward which African-American experience has compelled us all along.

Notes

1. Claudia Tate (ed.), *Black Women Writers at Work* (New York: The Continuum Publishing Company, 1983); Barbara Christian, *Black Women Novelists: The Development of a Tradition, 1892–1976* (Westport, Conn.: Greenwood Press, 1980); Mary Helen Washington (ed.), *Black-Eyed Susans: Classic Stories By and About Black Women* (New York: Anchor Press/Doubleday, 1975) and *Midnight Birds: Stories of Contemporary Black Women Writers*, with an Introduction by Mary Helen Washington (New York: Anchor Press/Doubleday, 1980).

2. Margaret Walker, *Jubilee* (Boston: Houghton-Mifflin, 1966); Gloria Naylor, *The Women of Brewster Place* (New York: Viking Press, 1982); Alice Walker, *The Color Purple* (New York: Harcourt, Brace, 1982); Paule Marshall, *Praisesong for the Widow* (New York: G. P. Putnam's Sons, 1983); Ntozake Shange, *Sassafrass, Cypress, and Indigo* (New York: St. Martin's Press, 1982).

3. Marita Golden, *Migrations of the Heart: A Personal Odyssey* (New York: Anchor Press/Doubleday, 1983); Audre Lorde, *Zami: A New Spelling of My Name* (Watertown, Mass.: Persephone Press, Inc., 1982).

In a review of Claudia Tate's *Black Women Writers at Work*, Michele Wallace makes passing reference to her own novel to come and to a recent novel by Gayl Jones, *Song for Anninho*, which, along with Wallace, I also have not yet seen. *The Women's Review of Books* 1:1 (October 1983), pp. 7–8.

4. The term as I use it here refers to René Girard's discussion of the phenomenon of scapegoating in *Violence and the Sacred*, trans. Patrick Gregory (Baltimore: The Johns Hopkins University Press, 1977).

5. Zora Neale Hurston, *Their Eyes Were Watching God* (Philadelphia: J. P. Lippincott, 1937).

6. For a full discussion of scenic devices, of which the "god-term" is preeminent, the reader should see Kenneth Burke's *Grammar of Motives* (New York: Prentice-Hall, 1945).

7. Edward Said's discussion of "civil culture" (after Gramsci and Vico) is a point of reference in the argument I make here concerning the dynamic relationship, or the dynamic potential of relationship between human will

and the products of society. "Opponents, Audiences, Constituencies, and Community," "The Politics of Interpretation," *Critical Inquiry* 9:1 (September 1982), pp. 1–26.

8. Ann Petry, *The Street* (New York: Pyramid Publications, 1961).

9. Alice Walker, *The Third Life of Grange Copeland* (New York: Harcourt, Brace, 1970).

10. Michel Foucault's discussion of discontinuity in the history of ideas and "influence" as a fiction of historiography is key to our understanding of relationships between texts and epistemes. *The Archaeology of Knowledge and the Discourse on Language*, trans. A. M. Sheridan Smith (New York: Harper and Row Publishers, 1972).

11. I borrow the term *gynocritical* from Elaine Showalter, who distinguishes between women scholars' "revisionary readings" of literature and a female-centered critical enterprise—" . . . the study of women *as writers* [emphasis Showalter], and its subjects are the history, styles, themes, genres, and structures of writing by women; the psychodynamics of female creativity; the trajectory of the individual or collective female career; and the evolution and laws of a female literary tradition" (pp. 14–15). "Feminist Criticism in the Wilderness," *Writing and Sexual Difference*, ed. Elizabeth Abel (Chicago: University of Chicago Press, 1982), pp. 9–35. I am suggesting a contrast between "black women's writing community" and the "gynocritical themes of recent feminist inquiry" because these markers still identify different cultural experiences among two groups of American women. Perhaps as we continue to extend the critique of culture from the woman's point of view, we will help to bring about wider consort between these powerful and contrastive alignments.

12. Some insights into the implications of the symbolic and political dominance of patriarchy for lesbian community are provided by Adrienne Rich, "Compulsory Heterosexuality and Lesbian Existence," *Women: Sex and Sexuality*, eds. Catharine R. Stimpson and Ethel Spector Person (Chicago: University of Chicago Press, 1980), pp. 62–92.

Barbara Smith's "Toward a Black Feminist Criticism" addresses specifically the absence of a "consistent feminist analysis . . . about Black Lesbian literature" (p. 157). Smith goes on to argue how such an analysis might be achieved against the long view of a corrected and revised politics of feminism in the United States. *All the Women are White, All the Blacks are Men, But Some of Us are Brave*, eds. Gloria T. Hull, Patricia Bell Scott, and Barbara Smith (Old Westbury, N. Y.: The Feminist Press, 1982), pp. 157–76.

13. This term is adopted from W. E. B. DuBois's discussion of "Negro literature" as the "drama of a tremendous striving" in pages of the *Crisis Magazine*.

The Contributors

BERNARD W. BELL, Associate Professor of English at the University of Massachusetts, Amherst, is the editor of *Modern and Contemporary Afro-American Poetry* and author of *The Folk Roots of Contemporary Afro-American Poetry* and *The Afro-American Novel and Its Tradition*. His articles and reviews on black American literature and culture have appeared in numerous journals.

BARBARA CHRISTIAN, Associate Professor of Afro-American Studies at the University of California, Berkeley, is the author of *Black Feminist Criticism: Perspectives on Contemporary Black Women Writers* and *Black Women Novelists, The Development of a Tradition*. Her essays on Afro-American writers have appeared in numerous published collections as well as journals.

FRANCES SMITH FOSTER, Professor of English and Comparative Literature at San Diego State University, is author of *Witnessing Slavery: The Development of the Antebellum Slave Narrative* and several articles on black American literature.

MINROSE C. GWIN, Assistant Professor of English at Virginia Polytechnic Institute and State University, has edited a collection of Civil War reminiscences, *Olden Times Revisited: W. L. Clayton's Pen Pictures* and is the author of the critical study *Black and White Women of the Old South: The Peculiar Sisterhood in American Literature*.

GLORIA T. HULL, Associate Professor of English at the University of Delaware, is the co-editor of *All the Women are White, All the Blacks Are Men, But Some of Us Are Brave: Black Women's Studies* and editor of *Give Us Each Day: The Diary of Alice Dunbar-Nelson*. Her articles on black American literature and especially black women writers have appeared in numerous journals.

DEBORAH E. McDOWELL, Assistant Professor of English at Colby College, is currently at work on a critical study of black women novelists, forthcoming from Indiana University Press. Her articles and reviews on the literature of black women novelists have appeared in *Black American Literature Forum*, *College Language Association Journal*, *In These Times*, and *Centennial Review*.

MADONNE M. MINER, Assistant Professor of English at the University of Wyoming, is the author of *Insatiable Appetites* and of various essays on women writers, characters, and readers. She is currently working on a book-length study of the reader's role in feminist fiction of the 1970's.

MARJORIE PRYSE, Associate Professor of English at the University of Tennessee, is author of *The Mark and the Knowledge: Social Stigma in Classic American Fiction* and editor of *Selected Stories of Mary E. Wilkins Freeman*. She is currently working on a study of American women regionalists and has published articles on American literature in numerous journals.

ELIZABETH SCHULTZ, Professor of English at the University of Kansas, teaches Afro-American fiction, fiction by American women, and nineteenth-century American fiction. Her numerous essays on these subjects and on Japanese culture as well as her short stories have appeared in a variety of journals.

THELMA J. SHINN, Associate Professor of English, was founding director of Women's Studies at Arizona State University. She is working on a book-length study of women science fiction writers to be called *Worlds Within Women*. She has published literary criticism, poetry, and reviews, and has written a play called *Don't Worry—Mary's Pregnant Again*.

JOSEPH T. SKERRETT, JR., Associate Professor of English at the University of Massachusetts, Amherst, has published articles on twentieth-century black and white American writers in *American Quarterly*, *The Massachusetts Review*, *Melus* and other journals. He is currently the President of Melus, the Society for the Study of the Multi-Ethnic Literature of the United States.

HORTENSE J. SPILLERS, Associate Professor of English at Haverford College, teaches literature and writing. Her articles and stories have appeared widely in journals. For one of her short stories she was the recipient of the National Award for excellence in Fiction and Belles Lettres in 1976.

CLAUDIA TATE, Associate Professor of English at Howard University, is the author of *Black Women Writers at Work*. Her articles on black American literature, women's literature, and criticism appear in numerous journals.

Index to Authors and Titles